OUT OF THE PARK

OUT OF THE PARK

The Craig McMillan Story

with Neil Reid

Hodder Moa

National Library of New Zealand Cataloguing-in-Publication Data
Reid, Neil.
Out of the park : the Craig McMillan story / with Neil Reid.
ISBN 978-1-86971-138-2
1. McMillan, Craig, 1976- 2. Cricket players—New Zealand—
Biography. I. Title.
796.358092—dc 22

A Hodder Moa Book
Published in 2008 by Hachette Livre NZ Ltd
4 Whetu Place, Mairangi Bay
Auckland, New Zealand

Designed and produced by Hachette Livre NZ Ltd
Everbest Printing Co. Ltd., China

Jacket images: Photosport

Contents

Foreword

I have been an avid follower of the fortunes of Craig McMillan since I managed the under-19 New Zealand team to Pakistan in 1994. And I was also able to assess him further when he captained the Under-19 New Zealand team to England in 1996, again when I was the team manager.

So I am in a unique position to write a few words as a foreword to his book, which I feel very honoured to do.

Craig is one of the very few batsmen in world cricket who can, and has, changed the direction of a match with his dynamic batting ability. But when Craig went through the period of being in and out of the national team, I was mystified as to the selectors' thinking.

Over the years I have done my stint at selecting the national team. The basis of good selection is to select your best side and stick to it. At times you should expect some performance failures. But that doesn't mean you should chop and change selections on the basis of a couple of poor performances. If changes are too frequent, the player is forever on trial, playing for his place.

During his early years in the New Zealand team, a few of the players had an overly aggressive attitude. And some of it unfortunately rubbed off on Craig for a while. But his ready smile dissipated any lasting effects.

On the two occasions that I was manager of the under-19 side it gave me a close insight into his health problems with diabetes. He controlled it by self-medicating with injections, which meant he had to leave the field before the lunch break to administer. For me, I held a life-saving injection pack in the team's dressing room fridge, just in case. How he was able to play and captain the 1996 team so well is beyond comprehension.

In my last book, *A Cricketing Life*, which came out in 2000, I wrote a little about my experiences with Craig and said that I could see a potential New Zealand captain waiting in the wings. Well, that did not happen – but it should have!

Craig is a pretty forthright character, both on and off the field. So I guess he trod on a few toes here and there along the way.

But New Zealand Cricket needs the cricketing abilities of the Flemings, the Astles and the McMillans. And I feel that their careers were cut short, and this was well before the Indian league monies arrived.

I am sorry that it seems that I will not see Craig on the field wearing a silver fern again. But he will carry my admiration and best wishes with him wherever he goes.

John R. Reid, OBE
Taupo, July, 2008

Writer's note

I've watched Craig McMillan's career with interest since his test debut against Australia at the Gabba in 1997, raising my glass along with other punters in a Wellington sports bar when he smashed Shane Warne for six to bring up a half century in his first-ever test innings.

Three months later, I was stretched out on the Basin Reserve's iconic embankment with mates, cheering him on as he posted his maiden test century against Zimbabwe. Those innings helped signal the arrival of a great talent onto the New Zealand cricket scene, one that was to be instrumental in many future successes.

Several years later and I first got the chance to interview Craig. Right from the start I was impressed by his openness and willingness to tell it like it is. For him, the party political line when dealing with the media wasn't the way to go.

I enjoyed interviewing Craig whenever we spoke, due largely to his honesty. He was refreshingly candid at a time when others didn't want to rock the boat when dealing with the media. And that was a trait he displayed even during the dark times which followed his omission from New Zealand Cricket's list of 20 contracted cricketers in 2006.

But as time went by it was an approach which irritated certain members of the media, because they were finally confronted with a bloke who wasn't prepared to simply take some of the cheap shots directed his way.

Just as he did on the field, he hit back. And who could blame him when things went beyond merely criticising his cricket skills to the personal?

As a journalist, one of the refreshing things about Craig is that he did read what was written about him. If he was going to shoot back, he wanted to know exactly what had been said.

It is with that same brutal honesty that Craig has approached this book. I've always struggled to comprehend why some fellow members of the media and a section of the cricketing public have directed vitriol in McMillan's direction. Some have labelled him arrogant, but anyone who has had the chance to talk to him will say that is far from the case. If anything, Craig is a very private person. He isn't one to blow his own trumpet. And at times that private demeanour has seen him portrayed as being aloof from the public.

Out of the Park — the Craig McMillan story will hopefully give an insight into the real Craig McMillan, the player who has the respect of his former team-mates and coaches, the committed family man who sacrificed a lot to ride the international roller-coaster for more than a decade.

Throughout his career, Craig has fought a battle with debilitating Type 1 diabetes. But he confronted his health situation with the same courage and determination he showed in the heat of battle on cricket pitches around the world. Given this kind of resolve, it probably isn't surprising that he made it back into the Black Caps in the months leading up to the 2007 Cricket World Cup, despite initially not being contracted to New Zealand Cricket.

His stunning innings against Australia in the 2007 Chappell-Hadlee Trophy series again showed the outstanding power, and at times brutality, he could dish out in the middle.

If he had been handled better by team management and the selectors in the intervening years from his debut, more of the same could have been seen from him more often on the international stage.

It's been a great pleasure to work with Craig on this project. He has been someone whom I have always respected as a person and an athlete, and those sentiments have been magnified by his openness and honesty throughout the process of compiling this book.

I would also like to thank everyone who has given their time for interviews about aspects of Craig's career. Their keenness to be involved just reinforces that he truly has the respect of those who really matter. Thank you, too, to Rebecca Milne, my family, the Milne family, the great team at Yahoo!Xtra, Craig's manager Leanne McGoldrick and, finally, Warren Adler and Hachette Livre NZ for their support and understanding.

Neil Reid
Auckland, July, 2008

The end of the road

I've been called a lot of things during my cricket career. Few have been as offensive as being called 'disloyal' following my signing with the Indian Cricket League. It's a tag which some have given to me and the other New Zealanders who have followed that path.

When you have played for your country for 11 years I find that tough to take. During that time, I put my heart and soul into it. Of course, playing for New Zealand did a lot for me and took me to places in the world I might never have visited. But I also made sacrifices to get there.

If anyone in any job, including the people who have bagged us, were suddenly offered twice or three times the amount they're paid to go and work somewhere else, most would jump at the chance. It is very easy to say, 'I would have done this or that', when you are not in that situation.

Over my cricket career there were many times when sport was put ahead of my family and relationships because of being away from home for prolonged periods. When you have two young kids, as Cherie and I have, you have a lot more to think about than just yourself. Family becomes your priority. And if you can create a better living for everyone involved, you will make decisions to achieve that. Creating a better life and future for my family was always my first consideration when I was deciding what I was going to do with my life and career after the 2007 Cricket World Cup.

I returned from the World Cup after nine long and largely unenjoyable weeks. It was great to have achieved my goal of making World Cup selection, especially after being well on the outer at the start of the season leading up to the tournament in the West Indies. But after all the work I had put in to get selected, the one thing that stuck in my mind when I was away was getting home to see the family and spending some proper quality time with them. I was also questioning whether I really wanted to continue with the touring life as an international cricketer.

There was also the question of how I would continue to manage my battle with diabetes. My thoughts turned more and more to retiring for the sake of my health and to spend more time with the family. Then the opportunity came up with the ICL to continue playing cricket, and to make a good living out of it.

When I did lose my New Zealand Cricket contract in 2006, one positive result was that it gave me 12 months with my family. I was still playing for Canterbury but I spent a lot more time at home. When you are playing for the Black Caps, through necessity you are all over the place.

While I was elated when I was reselected to take on Sri Lanka in December 2006, following a 12-month absence from the national team, I found it difficult when I got back into the side and started touring again. It was as if the landscape had changed. And I had probably changed as a person. Those feelings increased in magnitude when I was away at the World Cup. Everything had been geared towards me getting to the World Cup; that had always been the light at the end of my tunnel. I felt that goal had been achieved and I didn't know if I had anything else to chase — I felt flat.

Leanne McGoldrick (Craig's manager): Very soon after he was recalled to the national side, he started talking to me about retirement. It is ironic, really, but amid all the celebration of his selection and the success of his return, he was already thinking about giving it away. A settled lifestyle meant that his health prior to the Sri Lanka tour was better than it had been in a long time, but after the tour it deteriorated. He was very determined and had worked very hard to regain a position in the team, but there was an underlying insecurity about his place in the side. While I don't think that is uncommon at times for players, Craig found it really tough. The reality was that the worst possible thing for him in his professional cricket career had already happened. Some of the passion was gone. He seemed to have lost the desire to play.

Spending some decent family time wasn't the only plus for me on our return from the World Cup. It also looked like I was going to pick up one of New Zealand Cricket's top 20 contracts. That in itself was pleasing. After missing the cut at the start of the 2006–07 season I had played myself back into reckoning as one of New Zealand's top 20 players. And all the while I was trying to rehab the groin injury I had suffered in our World Cup semi-final loss to Sri Lanka. It took nine weeks to finally get it right, delaying my departure to England with Cherie and the kids to play for the Nelson Cricket Club in the Lancashire Leagues.

Before I could go I also had the Black Caps' season review to go through, something which ended with me being handed a contract. While it was gratifying to again be among the selectors' top 20, where I ended up in their rankings left a lot to be desired. Sure I was glad to be offered a contract, but to be offered contract No. 16 for the 2007–08 season was something I was pretty gutted with to be honest, especially after the season I had had. As I was only viewed as a one-day player, the system actually worked against me because the ranking points you gain in regards to the test arena are weighted more heavily.

I rang Lindsay Crocker about being ranked at 16, expressed my dissatisfaction and asked for an explanation, as you are entitled to under the system. It just seemed to be another example of how I didn't get too many favours from the national selection panel. He gave me the unofficial numbers and I was actually No. 12 in the one-day set-up. So I wasn't even in the top 11, despite the fact that I had pretty much played all season, including at the World Cup.

Even more alarming was when I was given my test ranking — out of the 20 players I was ranked No. 18. That's how I got ranked at No. 16 overall. I'm not having a go at any of the blokes who were ranked ahead of me; good luck to them if they were the benefactors of the contract system. But the fact remained that one of the guys who had been ranked ahead of me in the ODI ratings hadn't played much cricket in the previous season for the Black Caps. I was scratching my head asking myself, 'How does that work?' It showed yet again just how selective the whole contract process can be.

The review process also made it very clear to me that both Black Caps coach John Bracewell and New Zealand Cricket didn't want me to go to England. Bracewell talked to me about how he saw things, including how he wanted me to stay at home, put me on a fitness programme and for me to get seriously fit — they wanted me to be under their control. I said, 'No.' I wanted to take the family to England and just chill out and have some quality time.

Braces said that in the following season he saw a big role for me, especially in the Twenty20 scenario, with the ICC World Twenty20 tournament coming up in South Africa in September. He saw me as being a match-winner when I was at my best and in good shape. He talked about putting a system in place where I would be fined if I didn't reach a certain fitness level, such as $2000 if I couldn't run three kilometres in a certain time.

They didn't want me going over to England even though I was going to stay very active with my cricket. They felt they needed some recourse, something that would hurt me if I couldn't live up to their expectations. Fining me was just ridiculous. To my mind, if you are not doing what you are expected to do then you won't be selected for your country. That would hurt me more because I wouldn't be playing. Eventually, Bracewell agreed that he could see from a family point of view that he thought I needed to go. But from a fitness point of view, he wasn't overly happy at not having me in his sights.

While I wasn't happy with my ranking, what I had been offered from NZC was better than nothing. But I still wasn't sure what I wanted to do — I was in two minds, juggling up whether I still wanted to be available for the Black Caps 12 months a year or whether I wanted to retire. With the tight schedule we were operating under, I had little time to really digest everything. I had the contract offer for just four days before we were to fly out to England. I felt rushed, and talked to Leanne McGoldrick about not accepting. It was a big season of cricket coming up and I didn't know if I could commit to that. In the end we decided to sign the contract for the 2007–08 season before I flew out to England, see how I felt about things once I was in the UK and then make a definitive decision either over there or when I got back.

With that the McMillan family headed to England. It was a stint I really enjoyed, doing a lot of batting and bowling. While the standard of cricket isn't great, the best thing about it is that you have to do the job; you have to take responsibility to see the team through. You have to bowl your overs — and if you don't score runs then your team won't win. They are useful disciplines to have when you come back into the New Zealand team, in terms of doing the job and not relying on other guys.

Being over there and being able to spend three and a half months with Cherie and the kids basically confirmed to me what I was thinking: that I wanted to retire from the touring lifestyle. I didn't want to be on the road for nine weeks again, and I couldn't commit the amount of time needed if I was to stay in the Black Caps and continue to be successful. I would push hard for selection in the Black Caps' team for the ICC World Twenty20 tournament and then step aside.

Then I got a phone call out of the blue that changed everything, complicating what I thought had been a very well-thought-out plan. About two weeks before our time in England was up Leanne called regarding the ICL. It was perfect timing — it was also very bad timing. I thought it was only right to ring New Zealand Cricket's new chief executive Justin Vaughan to tell him I was considering both retirement from international cricket and also an offer from the ICL. I wanted to be up-front and state my position.

I was named in the 15-man squad for the ICC World Twenty20 in early August, then I would have a few days at home before I went to South Africa with the Black Caps. By the time I turned up at camp my mind was made up that this was going to be my last campaign with the Black Caps. Nothing was going to change that. I wanted the campaign to be successful, both for myself and the team.

They were feelings I expressed to Justin Vaughan when he came to meet me at our Auckland hotel the day before we flew out to South Africa. We went for a walk for about 45 minutes, discussing the various options that could be taken. He understood my reasons, for family and health. At the same time he was pretty keen for me to join the Indian Premier League, but at the time, the key to the IPL contract was that I had to continue to be available for international cricket. Later that stance changed and I would only have to be available for Canterbury. But the whole reason for me retiring was to be able to be with my family. Playing domestic cricket is still a solid five months of the year when you are touring locally. So I didn't really entertain the IPL offer too much. The ICL gave me more flexibility and freedom.

Justin urged me to go to South Africa and not to make a decision until I had been back in the team environment for at least a week. But I knew in my heart that I had made my decision; I was happy with it. I went to South Africa and after three days I knew that nothing had changed and wrote Justin an email on 6 September to notify him of my intention to resign. I told him that I could no longer commit to touring for six months a year — my wife and my kids needed me at home just as much as I wanted to be there with them. If anything, being back in the team environment made me want to be back home even more. In my earlier international cricket years I always looked forward to going on tour and catching up with my mates in the team. But that had changed quite markedly over a number of years.

Justin's reply came a day later, telling me that I had taken him by surprise and that hopefully he could talk further with me about my intentions when he visited the next week. His email also stressed the fact that my resignation alone was not enough to allow me to take up the ICL contract. For that, I would need a full release from New Zealand Cricket. And again he told me that I should also consider making myself open to an offer from the IPL.

Throughout this whole process I hadn't talked to anyone outside of my family, my manager Leanne McGoldrick, Heath Mills of New Zealand Cricket Players' Association or Justin about what I was going to do. Halfway through the ICC World Twenty20 tournament I told Daniel Vettori. He was surprised, but at the same time he understood where I was coming from. It was funny because the test team for the tour of South Africa was due to be named and I thought I might have been close to making that side. Dan knew the side and I asked him if I had made the cut. He told me no. I then asked whether I had even been talked about as a possible selection and his reply was, 'No, not really.' That confirmed to me that I wasn't on the radar. It gave me peace of mind that I was making the right decision.

I then set about playing the tournament and I am very proud to have finished on a personal high. The Twenty20 World Cup was an enjoyable event, more so than the Cricket World Cup. Everything was great for the spectators and I liked the general way the tournament was organised. And I enjoyed my cricket again, something that at times I haven't done. I suppose I also had a touch of freedom, given the fact that I knew this was going to be my last tour for New Zealand.

Daniel Vettori (Black Caps captain): It was a tough time because we weren't allowed to talk about it. I would have loved to have given him the send-off that he deserved within the team. All I could say to him at the end of our last game against Pakistan was, 'It has been a pleasure playing with you.' It had to be as quiet as that because all these other things were going on. It was a sad time for me, losing a guy I had played international cricket with for 10 years.

He was adamant he wasn't going to play on until 35 or 36. It would have been nice for him to push even harder and go and get his test spot back as well. But obviously with the ICL offer and other things going on in his life, having a young family and his health, you can understand his option to take some financial security.

The talks continued with New Zealand Cricket on my return from South Africa. Although I had made it very clear that I was going to retire, NZC didn't want to release me from my contract. The funniest thing was that they wanted to keep paying me, keeping me on the contract, for the full year. But it would have meant that they could have a hold over me in terms of what I could and couldn't do.

The negotiations certainly kept Leanne and Heath busy. After a few days we thought we had reached an agreement and a media release was drafted up by New Zealand Cricket. The day that the press release was due to be sent, I got on my computer at home at 8.30 am, sending an email to my team-mates and team management to let them know what was about to happen. It was out of courtesy; I wanted them to hear from me rather than through the media. I said: 'Thanks for everything. I am moving on. An announcement will be made within the next hour and I just wanted to give you all a heads up with what is going on.'

Half an hour later I got a call from Leanne to say the release was not being issued as New Zealand Cricket wouldn't alter the statement. We had an issue with one line in it and we wanted it either taken out or clarified because it didn't recognise that I had been released from my contract. But NZC weren't going to do that. So I frantically had to email all the guys again to say, 'There has been a bit of a hitch. There will be no announcement today, it might happen tomorrow. But I would appreciate it if you just keep the news under your hat.'

Within 10 minutes of me sending the email, it had been forwarded onto cricket commentator Bryan Waddle. Soon after, Radio Sport was forwarded a copy by someone who had received it from me in confidence.

Leanne McGoldrick: I had missed a call on my phone from Bryan Waddle 10 minutes after Craig had sent his email. Fifteen minutes later I got a call from Radio Sport. They said they had heard that Craig was retiring and proceeded to read out parts of the email. Craig was hugely disappointed. His loyalty is unwavering. You can trust him with anything, and he expects nothing less from you. So for something like that to happen was a blow for him.

Despite the leak, we were still negotiating in the background over the media release. It got to the point where we had gone backwards and NZC weren't happy to release me from my contract. Eventually, we got Queen's Counsel Hugh Rennie involved and we talked to Justin. The hardest thing I struggled with was that they recognised me retiring for family and health reasons — they had no issue with that — but they had no interest in releasing me from my contract.

I was prepared to go as far as I needed to go to get the release, even to court if it was required. Soon after Justin called a meeting, one that we thought was going to have a happy ending. But it ended up being fruitless and we left dumbfounded and confused. Within three days of that meeting, we were still at a stalemate. I got a call out of the blue from Justin telling me he thought he had found a way out of it and arranged a meeting at the start of the next week. Just days earlier there was no way they were going to give me a release. It was weird to get that call, telling me the last thing I expected to hear from New Zealand Cricket after our earlier meeting.

I did a lot of thinking over the weekend, comparing the different scenarios. I turned up to meet Justin on the Monday and he said they had agreed to everything and would release me from my contract for health and family reasons. It was a good meeting, a nice way to finish. We also decided that in two days time we would make the media announcement and have a press conference.

Throughout it all Leanne played a crucial part; I can't overstate what she did for me. And I don't think it would have ended up as well as it did had it not been for her input and help. It was enormous. So too was the work of Heath Mills, Hugh Rennie and Andrew Scott-Howman.

When the announcement was finally made official, I am sure people thought I retired just because I had been offered a contract with the ICL. And I am sure that some people still feel that way. It might seem like a good conspiracy theory, but I can categorically say it is far from the truth.

One reporter in particular at the press conference seemed to doubt my motives: TV3's David Di Somma. He kept hammering the same questions about ICL and wouldn't let go, even to the point of questioning why I was citing health reasons because I was looking healthy. What that had to do with anything, I don't know.

My reply was: 'I have been a diabetic for 15 or 16 years. OK, in appearance I might look fine to you. But I take four injections a day of insulin. You have no idea what I go through day in, day out — and not just to play cricket, but to live.'

There were some who thought I was using my medical status as a quick way to get out of my contract. But that wasn't the case. My health did create pretty serious problems after I came back from South Africa, including being hospitalised. What started out as a simple case of the flu turned into something more serious. The way my diabetes works, whenever you get sick the illness compounds everything.

Three days after first getting ill, I literally could not move off the couch. I ended up going to the local 24-hour medical clinic. At the time I was badly dehydrated and was put on a drip for three hours. The medical staff wanted to admit me to hospital overnight because of the amount of liquid I had lost. Being a bit stubborn, I said, 'I will go on this drip for three hours. Then when I get home I will drink a lot of fluids and see how I am tomorrow.'

They told me I had to drink six litres of water through the night. I only got through three and a half litres, going to the toilet every half hour, and I woke up in the morning feeling exactly the same. I took myself back to the clinic, told them I was no better and I was sent straight to A&E. I was admitted to hospital where I stayed two days. While I was suffering the flu, my diabetes had put everything out of kilter and my blood-sugar levels were all over the place. It took me about a week and a half to recover.

Heath Mills (New Zealand Cricket Players' Association boss): It was absolutely unfair for Craig to have his character questioned when he explained his reasons to retire. There is absolutely no doubt in my mind that Craig McMillan would have retired from international cricket at the start of the 2007–08 season, whether he was playing for the ICL or not. Certainly I can see how it might look to some people, that he retires and then takes the ICL offer — they see some sort of conspiracy there. But I can absolutely say that he was gone either way.

I look at him and see this guy who has been on the international merry-go-round for more than 10 years. He got to 30, he hadn't yet got to his prime years, but he had spent more than a decade in international cricket. I don't think people really understand how hard that life is. It is not to say guys shirk or moan about it, but the fact is that these guys are away from home 10 months of the year. There is huge pressure on them with family when they are on the international roller-coaster.

Craig and Cherie have two young ones. Cherie has been at home a lot of the time with the two of them. Craig has had his medical issues with his diabetes which has really tormented him the last couple of years. He really needed to weigh up what life was about and his health was deteriorating.

John Bracewell (Black Caps coach): You have to be realistic that this is a one-off opportunity. I don't begrudge Craig for making his choice at all. In fact, good on him. He had made it clear that he was retiring, saying: 'These are the reasons I have retired, this is what I can now fit in given my health and family. I can't do it 24/7, but I can do it for six weeks in the year.' A contract in New Zealand is 24/7 — it is as simple as that. You are never not a Black Cap. Once you sign that contract you are a Black Cap in your behaviour, the way you train and everything you do. Craig can now go and be who Craig wants to be in India, get paid bloody good money for it, and no one over here is going to give a toss and everyone can remember the good times. So good on him!

We are bottom of the pay table — it is as simple as that. So of course we are vulnerable. That is just the way of the world as a New Zealand cricketer. And we have been the bottom of the pay table for quite some time. That is why it was sometimes frustrating with the 2004 England tour, when guys spent most of the tour touting for positions and meeting up with agents and clubs. But then on the other hand you think, 'Well I can't really blame you because this is an opportunity to clear a major part of your mortgage, be able to buy a rental and set yourself up as a business of some sort to secure you after cricket.' As a New Zealand cricketer, we are not the same as Australia or England — we don't get paid anywhere near as much. Sometimes you have to accept reality regardless of how frustrating it can be.

Steve Rixon (Black Caps coach 1996–99): I think it is absolutely imperative that someone like Macca takes up the opportunity they have been offered in India. I would love to have seen him play another three or four years for the Black Caps, but he has done his time. And if New Zealand Cricket wanted so desperately for them to play here, they would find extra money for these guys to stay in the game longer. Yes, player wages have improved in New Zealand, but that was to do with the players' association coming in several years ago.

While New Zealand Cricket have made more of a contribution in terms of wages than they previously have, it is not acceptable that you could be an international cricketer for the Black Caps and you could actually be earning more money playing state cricket in Australia. It doesn't make a lot of sense to me if you're trying to get your best team on the park. If you are looking for a fault in the whole system, maybe New Zealand Cricket should have dug a bit deeper. These guys have a job to do and if you look after someone well enough in business, they don't go anywhere.

John R. Reid (former New Zealand captain and ICC match referee): I have no problems with Craig and the other guys signing to play in India at all. They are professional sportsmen, they have a limited life and have to go where the money is — it is that simple. It is the same thing with the yachties; it is the same thing with rugby players. If you are running around and good enough to earn that money, go and earn it.

It's not being disloyal to New Zealand Cricket at all. He is just using his ability to earn some money for his family. If you're good enough, go and earn it. These people who say something else simply don't know what they are talking about.

I was granted a release, but that wasn't entirely the end of the issue. Instead, a couple of very comical side issues ensued. First, New Zealand Cricket came out and effectively banned the so-called 'defectors' — me, Nathan Astle, Chris Cairns, Daryl Tuffey, Chris Harris and Hamish Marshall — from playing for the Black Caps. However, Nathan and Chris [Cairns] had retired from cricket. Hamish Marshall was also playing County cricket in England and wasn't eligible for New Zealand.

For a start, New Zealand Cricket can't ban us. That is the funniest thing about it. As a player, if I didn't want to retire but still wanted to sign with the ICL, I could still legally play for New Zealand. It would probably go to court, but judging from the discussions I've had with my lawyer, I'm sure I would have won that case. New Zealand Cricket obviously don't want it to go that far, because if the player won the case against them it would set a precedent for all the other players to challenge them.

The other side issue saw us being banned from our planned involvement in a blockbuster Bollywood movie. Soon after signing with the ICL, I got a call from Nathan saying he had been approached to star in a Bollywood cricket movie. He said they wanted two other New Zealanders involved, Daryl Tuffey and me. It would involve a couple of days filming after the Australia–India test in Sydney in January 2008. It was reasonably well-paid for a couple of days. And it was quite exciting to consider that you were going to be involved in an Indian cricket movie. It would have been huge. The Australians who were going to be involved were Michael Hussey and Brett Lee. There were big names in the movie and to have a New Zealand input was great.

We signed the contracts and organised our flights. But four days before we were due to go I got a phone call from a woman in the production company to say unfortunately we couldn't be used in the movie. The Board of Control for Cricket in India had instructed them that anyone who had an association with the ICL was not to be used in the film. From the production company's point of view, the BCCI were helping them out with grounds and a few other things in India. So they couldn't jeopardise that assistance by having us in the movie.

NZ cricketers upset after Bollywood roles canned
NZPA, 3 January 2008

Three former New Zealand international cricketers are upset after they were barred from featuring in a Bollywood film because they have signed with the rebel Indian Cricket League.

Nathan Astle, Daryl Tuffey and Craig McMillan were to have supporting roles in the film Victory *but the Board of Control for Cricket in India has wielded its significant influence to have the trio cut from the cast, effectively costing them a combined AU$40,000 (NZ$46,000) in side earnings, Melbourne newspaper* The Age *reported today.*

The film needed the backing of the BCCI.

The ICL is running in direct competition with the International Cricket Council's own Twenty20 tournament, the Indian Premier League, which is a brainchild of the BCCI.

The newspaper said it was understood each of the NZ players stood to make up to AU$13,000 for one and a half days' filming.

Astle blasted the BCCI for interfering with his off-field income. 'To me it's a bit farcical, really; they're just being silly. It is out-and-out wrong,' he said.

'The thing is it's starting to affect our earnings off the field. The big issue is that I don't think anyone, no matter how significant their standing in the game, should have a pull over our capacity to earn off the field.'

Australian test star Brett Lee has a speaking role, while Stuart Clark, Michael Hussey and Shaun Tait will also make cameo appearances in the movie, described as cricket's version of Bend It Like Beckham.

'We had been in discussions (with the producers), that started four or five months ago,' Astle said.

'They have had the hard word put on them by the BCCI to stop us from playing. I understand if they want to take that stance on the cricket field but this goes beyond that, and I think it's quite ridiculous, actually. I mean, this has nothing to do with playing — it's a movie about cricket. I was just supposed to rock up and bowl a few deliveries.'

The movie producers were gutted about it. But it was out of their hands and we were scrapped. They ended up replacing us with Kyle Mills and Chris Martin, but they didn't get to go over either. The days they were supposed to be doing the filming it was raining in Sydney so it was postponed. The guys were unavailable due to playing commitments when the shooting was rescheduled. It ended up being a sad story all round. It just shows the political world that cricket revolves around at times, especially when you talk about India.

> **Daniel Vettori:** The advent of the ICL has been a lucky thing for a lot of guys, giving them financial security for a number of years. And with all of the guys who have signed, I don't think you can begrudge them anything — this is just the

world we live in. It would be great if one day we could see Craig McMillan playing Twenty20 cricket for New Zealand.

I look at the guys who have defected, and Craig McMillan and Shane Bond are the two guys who I would most love to have back in the side. They still had a number of years left in their careers which could have been hugely productive. It is sad you don't get to play with your mates, but you don't begrudge them anything and you understand the rationale behind it. And so should everyone else!

Sadly, I can't see any of the guys who are signed to the ICL ever playing for their respective nations in the present state of cricket. But I think New Zealand Cricket would be in a stronger position if a policy allowing that was in place.

Until New Zealand Cricket or even the England and Wales Cricket Board get taken to court over it and a player wins a restraint of trade case, nothing will change. Until someone has the gumption to do that, the powerful boards such as the BCCI will continue to decide where and when you can and can't play. At some stage it needs to be brought to a head — and the only way for the players to win is for it to go to court.

The game of my life

My introduction to cricket was a world away from the exciting and ground-breaking times that were involved in the debut ICL Twenty20 competition. My first cricketing memory is of my mum and dad taking me down to Burwood Park in Christchurch, when I must have been about five or six. There was an old fella there with white hair, and that was Bill Duncan. He always used to wear this rep floppy Canterbury junior cricket hat — and 25 years on he still stands out with his red hat down at the East Christchurch-Shirley Cricket Club.

My parents were massively supportive of me right from the time I started playing cricket. They took me to sport every Saturday — they've probably watched just about every match I have ever played in Christchurch. And they were just as supportive of my sister Kathryn when she played tennis and netball. But at the same time there was never any pressure from my dad, Lindsay, or my mum, Judith, to play any particular sport. My dad's number one sporting forte was golf, and he went on to play for Canterbury in the Tower Interprovincials.

It wasn't just my parents who used to follow me around Christchurch to watch me play. Quite often my grandparents would be there too. Many years on my nana even travelled to Brisbane with mum to watch my test debut against Australia in 1997. I always had a good support team from an early age, which was fantastic, and they have been continuously supportive. I have always been aware of that support and it has been a big part of me.

After playing cricket for a year, I thought I would give something else a go. It was a decision which saw me take up tennis — but it was a career which lasted just two weeks, with Bill getting wind of it, turning up at the local tennis club and dragging me back to Burwood Park. Since then cricket has pretty much been it for me. And the relationship I built up with

Bill Duncan lasted for most of my formative years, as he coached most of my under-age rep sides — teams that included guys such as Shane Bond and professional footballer Ryan Nelsen.

Bill Duncan (Craig's schoolboy coach): Even now people will ask me if there is any kid playing in Canterbury who was like a young McMillan. And the reply is simple: 'Hell, no.' I have been involved in kids' cricket for so long and I have never seen anything like him. He was really, really special. His cricket came along nicely and I think the fact he was a little bit bigger than kids his age helped him out too.

And he didn't just impress with the bat either — his bowling was also far too good for a lot of the kids he was playing against. If someone had the good fortune to get Craig out for a low score, something that didn't happen too often, he normally came back and got lots of wickets. There was no game he played that he didn't do well in. He basically had a reputation of having a golden arm.

There was one game at Burwood Park where a young Craig McMillan wore out three cricket bats in one innings. He finished up with 185. In those years that Craig played in primary school cricket there were so many times when the opposition umpire cut him off at the ankles. There was one game when he was given run out even though he was standing next to the umpire, level with the wickets. He would be given caught behind despite missing the ball by a couple of inches.

In 1990 he was the star of the South Island Primary School championships in Gore. On the first day McMillan thumped South Canterbury — during the innings he peppered a few cars with sixes. The next day he opened and the partnership for the first wicket was over 100. By the time it was broken, Craig had scored another century and the other kid he was batting with had scored about four runs. Craig still has the highest score in that tournament's history with 152 not out off 145 balls. He also has the highest average, a staggering 154. He was absolutely ruthless. He just kept doing the damage. He got about eight centuries in the 1989–90 season — there was nothing else like him! Even at a young age he showed the character of a fighter who hated to be beaten.

Judith McMillan (Craig's mum): He always loved being outside. He wasn't one to sit inside with a book; all he wanted to do was go out and kick a ball around or play some other sport. And he was quite happy to do it by himself. He would spend a lot of time on the trampoline, getting Lindsay to throw the ball at him so he could dive left or right to stop it. Plus he had the sock with a cricket ball on the clothes line which he used to practise his batting with. He just loved any sport.

We just thought all kids played sport like that, until Bill Duncan came and saw us and said he believed Craig was something special. But over time we saw that he did have a good cricketing brain for his age. Craig didn't think he was anything special when he was a kid; he just loved playing with the other kids and being involved.

The support Craig has had hasn't just come from Lindsay and me. He's had aunties and uncles, grandparents and his sister Kathryn supporting him too. Every weekend was going to the park, either for soccer or cricket. He has given us a lot of pleasure too; we have enjoyed it.

Lindsay McMillan (Craig's dad): We went to a school sports event and they had a cricket ball throwing competition. They had a teacher standing where she thought the appropriate place was and he just about cleaned her out. He was quite strong at throwing the ball and could throw further than any other kids.

I don't think anything ever comes easily, but when I was young I used to live to play cricket. I wanted to play it every day of my life. I just loved playing the game — whether it was batting or bowling didn't matter. I used to be a fast bowler when I was a kid. I was lucky because I had matured quicker than some of the other kids at my age. Because I was taller than the other kids, I could scare them a bit. At East Shirley we had concrete strips in the nets and we would use the composite balls, which used to skid on and gather pace off the surface. I suppose I had a perverse pleasure in seeing kids ducking and weaving, even at an early age.

Going through all of my age-grade teams, I always used to be a little bigger than everyone else, so when I bowled I was always a bit faster than them. And I could hit the ball further. I probably dominated from an early age in a lot of those teams. I tended also to always be captain.

I made the First XI at Shirley Boys' High School in fourth form, playing with guys who were three or four years older. That was different both in terms of sport and socially. You had seventh formers who were out partying. It just made me grow up a bit quicker. Even back then, it was something that really helped me. Our First XI ended up playing in the second grade competition in Christchurch, one step down from seniors. And a lot of those players had played senior cricket and were at the stage of winding down. It really was a great experience and meant that from the age of 15 I was playing against grown men. As schoolboys we got sledged — but we had a really good side and we did very well.

Shirley Boys' had produced cricketers like Nathan Astle, Michael Papps and Gary Stead. Former All Black lock Chris Jack also went to school there. That was the thing I liked about the school. Generally, I went there to play sport. I was one of those kids who just loved playing sport — it didn't matter what it was. I don't really know why, but there was never any doubt for me that I was going to be a sportsman.

I also played soccer right through to seventh form. That was until I broke my ankle at a secondary school tournament in Auckland. I was 18 at the time and it meant I missed the start of the next cricket season, which really forced me to decide whether I wanted to keep playing football. The fact that it interrupted the start of my cricket season pretty much sealed it for me: I didn't want to miss cricket games for anything, so I made the decision give up soccer.

I had a lot of reasons to be encouraged about the direction my cricket was heading, including making New Zealand Youth teams. The first tour was a trip to Pakistan in 1994 when Chris Kuggeleijn was coach and the great John R. Reid was our manager. I was 16 at the time and I ended up having four years playing in the youth team. On that first tour there were guys like Andrew Penn, Robbie Lawson, Kerry Walmsley, Richard Jones — who was captain and the star — and Martin Croy. Two years later and I captained the side to England, by which stage I had already played first-class cricket for Canterbury. John Bracewell was our coach.

John R. Reid: I took him to Pakistan in 1994. I didn't know any of the guys at the start of the tour but Craig McMillan really was one of the better players in the side. Richard Jones was the captain and he scored so many runs that he constantly got the team on the front foot in most of the games. And Craig wasn't too far behind.

Our second tour together was in 1996 to England. Some of the guys on that tour went on to make the big time — Craig, as well as Daniel Vettori, Jacob Oram and Matthew Bell. I was manager again and Craig was our captain. What I saw from him as a leader on that tour, and how he developed later, has made me say and think many times that he should have been the next New Zealand cricket captain. And I still think that. He had a tremendous tour: he scored a lot of runs and handled the captaincy very well. To be a captain you have to have the ability to lead from the front, something that Craig always did.

John Bracewell: It was probably one of the most enjoyable tours that I have ever been on, even as a player. It had such a variance of players in terms of where they were in their maturity, their cricket and their life. You had a guy like Dan who was still thinking about what he was going to do at university. Then you had a guy like Craig who was so much older than the other guys, in terms of not only cricket experience but he had that gambler's attitude then — he had that almost bulletproof mentality.

One of the reasons we won that series was because of the gambler in Craig, the willingness to take a punt, the willingness to back himself and his team. And it brought through some cricketers that perhaps would not otherwise have emerged in New Zealand's conservative style. I think a guy like Dan emerged a long time earlier than he would have done otherwise because Craig was willing to back him — as a 16 year old — to win a series.

He was certainly a good leader on the field. He had a very good cricket brain. There was always that Christchurch, Canterbury detachment from the social world. Because of his health he was never a big drinker. He didn't mind sitting and having a night punting, whereas a lot of young guys weren't even up to that stage. I enjoyed that under-19 tour so much that I kept an eye on all of those guys. Seeing him, Dan and Jacob develop was quite a rewarding thing for me.

Daniel Vettori: I had seen Craig play on TV a couple of times and I knew that he was a pretty good player, an aggressive player. When I got selected on that tour in 1996 I was pretty excited to be able to play with guys of his ilk and calibre. He had already played first-class cricket at a young age, which showed how good he was. Craig was the captain, John R. Reid was the manager and Braces was the coach — they were three very forthright people.

My first recollection of him was at an indoor training session where we umpired ourselves — if you were out, you were out. I was only 16, Craig was a couple of years older than me, and I gave him out. Craig wasn't too happy and as he walked past just said, 'What the f... was that for?' That was my first real impression of him. But after that we became close mates and have gone on to play a lot of cricket together. I have always enjoyed his company.

Craig is the spitting image of John R. Reid in a lot of ways, especially the way he attacked the game. So to have a guy like Macca, who went over and didn't bow to anyone and just wanted to get on and win games, was brilliant. The English had a lot of players who were playing first-class cricket and were well known. But Macca led by example in terms of, 'This is my team, I am coming over here to win, I am not coming over here to make friends'. That led to a confident group of guys.

The fact that I'd played alongside guys who were older than me while coming through the grades really helped with my confidence. And it was the same when I made it into the Canterbury side. It was a team which had some pretty seasoned campaigners, with Lee Germon, Rod Latham, Chris Cairns, Blair Hartland and Stu Roberts. I always consider myself to be reasonably shy; if I don't know someone I am not the sort of guy who will go up to them and make small talk. So going into that side I remember being pretty quiet and trying to take it all in. There were so many experienced guys, and one of them, Roddy Latham, took me under his wing. He went out of his way to look after me and make sure I felt OK, so much so that I got called 'JR' which stood for 'Junior Roddy'.

Denis Aberhart (former Canterbury and Black Caps coach): When Macca first came into the Canterbury side he had played under-age rep cricket and rep soccer as well. He was a confident wee fella then. He often gets mistaken for being arrogant, and I think that is far from the truth. He is confident and competitive, and was like that even at that young age, when he came into the dressing room in Canterbury which had some pretty experienced, hard-nosed players in the side. There were people like Rod Latham and Mark Priest. But he got their respect very quickly because he gave back what they gave him in his own way. He showed that he had real ability and talent right from the start — he never took a backward step and went out there and played with confidence and aggression.

I went straight from school to playing for Canterbury. I was never going to go to university and I left school halfway through my seventh form year. I really only turned up during that year to play sport. At the time I had a part-time job, working for a courier company in their warehouse. Freight containers would turn up and I would unpack them and put them in the bays. Some nights I would be called into work at midnight. Most days I started at 6 am and worked until 8 am. Sometimes I would go home, have a shower and go to school. Other times I would just go home and sleep. That seventh form was probably a non-event really.

I continued the job part-time for a while. But once I got picked for Canterbury I had to give it up because we started travelling for the domestic season. When I made the Canterbury team something had to give and it was always the job that was going to get the flick. And that was the last job I ever had outside cricket.

We were lucky at Canterbury as we were one of the better-paid provinces. Five of the associations were contracted to New Zealand Cricket, but Canterbury already had a contract in place with Canterbury Draught. Looking back, I think my first contract with Canterbury Cricket was for $1000 a season, with match fees on top of that. We also got bonuses for each win. And that just seemed like a goldmine to me.

As a young kid I was living at home and it was all good. I didn't have too many cares in the world really. It was all about playing cricket and trying to do well. I was confident that this was where I was destined to be. I went about doing what I needed to in order to reach my ultimate goal, playing for New Zealand.

My biggest battle

My life changed forever when I was in fifth form. One night I felt really dry and thirsty and I woke up in the middle of the night with bad cramps — my hamstrings were screaming out; it was unbearable. About a week later, the same thing happened again.

At the same time I was falling asleep at school. In the afternoons I was at the back of class just dozing off. I would finish school at 3 pm, be home by 3.30 pm and then would sleep through to 6 pm. I had no energy; I was just so knackered.

Mum ended up taking me to the doctor and he told me that I had all the symptoms of being a diabetic. My blood-sugar level was 33 — the normal level is between 4 and 7. The reading is based on the amount of glucose in the blood and is expressed at millimoles per litre. It is an extreme level of sugar to have in your body and I was nearly hospitalised. Eventually, I was diagnosed with Type 1 diabetes, an autoimmune disease that results in the permanent destruction of insulin-producing cells of the pancreas. Type 1 is lethal unless treated with insulin via injections to replace the missing hormone.

John Denton (General Manager, Diabetes New Zealand, Auckland): One of the great things about the body is that it is designed to distribute insulin when needed, right to the minute. But when you have Type 1, we don't get that privilege, so we have to rely on insulin injections and ensure we eat at the right time. Normally, carbohydrates are turned into glucose and that gets absorbed into the blood. It then goes around the blood into the cells. The clever little thing that carries it out of the blood is a thing called insulin — it is like a truck that carts the stuff around and deposits it into the right cells so we have the energy we need to do all the things we want to do.

The problem is, if you are like Craig and have Type 1 diabetes, the only insulin you get is by external injections. That's because the body has given up making it altogether. The game in diabetes is to take insulin through injections, which tries to mirror what your body should naturally be doing. The warnings can be sweating, your eyesight beginning to go and getting confused. The trick is to spot it coming and deal to it really quickly. If you don't get it right you risk getting hypoglycaemia which has all these funny symptoms. First of all you get a bit foggy, then you get a bit dreamy, then you start to act drunk and then you fall over.

I remember going to the diabetes clinic with Mum in Christchurch and being shown what I had to do in terms of having to inject myself with needles. I burst into tears; my biggest thought was that this was going to stop me playing sport. I know now that there are bigger and more important things in life, but at the time that was all that I could think about. We were driving home and I broke down. Mum was crying too. We just couldn't believe it.

Judith McMillan: The tests came back saying Craig had diabetes and the doctor said that he couldn't believe that Craig hadn't been in a coma. They asked whether he could be put into hospital. I said no, as he had put up with it for this long I wanted to see if he could leave it for the next week so he could go to the New Zealand academy camp. The next week we went off to the diabetes centre. Within half an hour he was told how often he was going to have to inject himself with insulin — that was pretty traumatic for all of us.

Craig had a bit of time off school and his levels didn't come down fast enough. So he wasn't allowed to play any sport and he couldn't go to his cricket academy. That, for him, was a disaster. Craig eventually agreed to having four injections a day of insulin and then was able to start playing sport again. It was a shock for everybody. And as a parent you go through the guilt, asking: 'Why wasn't it me? Why did it have to be my child?' At the time it seemed just so unfair. But I thought he took it really well. He got on with it.

It was pretty shattering to be diagnosed as a diabetic while I was still just a teenager. In the early days I used to have to take a syringe, insert it into a bottle of insulin, inject it and then dispose of the syringe. Now I use an object that looks like a pen; I just carry it around and no one knows what it is. There are two things I have to be wary of: a 'hypo' episode when I have low blood-sugar levels and a 'hyper' when I have high blood-sugar levels. Having diabetes was something that I felt was pretty hard to tell my friends at school. But once I learnt that it didn't have to stop me playing cricket, that I was just going to be a little bit different to everyone else, things certainly started to look up.

But that didn't mean I was ready to tell the world what I had been diagnosed with. For one thing, I didn't want to gain any sympathy from being a diabetic. I also didn't want my health condition to be held against me when it came to various team selections. What's more, I didn't ever want my diabetes to be used as an excuse for any on-field error.

In my first season of first-class cricket for Canterbury, however, I learnt a pretty harsh lesson that it wasn't a great idea to keep things quiet. We travelled to Wellington for a Shell Cup semi-final, and on the day before the game we were warming up with a bit of soccer at the Basin Reserve. Because we had travelled during lunchtime, I hadn't eaten enough. So by the time we got to the ground and started running around and sweating, my blood sugar was low. I was goalie and just stood there and let someone run past me to score. Guys like Rod Latham were coming up yelling at me for letting them score. Then it happened again and Roddy was punching me because I had let a couple of goals in.

> **Denis Aberhart:** When he came into the side he didn't tell us about his diabetes. No one had told me that this fellow could all of a sudden fall over and die. We were playing soccer the day before the match in Wellington. Macca let in a goal and then started talking with a slurred speech. Roddy called him a useless bugger and he kept saying, 'We've got to get the one-twos going.' I said to Michael Owens, 'Is he alright?', and was told that actually Macca was a diabetic. I asked Macca what he had to help him, and he still kept saying: 'We've got to get one-twos going.' I later rang his mother and she said he didn't want to tell me because he thought he might not make the team. It was a fright early on, but we learnt how to manage it. It was amazing that before that day he was managing it by having several injections a day and I never knew.

I was pretty much in cloud cuckoo land because my blood sugar was low — Michael Owens was the only other person in the team who knew I had diabetes so the other guys didn't know what was going on. In hindsight, keeping it all quiet wasn't the greatest move. No one really knew what to do. I know they went back to my bag to get my insulin pen and give me a jab — but that is the worst thing to do. When you have low blood sugar, you need to get sugar into your blood-stream and you certainly don't want anymore insulin. They were going to get my pen and give me an injection which would probably have put me in a coma, or maybe even worse. Thankfully they didn't and in the end I got a hot chocolate.

> **Judith McMillan:** I got a phone call from Denis saying, 'Mrs Mac, why the f… didn't you tell me about Craig?' I made out I didn't know anything and said, 'What do you mean, Denis?' He replied, 'We have just taken Craig to the medical centre. I didn't know he had diabetes.' I didn't realise at that stage that Craig

hadn't told him. We didn't think it was our place to butt in and tell his coaches or anyone else; it was up to Craig to do that. But he hadn't quite got around to telling Denis. From then on Craig was a lot more open about it. I don't think he felt all that comfortable talking about it openly until that incident when he was away with Canterbury.

What happened in Wellington just showed me that if I missed out on eating during a regular lunch or dinner time, it could have dire consequences down the track. It was also a wake-up call to me that I finally had to let people know what I was suffering from, what brought on my blood-sugar level highs and lows and what treatment was required. But it certainly wasn't the only time my diabetes caused dramas for me while on the road.

After I scored my first test hundred against Zimbabwe at Wellington's Basin Reserve in February 1998 I went off to do some media work. It had been such a draining day, I got back into the changing room and really just needed to chill out and do my stuff. But I got whisked away to see the media straight off and I wasn't really in any state to be there. It was just one of those things. I was having a hypo and kept saying the same thing. I was just talking rubbish, repeating myself, and I came across as very vacant.

Lindsay McMillan: I can still remember him trying to speak on the TV. And it was surprising that there were so many people who didn't know he had diabetes, who said how badly Craig had spoken. But, in a way, it was good it happened because it got out there. And Craig was normally well-spoken. Even from the days he was going into the academy environment from the age of 15 he was getting media training like the rest of the young players.

One hypo in particular gave my team-mates something to laugh about during Pakistan's tour of New Zealand in 2001. Stephen Fleming brought me on to bowl but unfortunately I wasn't quite all with it and started running off Daryl Tuffey's run-up to bowl my medium-pacers. I just thought I was bowling normally. I remember Flem asking: 'Are you alright?' I told him I was and he told me he thought differently. I said, 'Bullshit mate, I'm fine. Just let me bowl.' I couldn't understand what he was on about until I saw it all on TV later.

Steve Rixon: I called Macca up to my hotel room in Manchester during the 1999 tour to talk about a number of issues in his game and how I wanted him to approach a certain match. And he looked at me like a drug addict who had just shot up — his blank face kept looking back at me. I kept talking and looking at him and I was thinking, 'This isn't right.' Then he started talking about something else and I had no idea what was going on. I didn't realise until later that he was having one of his sugar attacks — I had never seen it before. I looked at him and said, 'Macca, what is going on? I am not understanding you.'

When I realised, I got Dan up into the room and he gave Macca some jellybeans. It was basically a great impersonation of a man talking to himself; he didn't have any idea what I was saying and I had no idea what he was trying to say. I was trying to be serious, trying to get something back, but what I was getting back was coming in Chinese. What happened at Manchester really taught me that I should know about this as well.

Being around Macca helped me appreciate what diabetes is and what it can do to people. Every time before a lunch break we would have to make arrangements for him to come off the field five minutes earlier so he could test his levels and get himself right. He used to sit beside me and put this needle into his little love-handle on the front of him. It dawned on me just how difficult a time it was for him. He had to do it religiously. He couldn't miss having his injections, and there had to be a balance in everything he ate. That meant he had to be very wary of what was served, especially in places like India or Pakistan.

An appreciation of what Macca was going through really was dawning on a lot of people in the set-up — it was an awareness thing. And that awareness became a pretty serious part of the whole mental attitude of the guy too. He had to be very disciplined in what he was doing, not that he was always as disciplined with the bat or ball in hand.

John Bracewell: I have only experienced Craig going through sugar-level issues two or three times. Nathan Astle was always really good: in the New Zealand side he was one person who knew him inside out and knew when his sugar levels were down and things like that. The first time it happened I wondered whether he had been drinking — it was like that. Then he would start repeating things — it can be quite scary.

It is one of those situations where, as a parent, you think that you should do your St John's first-aid course just in case. With Craig, you recognised it and then wondered what you could do about it. The first time it happened I rang the physio and said, 'Look, I think we have a bit of an issue.' It was all because our team food was late and things started to drop for him.

I would say the great majority of the public still probably don't even know that he suffers from diabetes, but having said that I don't think it often affected his performance on the park. I think he controlled it really well and within the team there was a pretty good understanding of it. I think his attitude has helped him get through diabetes.

Sometimes you get warning signs: quite often I would get a sweaty top lip, double vision or pins and needles in my lips. That would let me know I was getting a bit low and I would go off the field and take my jelly beans. On occasions, as it did against Pakistan in Christchurch, it would just come up and hit me before I could do anything about it. It could take 20 minutes to come right, but even then you are not totally 100 per cent for the rest of the day. Your coordination and everything else is just down a little.

Over the years my team-mates have been able to pick up on some of the tell-tale signs that everything is not right. But probably the best judge of that is Cherie. When I get hypo, with low blood-sugar levels, Cherie says she can pick it straight away. She can tell by the look in my eyes or the by way I talk — she has got it down pat. There are times when I'll say she's wrong, but sure enough if I do a test on my sugar levels . . .

> **Cherie McMillan:** I can tell just by looking at him. He could get up to walk out of the room and I could tell by looking at him from behind that his blood sugar was low. And there have also been times when he has been batting when I have picked that his blood sugar is a bit low and question what he is going to do next.
>
> I don't think people, and I include myself, realise just how tough it has been for him. I see him have his injections four times a day and just brush it off — it is just part of life. I probably don't understand fully what he goes through. He could go out to bat and score two runs or he could be out there for 150 runs. A lot of people think he just gets up in the morning and goes out on the field. And with things like a day-nighter, all his meals are completely out of order. It is the same when he is travelling with all of the time zones. I don't know how he has done it and I can honestly say I've never heard him complain or use his diabetes as an excuse.

My health issue is something that is ongoing. It is not like saying to yourself, 'Right I am good at the moment, I can relax.' You have to be constantly thinking about it and that is very tricky. With normal people, their body regulates it. You just eat the food and your body reacts to the food you put in. But with diabetes, I have to try to guess with the food I have eaten just how much insulin I need. It is such a fine line. If I get it wrong, I will be too low. If I haven't given myself enough, I get too high. Throw in exercise on top of that, which can swing it either way, and it is an absolute juggling act. The tough thing is that with cricket, I don't know how long I am going to bat — whether it is going to be two minutes or three hours. And if I get it wrong, then it is an absolute nightmare.

One thing that made my condition even trickier was that from an early age I have been really fussy with food: I am pretty much your meat and three veg sort of guy. There might be sandwiches for us at the ground but I wouldn't eat them because I wouldn't like mustard or tomato in the sandwich. So it was my responsibility to go out and buy food that I would eat, meaning I would never put myself in the situation where I was going to be stuck. So I would go to the local supermarket and purchase things like bananas and muesli bars, and I would always get a couple of Moro bars and some jelly beans to leave in my cricket bag in case I needed a sugar fix.

Having diabetes, you are supposed to have your main meals of the day at a regular time, plus ensure you have snacks during the day. And at times that is very difficult when you are living a cricketer's lifestyle. Being a professional cricketer, we would sometimes not get back to our hotels until 8 or 8.30 pm — and if it was after a day–night one-day international, it would be a lot later. It meant I was eating after 9 o'clock at night, as opposed to 6 to 6.30 pm, which would have been my normal time-frame. That puts you out of whack. And when you are eating that late, it isn't ideal for weight issues and a whole lot of things. But, as a cricketer, that is just something you have to get around.

At times I found it difficult because my patterns were thrown right out. Sometimes we would do debriefs on other teams, having quite laborious meetings, and these sessions were always scheduled around dinner time. We discussed it a number of times and tried various things, sometimes ordering my dinner at the start of the meeting so that it would be cooked and ready as soon as the session was over. This was the juggling act that I had to go through to try to get on the park. Other issues to contend with were travel, including long-distance flights and time zone differences.

John Denton: When you jump on a plane, as Craig would have to have done a lot during his cricketing career, it can throw you around. With the time difference changes, you often have to spend a day or two getting back to normal. It is like steering an ocean liner with only the vision of your stern. When you are stuck with the travel that he has had to do, plus the times of games, your activity which you can't control and the fact your food could arrive late, I think it is remarkable what he has been able to achieve.

John R. Reid: Even on the youth tour to Pakistan in 1994 he used to have to leave the field shortly before lunch to check his blood-sugar levels and have an injection. That must have been terrible for him. I had to carry a life-saving injection to grounds and put it in a fridge in the dressing room or the ground manager's office. It was on hand in case Craig had a bad turn and couldn't self-medicate. I was the one that would have to give it to him — at the time I didn't know much about giving injections or diabetes. But I quickly became aware of just how dedicated he was. He continued playing, after being diagnosed at an early age, and didn't make a fuss about having injections every day. I am very aware of how brave he is.

Daniel Vettori: We just sat back and while we would never wish it on anyone, we admired the fact he could play international cricket while still combating what is a very tough illness. It wasn't easy and he got more admiration from the team for battling those things. There were obviously things he had to give up. He wasn't a big drinker and wouldn't come out for a few beers because his diabetes wouldn't allow it.

But Macca just got on with it, and it was just part of his life. He knew that he had to come off the field 10 minutes before lunch; he had a pretty good feel for what he had to do. It was a burden and you could tell there were some days when he was completely exhausted. Long innings really took it out of him too — he would ride the highs and lows of the illness and it would wear him down at times.

Gilbert Enoka (mental skills coach): I have marvelled at how he has been able to do it. He would get on aeroplanes and have to find a cooler to put his insulin in. So much planning went into it, especially when the Black Caps were going to some of the third world countries and didn't have some of the facilities we needed at the ground. A hell of a lot went on for him behind the scenes. The great quality about it is that he has never moaned about it. Never once in the 10 years I worked with him did I ever hear him whinge about his diabetes — it became part of the: 'This is my normal. This is what I have to do to manage myself.' I marvelled at his ability to do it in a normal way.

Diabetes was something I always thought would curtail my career. I never believed I would be able to play as long as other guys were able to, because the management of it just became too difficult. And I never envisaged being able to play fulltime until I was 34 or 35, to the point that I had a bet with Nathan Astle that I would retire at 30. I ended up being retired a month after my 31st birthday, so I was about a year out.

Maybe if I wasn't a diabetic, there might have been the opportunity to have a bit more longevity and play for a few more years. And while I was keen to keep the status of my health pretty quiet early on, there came a time when I had to go public. If I can get some awareness out there and if it helps other people with diabetes to see me playing cricket and doing well and that gives them confidence to go after their own goals, it has to be a good thing.

John Denton: It is hugely important that we have someone high profile like Craig McMillan who is prepared to talk about his diabetes. We have so few people who are on the public radar who will own up to this. This is the Cinderella of the health world — it has always been locked in the back cupboard and the closet door has never been opened. We desperately need this to get out, both so people understand how to treat someone who has got it and to dispel some of the myths associated with diabetes.

We urgently need people like Craig standing up and announcing that they have diabetes. In many ways, what he has done has put a human face to the disease — it is just like what John Kirwan has done for mental health. It is a huge step forward and we need more of the Craigs in this world to follow. Not only is Craig prepared to talk about it, he has also done a lot for us over the years. He has donated signed bats, playing gear and photos to our annual fund-raising auctions and they have proven to be popular items. He has been a great supporter!

If diabetes was bird flu or anything contagious, the government would know exactly who had it. So it is all based on estimates and they say there are about 180,000 people in New Zealand at the moment with diabetes, and about 10 per cent of them have Type 1. Diabetes causes more than half of the heart attacks in this country, the majority of renal failure and about 65 per cent of blindness. It is the biggest contributor to the amputation of feet and legs. For every person who is diagnosed with diabetes, there is probably someone else out there walking around with diabetes who doesn't know they have it. Then there is a whole armada of other people who are waiting to join the queue — the obesity epidemic and the lack of exercise is pushing people this way. That is why this is the biggest health problem this country faces in the next 20 years.

I would be lying if I said it hasn't been demanding to try to keep my health on an even keel during my international career. It has been a massive challenge. And I've got no doubts that there are a lot of sports where my diabetes would have been a lot easier to manage. But with cricket, where you have to regulate it for up to nine hours, it is bloody difficult.

And that is one of the real beauties of Twenty20 cricket for me. The game has such a short time-span, just three and a half hours, so it is much easier to keep my health in check. From that point of view, it has been brilliant for me. Twenty20 has allowed me to play good cricket and not compromise my health in the way I probably used to do when I was playing full days, sometimes for up to five days on end.

Entering the Rixon era

I've been lucky enough to be coached by some pretty impressive and supportive coaches during my career — my childhood coach Bill Duncan, who stuck by me throughout my career, my first Canterbury coach and future Black Caps mentor Denis Aberhart, and of course Steve Rixon, the first-ever Australian to coach the Black Caps and my first coach in the international arena.

Steve came onto the New Zealand scene during a fairly testing time for the Black Caps. Glenn Turner had left the coaching position in 1996, at a time when there were divisions in the team and when aspects of some players' off-field conduct were featuring in headlines. New Zealand Cricket brought in Steve as coach and former All Black captain John Graham as manager in an effort to turn things around both on and off the field.

Playing cricket for my country had long been my dream. And it was something which I felt I could accomplish after finishing my debut first-class season in 1994–95. I had a great year, defying my inexperience to post triple figures on a couple of occasions. But then I came crashing back to earth in the 1995–96 season, when I really did have what they call the 'second-year blues'. I struggled, didn't set the world alight at all and maybe some of the opposition had worked me out a bit. So when I was going into my third season with Canterbury I knew I had to play really well if I was to show that, even aged just 21, I still warranted consideration for national selection.

And that is just what I did, putting together hundreds for Canterbury and, at that time, I ended up with the most runs scored for the province in a first-class season. Because I had had such a good season, and my name had been mentioned as a possible call-up, I was hoping that I might make the Black Caps sooner rather than later. And the call I had dreamt of since I was a kid came with Rixon picking me for the Independence Cup in May, 1997

— a quadrangular tournament featuring hosts India, as well as Pakistan, Sri Lanka and us. To say I was ecstatic would be an understatement.

Steve Rixon ('Stumper'): My reaction to Macca when I first saw him was that he was a little bit different to the rest. When I say different, he had more character and freakishness about him. If I equate those things and put them together, I say he has a bit of flair. I like flair players; I always have done. Macca to me just seemed to push the boundaries to the length. I felt it was a challenge for me to make sure that we didn't lose that individual flair, but also to make sure he concurred which side of the barrier was right and which side of the barrier was wrong.

I loved him from day one. I loved everything about him. I realised that as long as we maintained that bit of discipline with him it was going to be a good association. As it turned out, that is what happened. Macca just really had to find his feet and see how international cricket worked. And I loved his attitude — some call it arrogance, some call it Aussie confidence. And I am one who would call it Aussie confidence. I very jestingly said to Macca that he was conceived in Australia. It was the way he went about the game, the way he talked, the confidence in him and the jovial way he worked with his fellow players. There was just a bit of difference about him — it made him special.

Gilbert Enoka: All the time I worked with Steve Rixon, I don't think I ever saw him as wide-eyed and connected with the talent as the first time he saw Macca play. He was a short, tubby and stocky wee fella who did things that made people flinch. He hit balls and played shots that made people take notice. And he was fiercely competitive. I don't think I have met a more competitive person. And when he got the ball in his hands he had this belief that he could bowl like Wasim Akram and he exerted that presence on the crease.

I had the pleasure of working with Craig for most of his professional cricketing career, right from when he first came into the New Zealand Cricket academy, through to when he retired. Craig is upfront, honest, together and he has those qualities where what you see is what you get — he doesn't hide anything, he puts it out there. And even from an early age, Craig had a perspective that no matter what the situation was, no matter how vulnerable things were, he could get people out of it. He would go into bat in different situations and there wouldn't be one seed of self-doubt in his mind. And that is really rare in a New Zealander.

It was an exciting time for me just for the fact that I had been named in my first full Black Cap side. It was also an exciting time for the team as a whole as Stumper hadn't been in the job for too long and he had a new captain in Stephen Fleming. And that excitement was evident when we went into camp in Auckland before heading to the subcontinent. We were at the right stage where everyone wanted to move forward and learn. I remember just fitting in and it was also a good learning experience meeting guys who I had played against and finding myself in the same national team as them.

Stumper wasted little time in instilling in us younger guys the qualities that he expected from us when we went into camp. We played a couple of warm-up games and then did some fielding work for about 40 minutes. I remember halfway through the session being pretty much out on my feet, thinking, 'I can't get through this. I don't know how I am going to survive.' I thought I was a fit lad at that stage. But the intensity of the fielding drills was something that some of us had never experienced before. I was also nervous about not wanting to make any mistakes and thinking, 'Shit, I don't think I can do this.' But the more you went along, the more you got comfortable with the pace and intensity at which he was doing things.

Stumper always made everything we did competitive and that was certainly an attitude that suited my make-up. Everything was at full intensity and there was no mistaking he wanted us to be fielding at a very high standard. There is no doubt that during his reign as coach, if we weren't actually *the* best, we were one of the very best fielding sides in the world. This strength was like our third leg really, because as we generally had a team of good players, but no superstars, we needed to rely on our fielding to win games.

I didn't play the first two games of the Independence Cup, finally making my one-day international debut against Sri Lanka in Hyderabad. It was a low, slow pitch, we were chasing 215 to win and we were struggling by the time I came out to bat. It's fair to say that I struggled too when I came out to the wicket, facing spinners like Aravinda de Silva and Sanath Jayasuriya who had employed fields like I had never seen.

I was trying to go through in my mind what I was going to do. I ended up really struggling, scoring just 10, and it opened my eyes to how cricket is so different over there compared to what we learn in New Zealand. It was all about rotating the strike and getting down the other end. That really is the most important thing for any batter, having the ability to get down the other end. In that game I didn't manage that — it highlighted to me that it was something I had to develop if I was going to go further.

Five months after making my sole appearance in India, I was on the road again with the Black Caps heading to Zimbabwe for the test and one-day international tour. And while I didn't figure in the test 11, I played another three ODIs, scoring my first international half-century in the third match at Harare. While I was pleased with my one-day form, I was really keen to fulfil my lifetime ambition . . . to play test cricket.

A month later and I was on my way to Australia for a massive tour that would see us playing there until late January. I was certainly looking forward to heading across the Tasman. When you are growing up, Australia is always the place you want to play. Touring over there, and playing on all of their great grounds, was really my dream. Australia was one of the top sides in the world, they had some great players and I enjoyed everything about that tour — the weather and the facilities were just so conducive to playing cricket and doing well.

And that was just what I had to do if I was to achieve my pre-tour goal: securing a test cap. During the warm-up games to the test series I realised I had to get at least two decent scores to try to force myself into the test side. I thought that if I scored well, I might have a good show at getting a test. And my timing was great, scoring 62 in the first innings of the final warm-up match against New South Wales. Then I got the news I had dreamt of since I was a kid, with Stumper confirming I was in the playing 11 for the first test of the 1997–98 series against Australia at the Gabba.

Before that test, my mind was working overtime thinking about who I was going to face. Their attack was Glenn McGrath, Paul Reiffel, Michael Kasprowicz and the great Shane Warne. It was McGrath and Warne who I really built myself up to face first. I was thinking, 'If it's McGrath it will be a bouncer, if it's Warne it will probably be a flipper.' So many different scenarios went through my head. They batted first and we had them in trouble at 108–5, then Ian Healey and Reiffel combined to help Australia post an impressive total of 373.

I didn't get to bat until the third day. Daniel went in as night-watchman the night before and I finally went in at No. 6. And after imagining who I was going to face when I went out to bat, it was a bit of a let-down to be greeted by the bowling of Greg Blewett and Mark Waugh. Those two guys hadn't even figured in the equation.

It wasn't long before Australia took the second new ball. And what struck me was just how hard even someone like Reiffel, who when seen on TV looked quite slow, hit the bat. They all got so much extra bounce bowling on their pitches. It didn't matter who you faced over there, whether he was a medium-pacer or not, they hit the bat hard. They put everything into it and bowled so differently from New Zealanders. I batted for two and a half hours, celebrating my first test innings by hitting Warne for six to bring up my first test half-century.

Shane Warne: One of the things you look for in younger players is the way they go about it. Are they aggressive? Do they sit in their crease and let you dictate? One of the things I was impressed with was that he was prepared to have a go and play his own way against me. There were a lot of times in his career in the future when that didn't work, but there were also a lot of times when it did work. My first impressions were that he was an impressive cricketer.

Steve Rixon: One thing we did discuss leading up to his test debut was with Warnie and how we needed to do something special to take him out of play. If you stay there and try to survive Warnie, you are out. That was my message to Cairns and Macca who hit the ball down the ground. I said, 'Get down the pitch, have a go at hitting him over his head and try to take him off his line.' It was about working on Warne's ego. That is exactly what Craig did. He had the freedom to do that, to play those shots. And for him to bring up his maiden test half-century in his first test innings was typical Macca. There was a bit of arrogance about it.

Gilbert Enoka: How he brought up his half-century was just so typical of his character. The biggest, boldest and best in the opposition are the ones he will target. And, more often than not, he would come off against them. He would target Warnie and back himself to be successful. Bolder people would become timid and then introverted. He would become positive and extroverted and away he would go.

That test was a very special one. I had both my mum and my grandmother over there at the Gabba. My family had always given me a hell of a lot of support and it was great to have them there for the biggest game in my career to that time. Both had watched a lot of my cricket over the years, so to have them present for such a special match meant a lot.

Judith McMillan: We weren't really expecting that he was going to get into the test team and Craig thought the only chance he had of playing was in the one-day team. We spoke to him in the build-up to the first test and he told us that he might be in the test team, but he wouldn't know until the day before the match. Mum and I decided that we would go if he made the team. I was at home waiting for the call from Australia, the plane was due to leave Christchurch at 3.30 pm and I got the phone call from him at 1 pm, with Craig saying, 'You are not going to believe it, but I am in the team.' I said, 'Right bye, see you soon.' With that we had a mad rush to get to the plane on time. Cherie, who worked at Young & Lee Travel, had organised the tickets and then we got on the plane with not long to spare. Also on the plane was Chris Doig and he was very nice in congratulating us on Craig's selection.

It was all a bit surreal at the Gabba. We waited and waited for him to bat and Mum was terrible; she was really nervous and couldn't watch. When it was finally Craig's time to come in, Mum just vanished on me. I didn't know where she was. She just said, 'I am going to the loo', and she never came back while he was out there. So I just sat there by myself watching, wondering whether she was alright, or if she had had a heart attack. But I wasn't moving. She was just too nervous, watching by peeping around a corner somewhere in the stadium. It was a really proud moment for me, and I had a tear in my eye. When he brought up his 50 it was a wonderful moment.

Lindsay McMillan: I didn't get to watch much of that test at all. I was down in Queenstown on business. I was lucky that one of my customers was able to tell me what was going on when I stopped off in Arrowtown. It was difficult: I was miles away from anything and couldn't really keep up to date with Craig's test debut. And that is why I made up my mind that when he played his first test in New Zealand I would definitely be there. That was great, seeing him involved in the test arena. The fact he scored a century in that test against Zimbabwe in Wellington in 1998 made it all the greater.

In many ways that first test summed up the things that were to follow for me in my career. There was the high of scoring 54 in my first test innings, hitting Shane Warne for six to bring up my half-century. Then in the second innings I got a first ball duck, lbw to McGrath. It showed me how you can go from hero to zero very quickly. Cricket is such a reality check: one minute you are on top of the world and the next — 'Boom!', it has kicked you in the arse and you are back on the ground. You can never get too far ahead of yourself.

It's fair to say we all loved Rixon's intensity in the remaining two months of that tour of Australia. Yes, he was a tough task master. If one of us was having a bad day or simply mucking around, he would be the first person to rip into you. But he was fair too. And while he demanded high standards, we still did have a lot of fun. It was just a great balance of enjoying ourselves and knowing when it was time to switch on and get serious.

One of the other great things about Stumper was that he didn't let things fester. If he had an issue, he would say his piece and move on. He would give you a blast, sort it out and the next day you would start afresh and it was like it had never happened. And he wasn't the sort of coach who would deliberately embarrass you in front of your team-mates. Instead you would get a call to his room — something that happened to me a couple of times in the Carlton and United one-day international series that followed the three tests against Australia. You knew that when you did get the call it wasn't necessarily going to be the nicest of meetings. But once he'd had his say you would both move on.

We all respected Steve and we also enjoyed having a beer with him. Quite often Daniel Vettori, Rixon and I would head off to a casino to have a punt. He didn't mind mixing with players and he had very good relationships with all of them, which showed his people skills, given the nature of the environment when he came on board. I really enjoyed my time with him and if you spoke to other guys who played in that era they would say the same thing.

> **Steve Rixon:** One of the things I tried to emphasise to that group of guys was that they shouldn't be afraid of making errors. My reaction to the culture of New Zealand cricket when I took over as coach was that they were always looking to save a game of cricket first before they were looking at ways to try to win it. When I looked at the likes of Cairns, McMillan, Astle and Fleming in that side, we had enough individual batting flair that we were better than our results were indicating. What I had to give them was some freedom of error. I remember saying to Macca and others, 'I don't mind if you make errors, but don't continue to make those errors. Learn from those errors as you go along.' I gave Macca a bit of licence, and as time went on some of the best innings I saw from him had exactly that quality. And they were match-winning and match-saving innings. Not a lot of people can do that.
>
> I had enough respect for Macca that it wasn't my place to berate him in front of his fellow players and belittle him in any form. But under no circumstances would I let him get away with average cricket. At times there were little reminders, just to say, 'Macca, this is why you have been good, this is how you become good, this is the way you want to play your game. Now in that there are a couple of guidelines and you are not following them. You have to give me a bit back for me to allow you to have the flair because I back you every time I go and do media after you have played a risky shot.' Macca was also a guy that if he didn't agree with what I said, he would confront me. And I loved that about him.

Stumper's coaching wasn't the only thing some of us enjoyed on that Australian tour. Our sponsor KFC also came to the party, and on arrival in Australia we were all given a special card which entitled us to $30 free KFC each day. It was certainly a great sponsorship, and one which it is fair to say some players enjoyed more than others.

It also provided for some pretty comical post-match scenes. We played Australia A at the MCG, and with about half to go in the game the 12th man came out with the drinks. But he also brought out a piece of paper to take our respective KFC orders for after the game — so we'd all be ordering our quarter-packs and Colonel burgers. When we walked off the ground we were greeted in the changing room by a massive pile of KFC. Everyone went over and picked up their respective order, sat down and had a feed. I have never seen anything like it — it was beautiful!

Of course, things have changed drastically over the last five or six years. With the amount of cricket we are playing, you have no choice but to look after your body. That means keeping a close eye on what you eat and drink. If you do over-indulge it will catch up with you. And when that happens, chances are you'll be struggling to hold onto your place in the side.

Nine years after last playing under his coaching, I have a heap of respect for Stumper and still see him from time to time. We also exchange the odd phone call, generally talking about rugby league. I went to Australia a few years back and he took me to a game at the Sydney Football Stadium to see St George Illawarra, who are his beloved side, play Cronulla. My team is the Bulldogs so we'd always be having bets throughout the season about who would beat who. Stumper also came to Cherie and my wedding in 2003 and gave me one of the best presents out of the lot. I haven't managed to take it up yet, but when the timing suits both of us he will arrange for tickets to an NRL grand final. For me, being a huge league fan, I can't wait. And now I have retired, hopefully in the next year or two I can take up that offer.

Better than before

A tour of England is widely regarded as the ultimate destination for a cricketer — and with good reason. It's the home of cricket and many of the grounds that you visit are steeped in incredible history. The 1999 tour of England came in my third season of international cricket. And it wasn't just any tour — it also included the Cricket World Cup.

It wasn't my first time touring England, as three years previously I'd captained the New Zealand under-19 team which went through the UK.

I'd say we were the best prepared of any of the New Zealand sides I have ever been a part of, both physically and mentally. The latter had a lot to do with Gilbert Enoka, our mental skills expert. All teams go away with goals, but often they can be without substance.

That wasn't the case in May 1999 when we left New Zealand for England. We were well coached, had a strong management and some classy players. But we also had a secret weapon that would play a major part in our eventual and historic success in the test series against England. This was the tour when we vowed to be 'Better than Before'. The motto and concept was Gilbert's master-stroke. It may have just been three words — but they carried a lot of weight with us.

But before we got the chance to take on England in the four-test series, we first had the Cricket World Cup to contend with. The tournament was scheduled for a mid-May start, pretty much the worst time of the year to be playing cricket in England, especially if you are a batsman.

The pitches are wet and the big Dukes cricket ball swings all over the place, aided by the overhead conditions which certainly help out the bowlers. It was one of those tournaments where opening bowlers had a lot of success. And we were no different, with Geoff Allott finishing up as the equal top wicket-taker, alongside Australia's Shane Warne, by capturing 20 World Cup scalps.

We warmed up for the tournament with a wins over Hampshire and Surrey, before taking on Bangladesh in our tournament opener in Chelmsford. It took just three balls before Allott had opened up his wicket-taking for the tournament, claiming Shahriar Hossain lbw as Bangladesh were dismissed for just 116. I contributed 20 in our eventual six-wicket win.

We were obviously stoked to start our campaign off with a win, but really it wasn't the most ideal preparation for what was in store for us three days later — the might of Australia in Cardiff.

But you would never know that the way we played against Australia, limiting them to just 218–8 in their 50 overs at Sophia Gardens. Again, Allott made a big impression early on, nabbing the wickets of Mark Waugh in the third over and Adam Gilchrist in the ninth.

We bowled brilliantly and, coupled with some helpful overhead conditions, restricted them to a modest total. A lot of dot balls were bowled, and it was during that period when the loudest applause of the day was unleashed by the crowd. All of a sudden the crowd stood up and started cheering, but we were just bowling dot balls and I thought the reaction was a bit over the top.

As it turned out, the applause wasn't for us. We found that out when we looked over and saw Graham Henry, who was Wales' rugby coach, walking past the grandstand. He was their new favourite son, having turned Welsh rugby around, and was there to see our manager John Graham.

We ended up beating Australia by five wickets, a result which was to be the eventual champions' sole loss of the tournament. Roger Twose and Chris Cairns both batted well, with each of them posting half-centuries. I chipped in with 29, but my diabetes was playing up and I needed a runner. I had too much sugar in my body and cramped up, and in that situation I can't run until I get my levels back down to normal. I just couldn't function properly. When I went out to bat I had to blast it while I could. It certainly wasn't ideal.

Next up was the West Indies in Southampton and this time it was us who felt the brunt of an impressive bowling line-up, aided by the conditions. We were in trouble early on, with both our openers Matthew Horne and Nathan Astle gone inside the first five overs.

I came in at No. 3 and it provided me with the first and only time that I faced Curtly Ambrose. I made 32, the highest score in our total of just 156, and ended up batting through his 10 overs. He was so hard to face that day. Of about 25 balls from him I managed to hit only three. And all were nicks down to third man — the ball was going all over the place. He was just way too good for me.

We followed our seven-wicket loss to the Windies with a 62-run loss to Pakistan in Derby before ending our pool-play phase by beating Scotland by six wickets. A five-wicket win over India at Trent Bridge, Nottingham, in the Super Six stage was then enough to secure us a semi-final berth, following an earlier loss to South Africa and a rain-out against Zimbabwe.

We travelled to Old Trafford, Manchester, for our semi-final against Pakistan. But you could have sworn the match was being played in either Lahore or Karachi, given the level of support that they had. I have never seen so many Pakistani flags at a cricket match outside their home nation. We scored 241–7 after being put into bat on a wicket that did a bit early on. My lean patch continued, scoring just three.

Shoaib Akhtar bowled at the speed of light and he ran hard that day. Flem batted well and scored 41, but he ended up getting knocked over by Akhtar and there were stumps flying everywhere. We thought 241 was pretty good, especially considering that the pitch was pretty wet at the start. But Pakistan knocked it off inside 48 overs with the loss of just one wicket. While Akhtar had proved to be their hero with the ball, it was Saeed Anwar who starred with the bat, scoring an unbeaten 113. Wajahatullah Wasti chimed in with 84.

The Pakistan supporters certainly put on quite a show throughout their side's run chase. Late in the game they needed six to win and Anwar hit a four which led to a ground invasion from the Pakistani supporters. It was actually quite scary because their fans were in such a frenzy. The ground was eventually roped off, there were fireworks going off and it was just like being in Pakistan. Eventually, Nathan Astle bowled the third ball of his over, it was hit by Anwar and we all just turned to run off the field. No one was worried about stopping the ball; we were just worried about getting off the field as quickly as we could. It was carnage!

Cricinfo, Live Scoring, 16 June 1999
47.1 Astle to Saeed Anwar, no run.
47.2 Astle to Saeed Anwar, FOUR, slogged over the bowler's head, 2 to win.
47.3 Astle to Saeed Anwar, two runs, edged in the air, Twose may get a catch at long on, but no, terrific fans, a credit to the human race, storm onto the field. Twose aborts going for the catch and instead seeks out some protection.

I had a poor tournament, a really bad tournament. I was inevitably early into bat at No. 3 and struggled to deal with the moving ball. I was fairly new in the side and that was just where I batted. I played a few games at No. 3 and it is probably fair to say never performed or scored as I should have in that slot. I think my best slot ended up being No. 5.

Steve Rixon: Macca is a guy who, given a big situation like the World Cup, he rises. Had we got to the final he could have been the match-winner. I was disappointed because I thought we were a better side than a couple of teams in the top four. With Macca and Cairnsy at their best we could have been a better rival for Australia in the final.

Macca obviously tried risks sometimes with his shot selection and I don't think he did that particularly well during the 1999 Cricket World Cup. That might have cost him. Having said that, I didn't see at any stage that Macca was the sole offender there.

We didn't play bad cricket, we were in the semis. And I still say to this day, for New Zealand to get through to a final and win a World Cup, they are going to have to have a lot going for them. Unfortunately, right now, their grand final is making the semis. I don't really believe they think they can win the final.

We had little time to lick our wounds after our World Cup exit. It was time to launch ourselves into our warm-up matches before the four-test series against England just five days after losing our semi-final to Pakistan. As we prepared for the first three-day match against the British Universities in Oxford it was time for the best motivational tool I have ever seen used in the Black Caps to kick in.

The tour motto, 'Better than Before' was the brainchild of Gilbert Enoka. He also compiled a motivational movie, complete with clips from the Robin Williams movie *Dead Poet's Society* and images and clips of Walter Hadlee's 1949 New Zealand team which toured England and drew all four tests. It was a brilliant video montage — the first time we watched it, which was before we even left New Zealand, everyone just sat quietly in this room. We were totally spellbound by Gilbert's creation and took that video right through our tour of England.

For some of the guys it was their one and only chance of touring England, a trip which is probably the most special cricketing tour that there is. Everyone in that team had a determination to be better than the New Zealand teams that had been to England before, to create our own part of cricketing history. And we thought we had the team to do just that.

Gilbert Enoka: I introduced the team to a vision of values-based culture. I had come out of working with the Crusaders, where we'd started that run of winning four Super 12 championships. Once people had agreed that this is the way we do things around here, with the values sense and we had a vision that drove everything, it inspired people to perform. Hence, in 1999 'Better than Before' was the theme for the Black Caps in England.

We had a video done for 'Better than Before' which we played at various stages. The aim was to head to England in 1999 and do things that no other New Zealand cricket team had done. Our video had clips from *Dead Poet's Society* featuring Robin Williams talking about having a look at the faces of people who had gone before. We reflected on cricketing history — it was emotionally moving and connecting for the players. We were careful about when we showed it so we didn't overkill it.

The tour in 1999 was just so special. We had 'Better than Before' pledge cards which had the values on them that we were driven by. We had a pledge and we would recite it after every win in the changing sheds. The players came up with those values.

Those values cards weren't just given to the people, they had to earn them. One of the players was responsible for giving the cards to the management; one of the management members was responsible for giving them to the players. The players got them when they exhibited those qualities. At the end of the training you'd be given your card for displaying the qualities that the team was built on. As you went on, if you did something which was against those values, you handed your card back in. Then you earned it back again.

We worked through that, and it gave us such fantastic leverage, inspiration and nourishment through the World Cup and going on to win a first test match at Lord's. No one had done that, so that was better than before. We won two tests, and that was better than before. Even if someone got the highest test scores, that was all part of being 'Better than Before'.

'Better than Before' would prove to be a real gem as the test series progressed. But it wasn't the only initiative which helped bring us together in a way few sports teams can speak of. We also had a tour bus for the duration of that tour. It was great from a team point of view, sitting in the same seats. We had tables at the back so quite often when we were travelling for three or four hours we had card schools going on. There was a really good feeling about it.

Our second warm-up match was against county side Somerset at Taunton, somewhere always regarded as a great batting ground. We talked as a batting unit about how the World Cup had been tough on us, with the big white Dukes ball swinging around early in the season. Not many of our batters had a good time of it. We discussed how we had to step up and put some totals on the board that our bowlers could bowl to. And we had a good bowling attack, probably our strongest for a while.

The nature of the batting conditions was highlighted by Somerset's first innings total of 554. This was a game which I had picked out as being one I had to score runs in. I was totally focused on posting a decent score, although you might not have realised that given the scenes during my build-up to going into bat at No. 5.

Leading up to the match I'd broken a bat. So the timing of going to Taunton couldn't have been better as it is home to the workshop for famous bat makers Millychamp and Hall. I remember going over and seeing a bloke in the workshop and talking about getting a bat made up for me. I went over at the start of lunchtime and I must have been talking to him for about 45 minutes about the bat and how I wanted it shaped. Then I looked at his watch and couldn't believe the time; the game had actually been going for the 10 minutes. I was next in to bat and everyone was looking for me.

The only gear I had on was my whites and my thigh pad. So I had to race back to the sheds and quickly chuck my pads on. The guys were just wetting themselves with laughter, but I remember getting quite a stern look from Steve Rixon. It was the worst feeling, looking at the bat maker's watch, realising the game was underway and thinking, 'Oh god, I hope no one has got out'.

I ended up getting 121 so it worked out alright, and we beat Somerset by six wickets, heading to Edgbaston for the first test in pretty good spirits. But we were soon in for a reminder of just how demanding a tour of England can be for a batsman.

For Twosey, the first test was very special. It was a bit of a homecoming for him after all the seasons he had spent playing at Warwickshire. But it wasn't the homecoming he would have dreamt about — he got a pair, facing just four balls in the test which we lost by seven wickets inside three days. Needless to say, he was totally gutted.

It was the first time I had ever played at Edgbaston and the ball swung all over the place. In fact I'd never see the ball swing so much anywhere before. We batted first and got 226 — Adam Parore top-scored with 73, but the rest of us didn't get too many. But it wasn't a bad result considering the way Mullally and Caddick were bowling. Even Mark Butcher, who was a part-timer, came on and got a couple of wickets bowling big banana balls.

We bowled England out for 126, giving us a 100-run lead, which you would never have imagined possible considering we had scored just 226. Our guys just bowled beautifully; they all swung the ball and chipped in with wickets. At one stage we had them at 45–7. There was a full house for the test and one of the things I will always remember about that ground was the singing. It went around the whole ground and made for an amazing atmosphere.

Unfortunately, we had a total shocker in our second turn at bat, being dismissed for just 107. No one could stay in for that long as the ball swung all over the place. Funnily enough, after we got bowled out the sun came out and that was the end of the swing movement. England needed just 211 to win and did it with seven wickets to spare.

The strangest thing about their run chase was how night-watchman Alex Tudor was left stranded on 99 not out. At the other end was Graham Thorpe, who finished on 21 not out off 21 balls. It was pretty clear when

Thorpe came into bat that he wanted the game over as soon as possible; he wasn't interested in easing off, even if it would help a regular No. 9 test batsman record a century. It was certainly interesting to take note of that out on the field and we were chipping away about it. Thorpe was worried about winning the match, but he wasn't too interested about any other milestones. I understand that: at the end of the day the team win was the most important thing. But it did seem a little bit strange when he ended up stranded on 99 not out and they were just seven wickets down.

Next up were a couple of county teams in Hampshire and Kent. I struggled in both of those games, I felt badly out of nick. Despite it being just a couple of games since my century against Somerset, my feet weren't moving and I tried working on different stances. I was playing across my pads and getting out lbw. I tried various things in the nets which were unconventional. They felt alright in the nets but once I got out to the middle it was just terrible — I couldn't middle the ball and felt like I couldn't bat.

The second test of the tour took us to the spiritual home of cricket, Lord's. For many of the guys it was their first chance to have a look at the honours board in the away dressing room, something which truly is a big focus for all touring teams. Our guys looked up and could see other New Zealanders' names up on the wall — there are only a select few up there.

We won the toss and bowled in overcast conditions. Our guys bowled well again and we had England in trouble, getting them out for just 186. Cairnsy was a star for us, taking 6–77. His wicket haul included Thorpe, who was given a pretty intensive send-off. He talks with a bit of a lisp, so a few of us thought it would be a bit funny to mimic some of the things he used to say, complete with a lisp. He didn't take some of our ribbing too well.

We responded with 358 and Matt Horne scored a really gutsy hundred. He got hit on the arm towards the end of his innings by Caddick and couldn't hold the bat properly. For a while there he was batting one-handed, he got to 100 and soon after got out because he couldn't bat. It was a huge knock for us, to give us a lead of 172.

But, for me, the first innings was one to forget. I got just three off 36 balls and was dismissed by Caddick in the last over of the day. I felt out of nick and was just trying to survive through to the next day. Three runs in 36 balls just isn't how I play. I was fighting a real battle, trying to leave the ball and trying to survive. After I walked off I went and sat in the toilets for 40 minutes, thinking, 'Where has my game gone?' I felt low — I had really wanted to do well at Lord's.

England only managed 229 in their second innings. Again our guys all chipped in with the ball. It meant we needed 60 in our second innings to win. Being on the balcony when the winning runs were hit was a great feeling. It also felt great to bounce back from the first test loss. Straight after the win we sat in the changing room, had a few drinks and enjoyed the moment.

It was only our fifth win in the 80 tests we had played against England to that point, and our first win at Lord's in 13 attempts. The dirties, the non-playing reserves, went down on the ground and performed a haka led by Shayne O'Connor. From his first XV days he enjoyed taking his shirt off and doing the haka. There were a lot of Kiwi supporters still around and it was a very special moment to savour at a very special ground.

Next we went to Derby for a one-day game and I scored 86 and took two wickets. I got rid of the silly stance, went back to batting normally and generally hit the ball really well.

Our next stop was Leicester and by that stage we started to be hindered by injuries to Simon Doull and Geoff Allott, two of our best bowlers. Doully was a magnificent swing bowler on his day but he was so fragile, his knees were shot and he wasn't really built for bowling. For Allott, it was really the beginning of the end as far as his cricketing career was concerned. We called in Andrew Penn, who was in England playing club cricket. He got six wickets and 69 and performed really well. I got 85 not out in our second innings and I started feeling a lot better.

My form continued into the third test in Manchester where I managed 107 not out, later being named man of the match in a test that was ruined by bad weather. Again our bowlers did well, chipping England out for 199 in their first innings. This was probably the first game where we took full advantage of the great work of our bowlers, replying with 496–9 declared.

Nath and I both scored hundreds. It was special for many reasons. The girls were both over and so were their parents — it was a really good time. England were 181–2 when bad weather set in again on the fourth day, putting an end to that test. But it was a good continuation from the Lord's test, and we were on top again. At least now some of our batters were in form — our bowlers had been in form the whole time.

We had a couple of county games before we headed to the final test. And this was probably the turning point of the whole tour. We played Middlesex in a 50-over match and lost. They made 239 and we got bowled out for 200, including an innings of 42 from me. It was a game we should never have lost.

Then we played Essex in a four-day game at Chelmsford and got spanked, losing by an innings and 40 runs. It was a really bad loss, especially after we'd been on a high in the previous two tests. In the changing room afterwards there was a bad feeling about the loss. Two things could happen at that point of the tour: we could either fall over or get things back on track.

It was with that knowledge that we headed to The Oval, London, for the fourth and final test of the tour. This was the match where the benefits of the 'Better than Before' mantra saw the team of 1999 write themselves into the record books. It truly was an awesome test for us — but you wouldn't hear too many of us saying that out loud during the first three days.

We scored only 236 in the first innings, a total which really wasn't that flash. Flem scored 56, but batted for five and a half hours. It was one of those knocks where he was gritty and batted as long as he could. I charged Tuffnell and was clean bowled for just 19; again there was no respect for a spinner.

Yet again our bowlers came to the rescue, bowling England out for just 153, giving us an 83-run lead. But we didn't fare too much better in our second innings, being bowled out for 162. Cairns scored 80 and I chipped in with 26 — the next highest score was 10, posted by both Matt Horne and Dion Nash. We leaked wickets all over the place and were also bowled out in just 54 overs, something which was criminal in a test match.

England's target to win was just 245, with two days left, so there was no doubt who the favourites to win the series-clincher were. At the time I felt that we didn't have enough runs, and I certainly didn't think a total of 245 would be enough with their batting line-up. Those concerns were magnified when England finished at 91–2 at stumps on the fourth day.

After we got off the field we had an emotion-charged team meeting. Nash was the main spokesman, talking about how we needed to be true to what we'd committed to in terms of 'Better than Before' and how guys had to put their hand up and make the difference. He said there would be opportunities, but we had to take them.

The management didn't really say anything; they just let the players take charge. The message was clear for everyone to soak up: we had one game left on tour, one test left to create the history we had talked about, and we didn't want to leave England with any regrets.

Gilbert Enoka: England were two down at the end of the fourth day. We needed eight wickets to win, they needed 154 runs. We walked into the dressing room and Stumper had talked to me about just letting the boys take the session. Dion Nash is a player I would hold up as one of the top five New Zealand athletes I have ever worked with — he is just outstanding.

He stood in the room, pointed at Cairnsy, Dan Vettori, Shayne O'Connor and Macca and said: 'If we are going to win this test match, then one of us is going to have a great day.' With that he turned around and said: 'And it is going to be me!'

> What Dion said created one of the most moving and inspirational changing rooms I have ever been in. His speech wasn't long; it was short and to the point. It really captivated his team-mates. History shows that he went out the next day and started the rot for England.

When I arrived at The Oval the next morning I was thinking that it was amazing we had been on tour for four months and it was all coming down to the last day. It was a pleasant day, with a big crowd turning up expecting England to win.

And Nashie proved the substance behind his words, grabbing the wickets of Mike Atherton, Mark Ramprakash and Alec Stewart. The big wicket was Graham Thorpe's, dismissed by Shayne O'Connor with an out-swinger which he nicked to Flem. After that the English just fell over, eventually dismissed for 162. There were wild celebrations for us — we had done what we had set out to achieve.

It was an amazing series, one that I will always look back on very fondly. And the guys who were over there all talk highly of that series. Throughout it everyone chipped in at different times; everyone played their part. Part of our belief came from Steve Rixon. He made it plain there was never any doubt in his mind that we would win that series. It was a belief which we all fed off. It wasn't quite the typical New Zealand way of going about things, but it gave us the confidence.

> **Steve Rixon:** Macca played a big part on and off the field during the test series. Keeping things light is important, that is why I was so impressed with him and Dan. As a unit they kept it at a level where people could blend. You had some quite intense people in that series. You had Nashie who had a back injury who didn't know what to do with it and was so desperate to play. So we needed to have a few guys having fun around the place, even though those two guys were the most competitive.
>
> Dan and Macca might have been having fun, but at the same time having fun meant winning. And they would do anything to win. They got on board very quickly with the mentality that winning was a lot better than its opposite. In that series there were guys who needed to be brought down to a nice relaxed level. Therefore the dressing room was a very important place. Macca and Dan were important in the settling of the dressing room along with the main man, the captain.

We were later recognised at the Halberg Awards, a really nice reward for the pretty successful year we had had. I don't think there were a lot of people at the ceremony who thought we were going to win it. I've found that cricket is underrated a lot of the time in terms of those awards.

Steve Rixon: Winning the team prize at the Halberg Awards was a massive thrill for everyone. When I first came to New Zealand Chris Doig asked me to go along to the Halbergs with three players. I just remember sitting there and listening to the compère and the guest speakers — it seemed that everyone on stage used New Zealand cricket as their cheap line. I looked at Doigy and said, 'Mate, is this normal?' He told me they were harsh on cricket. I told him, 'Well, you tell me when I can go because I don't particularly want to put up with this shit. These blokes don't deserve that.'

That stuck in my head until the day I was dragged back from Australia for the Halberg Awards after the 1999 tour. I asked Doig if we had won it. He said, 'I don't think we did, but I want you there.' I said, 'Mate, if you want me there I will be there. But remember what I said last time.'

Geoff Allott, Dion Nash and I went along to represent New Zealand Cricket at the awards. I got up and made this speech; I never missed one of the guys who had a crack at us last time around — it was payback time. I nailed them, nicely, but it was about not taking cheap shots unless they were prepared to cop something back. At the end of it I had 1000 people rise from their seats and they gave a standing ovation. I have a photo which still holds pride of place in my house in Australia from that night.

It was a great tour to be part of and one of the real highlights of my international career. Unfortunately, when it came time to return to England five years later things didn't run as smoothly either on or off the field.

My mate Warnie and other spinners

Spinners have been like a red rag to a bull for me since my early days in cricket. If there was one thing I loved when I was batting, it was dispatching a spinner to all parts of the field. That was the case from when I was a youngster coming through the grades, through to my introduction into the domestic first-class scene and right throughout my international career — even if it was an attitude that led to my downfall on more than a few occasions. I just loved whacking spinners!

Spinners have probably got me out a lot over my career, more so than they should have. Part of that is just because I had a general lack of respect for them. I think that improved as my career went on, in terms of realising that there actually are some good spinners out there. But early on I thought I could just hit them for six, and that is what I went about trying to do. There's no doubt that at times it has cost me my wicket, but generally it is the way I have enjoyed playing.

Early on I liked using my feet; I loved coming down the wicket and hitting the ball back over the bowler's head. I really saw that as a sign of dominance. And I liked doing it early on in an innings so the bowler knew he had a battle on his hands. Thinking back to the last 12 months of my international career, I didn't charge much. I tended to stay in my crease, still hit straight, but swing away and by doing that I took the risk of getting stumped out of play. I felt I could manipulate the length a bit by staying in the crease.

When I first came into the domestic scene during the 1994–95 season, the Shell Cup and Shell Trophy were packed with seasoned pros. And my attitude towards spinners, combined with my age, certainly managed to get on the nerves of some. I just felt that the spinners' part in the game was to bowl a few overs and get caned. When I was younger, on the first or second ball I always charged down the wicket. If I didn't charge on the first ball

I faced from them, it was coming on the second ball. And it didn't matter whether the spinner was a rookie or an international veteran.

It didn't take too long for me to find out that the attitude didn't sit too well with some of the veterans. In one of my early Shell Cup games for Canterbury I came up against Dipak Patel at Lancaster Park. The fact that Dipak was a test and one-day international veteran didn't make me change my policy to attack him; if anything it might have prompted me to belt him even further. Early on in my innings I charged down the wicket, intent on hammering him over his head, but missed the ball and was very lucky not be stumped. Dipak came down and gave me an absolute gob-full, telling me I should be back off to school and that I certainly didn't belong on the field. He absolutely gave it to me and it set the tone for numerous encounters against him.

Daniel Vettori: I think I have probably got him out 1000 times in the nets, so I have a good feel for what he is up to. But in saying that, in game-time he has got hold of me a few times. I remember he reverse-swept me for six in a domestic game; it was an amazing shot.

I always enjoyed his attitude to spinners. When you are a spin bowler, you actually want to see opposition spinners being smashed. You know when a guy like Craig goes out to bat, he has that at the forefront of his mind. And for the majority of the time, it is the right way to play the game. Craig would probably admit he may have come unstuck, but not that many times, by being overly aggressive and trying to get the better of spinners.

I always thought that when Craig was in the middle against good spin bowlers. He could not only dominate them but was also intelligent about the way he manoeuvred the field or got his singles. There were times where it didn't work, and he got accused of being reckless, but I always thought he had a good feel for how to play spin. He was always willing to learn; it wasn't all 'his way'. He tried a few things, as we've seen over the years, and he did question me about different options. The style in which he played never led to him being called an intelligent batsman. But when it came to spin bowling, I always felt that he wanted to learn more than a lot of other guys. And that is intelligent batting.

John Bracewell: I quite liked the way he played to spinners — I didn't have a problem with his approach. I think he was probably brought up in an era when there was a slight disregard for spin and a fall-off in the standard of spin. Then obviously the Warnes and the doosra bowlers arrived on the scene and made things more difficult and changed the balance of cricket.

He has always been an attacking bully-type batter, even as a kid he dominated physically. He was stronger than most kids at that age. I don't think he ever developed a strong defence. And the best way for Craig to defend was to be offensive in the way he went about it. He was basically saying, 'I am not waiting for you to bowl a good ball, I am going to knock you out of the attack.' It was a pretty simplistic approach and pretty effective if he got it right.

Shane Warne is by far the best spinner I have ever faced. He is just a magician. He has got so many subtle variations and really does have the ball on a string. But one of his greatest strengths is how impressive his cricketing brain is. He can work guys out very quickly, where they are strong and where they are not.

I always tried to attack him and in my first test I hit him for six to bring up my 50, which was quite an amazing thing. But he got me out about three balls later, lbw to his flipper. Again, he was a spinner, so I thought I would play him like I play every other spinner and tried to smash him out of the attack. I didn't think, 'Oh, it is Shane Warne, I have to be careful.' I just saw him as a spinner.

Shane Warne (former record test wicket-taker): Playing against Craig McMillan was always a challenge — and a challenge I looked forward to. I always held him in high regard as a player. You always knew you were in for a good competition; he was aggressive and always batted with a lot of intent. I thought he played the game in the right spirit. He was just a competitor, a natural competitor. When you come up against competitors in any sport, especially cricket, they never give in. They always keep fighting. And to me, Craig was a competitor and a fighter. Australians are regarded as are competitive people who fight and never give up. Craig struck me as one of those sorts of people.

And I always thought a New Zealand side with Craig McMillan was a stronger side than one without him. So it was definitely a surprise to all of us in Australia when he missed out on getting a New Zealand Cricket contract in 2006. Every time we played against New Zealand, we did think they were better off when he was in the team. He was unpredictable, a match-winner with both bat and ball. So any time Craig McMillan wasn't in the side, we thought it was a weaker New Zealand side.

Warnie had an impressive range in his bowling repertoire — he had the flipper, a big leg-spinner, a little leg-spinner and he could land the ball wherever he wanted to. If he wanted to tie you down, he would just bowl out of the front of his hand, the ball would skid on and you would play it. The same thing would happen again and you would play for no turn, but the ball would turn, grip your edge and you would be gone. He could always build up pressure and he normally had someone like Glenn McGrath bowling at the other end, so runs were always really hard to come by.

I talked to him at the 2007 Hong Kong Sixes in regard to attitudes different batsmen adopted when they faced him. He said he still believes that you have to attack good spinners. He said, 'That is why I like bowling to you.' He always knew I was going to attack him and said, 'It is about putting pressure on the bowler.' Shane said that if people are just too defensive, he knows he is eventually going to get them out and that he won't have many runs scored off him.

He always felt that you attack good spinners and just sit on bad spinners. That's a valid view. If a guy bowls you two full tosses an over, you want to take eight runs off it. You don't want to take 15 runs off his first over because you want him to bowl three overs for 35 runs, as opposed to one over for 15 runs. That wasn't only my method against him; generally, it was my method against any spinner.

One of the best things I learnt early on was the sweep shot. And it was probably the most important shot to have available to you when you were facing Warnie for the simple fact it allowed you to get down the other end. You can't let him bowl three overs to you on the trot because he will knock you over. You must have a shot where you can get a single, get down the other end and watch your mate struggle against him. That is the same with Murali as well.

A few years back the sweep was like a new shot. But there are so many different types of sweep now — the slog sweep, the fine sweep, the lap and of course the good old reverse sweep. It really is a shot that has been reinvented. To me, the sweep shot would get you a single, paddle it around for one run and get to the other end. If I was talking to youngsters, it would be one shot I would be encouraging them to play and have in their repertoire.

Warnie was such a showman and I used to love playing against him. You just knew that something was going to happen. He had a pretty good record against us, and generally we always struggled against him. At times we talked about it, whether we were being too aggressive against him. But I believed that you had to appear positive against him. Like any other bowler in the world, he does bowl a bad ball. But quite often he used to get away with it, because a lot of times the batters are playing the bowler and not the ball. If you get caught up in a mind-set of 'I am facing Shane Warne', you forget about what you have to do. You should remember that your job is to hit the red ball and go about it that way.

Not only was Warnie the greatest spinner I have seen, he is also the greatest cricketer I have ever seen. He made spin bowling an art form again. At one stage it wasn't cool to bowl spin. Everyone wanted to come in and bowl fast. But Shane Warne made it cool again. Now it is amazing that when you go to any cricket ground you will see people bowling spin, even kids bowling leg-spin which was a dead art before Warnie started.

One of the most enjoyable periods of my career was a nine-week County cricket stint I had with Hampshire in 2005, an opportunity which saw me captained by Warnie. I got a call out of the blue from Shane asking if I wanted to come over on a short-term contract to stand in for Simon Katich who had been called up for the Australian team. At the time I had no plans for the New Zealand winter and certainly didn't need a second invitation to go and play with Warnie in England. I jumped at the chance. In terms of cricketing experience, it was a very valuable period.

I would rate Warnie as the best captain I have played under. He showed just what a great captain he was in my first game for Hampshire, when we played Nottinghamshire at Trent Bridge. Stephen Fleming was captaining Notts. The game was pretty much dead and buried after rain delays, including no play on the first day, but that was no barrier for Shane as he displayed his attitude to play to win. He would rather lose trying to win a game than playing out a boring draw. A lot of captains these days let themselves down in that area. But because he is so great, he is prepared to risk things a little. And that's just what he did against Notts.

After some negotiation between Shane and Flem, Notts were set 267 to win on the final day. Considering that the pitch at Trent Bridge had flattened down, it certainly wasn't an arduous task. But Warnie had taken a punt and backed us to knock them over; he didn't want to play out a draw. Notts were going along very well: David Hussey got 64 and Flem was well on his way to a century. It got to the point where they needed just 40 off the final 15 overs, with seven wickets left — you aren't supposed to lose a game from there.

But then Flem holed out to long-off off Shaun Udal for 105, Chris Tremlett took a hat-trick and all of a sudden Notts were batting to save the game. They had the last pair in to bat out the last three overs. Warnie ended up knocking over Ryan Sidebottom and we won by 14 runs. It was one of the most enjoyable games of cricket I have ever played in — that's always the case when you win a match which at one stage appeared unwinnable.

There is no doubt that Shane Warne should have captained Australia. The experience and the cricketing brain he had meant he was the best captain I ever played under. That is hard to say because Flem has obviously been a very good captain and I have played most of my career under him. But there is just that X-factor about Warne — there is something special about the guy and I have no doubt that had he captained Australia it would have led to his leadership in the international arena.

Shane Warne: Getting to play with him at Hampshire, and at the Hong Kong Sixes, I got to know him pretty well. We share a lot of similar interests, we both like poker and having a bit of a flutter. In captaining him in Hampshire, I found he was really good player to have around the group. As a captain, I found to have someone like that in the team, someone who thought outside the square, was great. Craig always had an opinion or a thought. I really enjoyed playing with him and getting to know him even better.

To me, cricket should be fun. I don't do team meetings, I don't tell people when they should play — I leave everything up to them, everything is optional at Hampshire. That is the culture and environment I set up there. It is up to you to become the best player you can. In team meetings, I think all you do is talk around in circles, so I didn't do those. And I think that everyone just had a good time in that setting, including Craig. Having Craig around, we played a lot of poker, had a few beers and talked cricket. I would like to think that we created an environment where he was both able to play really well and enjoy his time there.

Every time I have come across Macca has been fun. He always seems to have a bit of a smile on his face. I enjoy his company over a beer or a water. He is a competitor and a person I like to play with or play against. I consider him a friend and it was a shame we didn't get a chance to play with each other more often.

Muttiah Muralitharan was a totally different kettle of fish to Warnie — he's an amazing bowler too. There were obvious question marks about his delivery, but to do what he has done over a number of years is amazing in itself. How he is viewed depends on the person. We as a team always felt there was something suspect about the way he bowled. But after the ICC changed the rules his bowling is OK — before that, there probably was a question mark.

I first faced him in the test arena in early 1998 when the Black Caps toured Sri Lanka. But my first test innings against him wasn't that memorable, being dismissed by Murali for a four-ball duck at Colombo's R. Premadasa Stadium. But it was a different story in the second innings, with Flem and me putting on a partnership of 240 before my dismissal for 142, again inflicted by Murali. In that second innings I just swept everything from him. I hit six sixes and they were all sweep shots. That is when I learnt I had to sweep — and if I couldn't sweep, I didn't have much to offer.

The thing I noticed most about him was his doosra. I always felt I could pick it because it came out higher, you could also see the rotation of the seam and it was a little bit slower than his offie. But what I noticed when I came back into the Black Caps for the 2006–07 one-day series against Sri Lanka was that he bowled the doosra at the same pace as he bowled his off-spin. Because it was quicker, the ball rotations were quicker, and it was harder to actually see something different. In my first game back in Queenstown I got caught at first slip for two off his bowling — he just had me mesmerised. I hadn't played him for a few years because I had been in and out of the side and I thought I was one of the better guys at playing him. Then I got back into the side and I couldn't pick his doosra.

He was someone I liked to attack as well. At times it was a bit of a guessing game if you aren't picking him. He had those big white eyes and he was like the smiling assassin — you would see him at the top of his mark, with his white teeth smiling at you and you would just want to hit him as far as you could. He would be smiling whether you had just pinged him for six or played and missed. He sets you up beautifully. He also bowls the doosra a lot to tail-enders because they don't have any idea of what he is bowling.

The Black Caps have played him poorly over a number of years. We talked about him and often said that in a one-day international if he could bowl 10 overs and finish with figures of 0–25 or 0–30 then we had done a really good job. That meant they would have to turn to someone else to take their wickets. We would try to bat conservatively and get those 25 runs off his bowling without conceding a wicket. But inevitably he would take 3–25. It would rip out our top or middle order and stop all our momentum.

The only time I have seen a New Zealander really get hold of him was Flem in the one-day international against the Fica World XI at Jade Stadium in January 2005. Murali was hammered all over the park, going for a staggering 57 runs in his 3.1 overs. Most of those runs were hit by Flem in his 57-ball knock of 106. It was just amazing hitting and I have often wondered if that actually was the best way to play him. Australia did the same thing in the 2007 Cricket World Cup final. The Black Caps did try different things against him, with a pinch hitter at times, but it isn't always the greatest scenario when you come in cold and are expected to hit him out of the ground when you are not entirely sure what he is bowling.

Murali's record is going to be phenomenal — he will smash all test wicket-taking records and will probably get close to 1000 wickets, depending on how his body holds up and how long he wants to go on. But I would still rate him a notch behind my mate Warne.

Innovate and invigorate

It's safe to say I probably wasn't the most technically correct cricketer during my international career. I don't think that's a bad thing — the last thing I believe you want in any cricket team is 11 cloned, classically correct players. And I copped a fair bit of grief for some of the innovation I brought to my cricket, both with the bat and the ball.

One thing I think some struggled with was the notion that some of the things I tried on the cricket pitch were purely spur of the moment. I can tell you that is far from the truth. Countless hours of hard work went into some of the different shots and stances I toyed with over the years, well before I used them in the international arena.

One of the biggest frustrations I suffered from was that there seemed to be an accepted way to get out — certainly that seemed the case among certain members of the media. That was particularly the case whenever I got dismissed while playing the reverse sweep, a shot that I think is hugely effective when it's pulled off properly. I think that was also the case for part of the cricketing public too; they would rather see someone hooking and getting caught at fine leg or driving and being caught at second slip than getting out reverse sweeping. I just didn't understand that logic. To me, it was exactly the same thing. I had practised it, played it well and it was part of my set-up. A lot of guys couldn't play the reverse sweep but had other shots they could play.

The biggest thing I found about the reverse sweep is that it is hard to set fields to. Generally, you only play it when you have certain fields, settings where there are gaps for you to hit. It is something I experimented with in the nets for a while before bringing it into my game. I played a match against Northern Districts at Seddon Park and hit Dan Vettori for six with the reverse sweep. It's certainly something that I've reminded him about over the years.

The best I ever saw the shot played was by Andy Flower. He used to reverse sweep guys like Chris Harris. You would have one or two players up in the circle in a one-day international and so long as you got it either side of the fielder, or over the top, it was four runs. And because you left it quite late, you surprised the bowler as well. Now it is even an option against medium pacers with third man being brought up inside the circle.

I practised the reverse sweep for many hours in the nets. I spent time on how I held my hands, where I hit it, how I tried to hit it — whether that was just deflecting it or trying to hit it for four or six. I went through all of that and once I had the confidence that I could do it well, I brought it into my game. To me it was no different from practising the hook shot — it was just another shot. And don't forget that the hook shot can be high risk as well.

> **Steve Rixon:** We have this standing joke about him and the reverse sweep. I didn't see that he needed it in his game because he was a good enough player without it and had the ability to score runs, at will, anywhere he liked. I would have liked to have seen the conversion of the ones being a bigger issue instead of just innovating a new shot that would maybe get him four or maybe get him out. In his risky style of game, he had plenty of other ways of getting out.
>
> If I am anywhere in the world and he has pulled off a big reverse sweep, Macca finds a way of letting me know. He hit a six in New Zealand domestic cricket over point which made the news over in Australia and I just knew it wasn't going to be long before I heard from him. And he didn't let me down, on the phone as quick as, saying, 'Hey Stumper, it's Macca here. Just letting you know that I got another one away. This time we cleared the picket fence.' I thought, 'You little smart-arse.'
>
> Because of his innovation and style, he would have been a major asset to the Black Caps in 2008 and beyond. They need people like Macca right now. They have a lot of players who are good technicians. But when it comes to winning that game of cricket, I am looking around and I can't find them. The Black Caps have to look at how they are going to win games of cricket. And batsmen with flair is how you win. If he had been allowed to continue to play his style, as long as it was fine-tuned a little bit, I don't think he would be retired from international cricket.

I suppose I was always looking for different ways of doing the same thing. It is just like the front-on stance I adopted to take on Warnie. I first did it during the 2001–02 VB Series in Australia, and I remember taking my stance and Warnie, who was standing at the top of his mark, saying: 'What the f... is going on here?' He was just twiddling the ball in his hands for about a minute and a half and I was in my stance waiting for the ball. He had never seen anything like it and didn't know what was going on. They just started chipping away after that.

The whole point of the stance was that I wanted to play the sweep shot. By standing like that, I had less movement compared to a conventional stance to get into the sweep shot position. It meant I could just bend my knee, get down and get over the ball.

Shane Warne: I always found it fascinating when people came up with different stances and all that sort of weird stuff. I just thought, 'You beauty, I've got him to change his whole game before I start'. I thought what Macca did was actually good. It was a bit weird but it didn't put me off my game. If anything it made my job easier. He was going into so much other stuff, worrying about his stance and all types of things, that I thought the percentages were in my favour. I didn't have to do anything different.

One of the things people probably did get frustrated about with Craig was that sometimes he did have a bit of a brain explosion. But to me, that was a bit like Mark Waugh. Mark Waugh had a lot of brain explosions as well. And when he did, which was every now and again, you just accepted it. It was because this bloke could win a game, this bloke was a match-winner. He might have the odd brain explosion, but he was better off in the side than out.

Again, the stance was something I had practised a lot in the nets and asked myself, 'Why can't I stand like this if this is the shot I want to play and it is easier to play the shot by standing like this?' I knew that it looked a lot different and I was going to cop some flak. That was certainly the case at the Adelaide Oval where I got caught and bowled by Mark Waugh. Rather than actually sweeping, I tried to play one square to mid-wicket and instead got a leading edge. I got the biggest send-off ever from Waugh; they were just laughing.

People probably don't realise but a new shot or stance is something you think about a lot when you practise. You think about how it works. So you get someone to throw the ball down in different areas, you go through all the scenarios, depending on whether the ball is short or right up to you. It is not until you are confident that you actually take it into a game — it wasn't like I just woke up one morning and thought, 'Right, I am going to stand front on to Shane Warne and see what happens'. That would be ridiculous. I wouldn't have the confidence to do that because I wouldn't have worked out what was right about it and what was wrong.

I also used the stance against Ashley Giles when England toured in 2002. He didn't really know where to bowl because people thought by standing like that they could bowl wide of off-stump and I wouldn't be able to hit it. But that is actually where you want them to bowl, to give you width. That was the other thing with that stance: it made the bowler think 'What the hell is going on here? Where am I going to bowl it? What is he going to do?' Part of that stance was about sowing some doubt in the bowler's mind. It was unusual but it was something I was prepared to give a go. If it worked, great; if it didn't, it just meant it was time to go back and work on other things.

> **Daniel Vettori:** I always thought Craig's innovation came from the right place. He took time to analyse his game and think things over. While it may not have looked particularly traditional, or the way most people interpreted the way the game should be played, in my mind it came back to the fact he'd gone back to the drawing board and had looked over a few things. It wasn't just the case of trying to do the same things, day in day out. I think if you want to stay in the game as long as Craig did, you have to be able to do that. If you don't, then people will just get used to what you do.

> **Denis Aberhart:** When you think back to when he decided to have that stance, people at times criticised Macca for not having a good work ethic. But he was a great thinker of the game and he thought outside the square. So he turned up with this stance and it worked OK for him. When he did that open-eyed stance, it was something that he had spent a lot of time in the indoor nets working on before he even brought it out. You have to give him credit for that. With his work off the park, he tried to make things happen that were positive for him. You have to respect him because he wasn't afraid to make it happen.

It wasn't just the bat that I used to try to make a difference in a game of cricket. I also backed myself with the ball to get things happening. As a bowler, I loved the confrontation and guys answering back or trying to hit me out of the ground. I am always amazed at how many wickets I did get. Generally, a lot of them were more through talk than anything else.

There was a period in the 2000 season when I actually thought I was a bowler. I was clocked bowling at 135 kph in South Africa. For around 18 months I worked on a long run-up with Ashley Ross. We went to Zimbabwe and I was coming off the long run-up and trying to bowl as fast as I could. Looking back now, I don't know what was I thinking!

At the time there was a bit of a battle between the bowlers about how fast they bowled. In South Africa, after each delivery the speed would be displayed on the sight-screen. My speed of 135 kph was displayed, and everyone was shaking their heads because they knew I wouldn't stop talking about it for the rest of the year. No one mentioned it; they had all seen it but knew best not to bring it up.

As a bowler I went through many stages. Tristy had me as a death bowler at one stage in the one-day arena. If I am asked to do something, I will do it in the best interests of the team. If I was asked to be the floating batsman who has to go in and up the run rate, I would do that. It was the same with bowling at the death. I would never question those sorts of things. To me it was an opportunity to get involved in the game. There are a lot of guys who probably wouldn't do that as it would take them out of their comfort zone.

> **Denis Aberhart:** I think Craig could have bowled a lot more. And I know he was quite frustrated at not bowling more in international cricket. He could bowl a reasonably heavy ball, he could do a little bit with it and he certainly had the ability to take wickets. He also had the ability to get smacked around the park as well, but so can anyone else.
>
> Macca was a very good thinker of the game and that really came through with his bowling. He could make things happen. Because of Macca's aggressiveness, his bowling brought the worst out of batsmen. I think they thought, 'How can this upstart come in and bowl like this, come in and bounce me at 130 kph?' But Macca could take wickets. Sometimes he probably tried too hard, you probably wouldn't want to bring him in to tie an end up but you would bring him on to make things happen.

In the 2001 test in Brisbane I was thrown the ball when Australia were none for 224. We were getting smashed, Flem called me on and I ended up getting 3–65 to help get us back on track. I was just itching the whole time to have a go and that was the perfect example for me. It didn't matter to me that they were 0–224 and with both of their openers well set out in the middle. I just thought, 'Right this is my chance now to get a couple of wickets'.

The thing I most remember about bowling in that test was bouncing Steve Waugh and telling him he couldn't play the short ball. I was saying all these things that I had no right to be saying to a guy who had played more than 100 tests and faced guys like Curtly Ambrose and Allan Donald. I remember hitting him on the shoulder and chipping away at him. Then I bowled a full one which he nicked through to Parore to be dismissed for just three.

I loved that competitive edge about bowling. It was me against Steve Waugh. And Craig McMillan the bowler had no right to win against Steve Waugh the batter. But bowling gave me an opportunity to do that.

I got really frustrated near the end of my career when I didn't bowl as much as I would have liked. Flem generally went to an Astle or a Styris more than me. I felt, in the one-day game in particular, Nath and I could have bowled eight overs a game between us. And that could have meant we had a better balanced side. I always felt I got thrown the ball when Flem had looked around the field and there was no one else to throw it to — all the other bowlers had been tried. At times it felt that I was the last resort in terms of bowling and I thought I could be a bit better than that.

We went through a period in the Black Caps where Flem believed the players should just concentrate on their core job — so if someone was in a side to bowl, they bowled regardless of how well they were going. He didn't want to use guys like Nath and me; he wanted the bowlers to bowl their overs. I understand the theory behind it, because if you are in the side to bowl you have to bowl. But when you have some other guys who can do a job, I think you are silly not to use them. And in some conditions, when we were playing on low and slow pitches, we were actually more effective than the quicker guys.

Enough is enough

No cricket tour I was ever involved in could come close to the on and off-field dramas which we were to experience during the 2002 tour of Pakistan. In many ways the omens were always bad for what was to follow in Pakistan.

For a start, the tour was delayed for seven months due to the 9/11 terrorist attacks in America. The tour was supposed to start in September 2001. The team was picked, we were outfitted and headed for a stopover in Singapore on the way to the subcontinent. But that was as far as we got.

We had arrived in Singapore late that night and Chris Harris and I were rooming together. While Harry went to sleep pretty much straightaway, I am a more of a night owl, I struggle to get to sleep before midnight, so I was just flicking between TV channels and ended up on CNN. They were showing a fire coming out of a building, then they showed what had happened earlier with a passenger jet crashing into the World Trade Centre. I woke Harry up and told him to look at it. It was pretty hard to take in; it was all surreal.

Martin Snedden was new to the position of chief executive of New Zealand Cricket, but he wasted no time in deciding that the right thing was for us to come home immediately. We were due to fly out the following morning to Pakistan. With all the uncertainty, and then the news the American military were looking at sending resources into Pakistan, it was totally the right decision to make.

Seven months later and the belated tour to Pakistan was back on again. But it wouldn't take long before hopes that the rescheduled tour would run smoothly, both on and off the field, were shattered.

The tour began with a three-match one-day international series, starting in Karachi. Due to injury and illness I was given the captaincy. Probably the most notable thing about the game was when we left the field for 24 minutes after stones and other objects were thrown onto the field. The match referee, Mike Proctor, had to try to sort it out.

Pakistan scored 275–6 in their 50 overs and for a while we were going along alright with the run chase. I was on eight and then for some reason I decided to try to pull Akhtar, which was not one of my shots. And it was a doubly crazy thing to do against someone bowling the ball that fast. Sure enough I ended up spooning the ball to mid-wicket. The next thing Akhtar ripped through our side, ending with figures of 6–16, and we got knocked over for 122.

The second match of the series was in Rawalpindi and is one I will always remember fondly, mainly for the fact that I scored my second one-day international century. We batted first and I was eventually dismissed for 105 in the last of our 50 overs at bat. It was one of my best-ever innings against Waqar Younis, Wasim Akram, Shoaib Akhtar and Saqlain Mushtaq. Make no mistake, the first three of that lot bowled very fast.

The match was played in 40-degree heat and I was wearing my short-sleeved jumper. I always had a bit of a superstition that it didn't matter how hot it was, I always liked wearing my jumper, regardless of whether I was playing one-day or test cricket. And once I started with it, there was no way I could take it off. Needless to say I was pretty knackered at the end of the innings, by which time we had put on 277–5.

Daryl Tuffey got a wicket with his first ball, as he did during that period of his career. His early strike rate was such that we could almost always rely on him to take a wicket in his first over. We had Pakistan in a bit of trouble after that until we lost the plot somewhat, with Abdul Razzaq smashing us everywhere. He has taken a real liking to our attack over the years and they won with almost three overs to spare. I felt great that I had scored a good hundred in hot and demanding conditions, but at the same time we felt deflated that we hadn't managed to win the game.

The final match of the one-day international series was played in Lahore. And it was in that game when I faced Akhtar and the delivery he fired down which broke the 160 kph (100 mph) mark. They had a sponsor's radar at the game and Akhtar was really playing up to the crowd. It was a very disconcerting atmosphere for a batter with Akhtar charging in, progressively getting faster, and the crowd going absolutely nuts. A lot of his deliveries were around the 156 kph mark. Then he bowled another one, which didn't seem too different and I blocked it, but it came up on the board as 160 kph. The crowd went wild — there was a massive celebration and Akhtar was clearly bowling on adrenalin.

We struggled in Lahore, losing a third successive ODI match following our 66-run defeat. The series could easily have finished 2–1 but it wasn't meant to be.

We had little time to lick our wounds after the one-day series, with the two-test series starting in Lahore soon after. Again Tuffey got a wicket in his first over, but we got little respite from some very dominant Pakistani batting. 'Tower' dismissed Shahid Afridi and, despite having lost the toss, we thought if we were able to get out three or four wickets we could have a chance. We ended up being made to field for the first three days of the first test. And again Inzamam-ul-Haq dined out on a New Zealand attack, scoring 329. Lou Vincent dropped him when he was on about 110. I remember at the time thinking, 'Jeez, that's gonna be pretty costly'. But little did I think it would cost another 200-odd runs.

Inzamam butchered us all over the place, including playing Dan beautifully. He was running down the wicket and hitting him for six — he was totally in control. In the end we were just like dead men walking and our bowlers were out on their feet. After three days in the field we had to go into bat against Akhtar, who was bowling in the high 150s and swinging the ball all over the place.

In that innings he knocked over all our left-handers, coming around the wicket and bowling big in-swinging yorkers. He just kept knocking our poles over. It was like nothing I had seen before: he was bowling thunderbolts and ended with figures of 6–11 off just 8.2 overs. We were rolled and absolutely no match for him. We followed on and things didn't get much better in the second innings. This time Danish Kaneria was the chief destroyer, ending with figures of 5–110 off his 32 overs.

It was a pretty disappointing way to finish the first test. Any hopes of us making up for it in the pending second test in Karachi were dashed in terrifying circumstances, with a horrific bomb blast outside our hotel just under three hours before play was to start on the first day, cancelling both the test and the tour.

My build-up to what was supposed to be the first day of the second test, on 8 May 2002, started off no differently from any other. We were staying at the Pearl Intercontinental Hotel, one of two hotels in central Karachi which were frequented largely by Westerners.

We had two buses that would take us to the ground, an early bus and a later bus. The early bus was always for Mark Richardson, who liked to go to the ground and have 1000 throw-downs before anyone turned up at the match venue. The rest of us, who liked to have more sleep, waited around for the later bus.

The early bus was originally scheduled to leave at 7.45 am and the second bus was set to leave at 8.15 am. It was about 7.45 am and I was lying in bed thinking that I would have to get out of bed soon and that getting ready was going to be a bit of a rush. I was struggling to get up that morning for some reason.

Five minutes later I was blown out of bed. I had been just lying there in bed and all of a sudden I was on the floor, with glass all around me. My first thought was that someone had let off a grenade on one of the floors of the hotel. I was lucky that I had my curtains pulled across the window. The blast, which was outside my window, blew all the glass in, which was then stopped by the curtains. It gave me something of a shield. My door was blown off its hinges and there was a haze of smoke hanging around.

Eventually, I heard yelling. I didn't know what the hell had happened so I brushed myself off and walked over to what was left of the window in my hotel room. What I saw shocked me — a bus up in smoke and a massive crater in the ground. There was no mistaking the carnage and at that stage I had no idea about exactly whose bus had been blown up. I looked at my watch and thought, 'Shit, the early bus was supposed to leave around now'. The bus was an absolute mess, there was a massive crater and apparently the motor from the bomber's car was found 300 metres down the road.

We had an Australian security expert with us, Reg Dickason, and the next thing I remember is him approaching and yelling at me to get downstairs and get to the car park as quickly as possible. I went to my suitcase and immediately grabbed my passport, thinking, 'If I am going to get out of this place I will need my passport'.

It was just chaos downstairs: people were in shock, running all over the place. I ran downstairs to get to the car park and saw mass destruction everywhere. At the top of the hotel was a Japanese restaurant where we ate most nights, which had glass all around its high ceilings. You could sit up there and look all around Karachi while you were having your tea. From the car park I looked up and saw glass panes hanging by a thread, some were dropping and smashing. It was unreal.

About 10 of my team-mates were already in the car park by the time I got down there. Everyone was in a state of shock. A few of the guys, including Flem, had been at breakfast when the bomb went off and had seen some pretty atrocious things. Members of the Pakistan cricket team, who were staying at the same hotel, were also in shock after seeing things that no one would ever want to.

If what had happened wasn't disturbing enough, there was still a lot of uncertainty about our remaining team-mates. Because some of us were at breakfast, some were meant to be on the early bus and some were still in their rooms, no one knew if anyone was injured or worse. We were all distressed about exactly what might have happened.

Reg was invaluable to us. What happened at our hotel was one of the things that he had been specifically trained for. He took control and did what needed to be done. But it was all too much for our local team liaison officer who had a heart attack and was taken to hospital. Eventually, everyone made it down to the car park and it was a massive relief — I don't think we've ever been as happy as that very moment to see all of our team-mates in the one place.

From the car park we were taken to the hotel pool for about an hour, a time when the hotel was fully checked for any other explosives. Quite often there can be a second bomb — there was concern about that. During that time a lot of phone calls were made back home, to let everyone know that we were alright. For me, calling my wife-to-be Cherie was a bloody hard call to make.

> **Cherie McMillan:** The person I remember having the most conversations with was Linda Harris, Chris' wife. I have always been very close to her; she always took you under her wing. I was at work when I got a phone call from Mum to tell me that a bomb had gone off. I was in shock; I felt sick and didn't know what to do next. But we were quickly reassured that they were safe and everything was fine. Obviously, the biggest relief came when I talked to Craig. Linda came over to our place that night and, having each other there, knowing that we were both in the same situation, was a comfort, just talking about how we were feeling.

As the New Zealand Cricket Players' Association's Black Caps rep, one of the other calls I made was to CPA boss Heath Mills.

> **Heath Mills:** Craig called me literally 10 minutes after the bomb went off. We had a chat and it was quite a surreal discussion over the phone — I am sitting there talking to this guy, who is acting on behalf of all of his team-mates who are effectively shell-shocked in the back of the hotel where a bomb has just gone off.
>
> He and I were working through the players' position and what we should be communicating to New Zealand Cricket and what we needed to do. He was very calm and very cool at a time of crisis. He wasn't thinking about himself. He was thinking about the team and New Zealand Cricket.
>
> He very quickly ascertained that the guys didn't want to be hanging around Pakistan for too much longer. We communicated that to New Zealand Cricket and, to be fair, Martin Snedden was excellent. He always placed the security of the players above everything else — he would never put them in a dangerous situation. It only took one conversation with Martin and he was pulling the team home.

Jeff Crowe was our manager and he was great in his role in the aftermath of the Karachi bomb. He was very proactive in terms of getting things sorted very quickly to enable an early return home that day. The Pakistan Cricket Board weren't happy for us to go — something which still defies logic. A couple of members of the Pakistan cricket team could well have been casualties too — they were down at breakfast with our guys.

New Zealand Cricket press release, 8 May 2002
New Zealand Cricket bring TelstraClear Black Caps home from Pakistan
Following the explosion of a bomb outside the TelstraClear Black Caps team hotel New Zealand Cricket has decided to bring the team home from Pakistan.

The team will fly out of Pakistan this evening and will arrive in Auckland at 10.20 am on Friday, 10 May.

Chief Executive of New Zealand Cricket, Martin Snedden, spoke with team manager Jeff Crowe and team coach Denis Aberhart within an hour of the explosion and confirmed with them that all members of the team were safe and well.

'From the information we have to date it seems that a bomb exploded in a commuter bus on the road outside the team hotel. The damage to the Pearl Intercontinental Hotel is confined to the front of the hotel where the windows were shattered.

'The explosion occurred close to the time when the team were due to depart for the National Stadium but, in line with the security plan, the team bus was situated in a secure car park. Most of the team had yet to leave their rooms although the team physiotherapist, Dayle Shackel, received a minor cut to his forearm from flying glass.

'The team management has indicated that the team would like to leave Pakistan and New Zealand Cricket has made arrangements for their departure this evening.

'I have spoken to Brigadier Rana of the Pakistan Cricket Board and conveyed our decision to him. Our main priority now is to bring the players home safely to their families,' Snedden said.

After the hotel was cleared we were told to go back to our rooms. There was a real unease about being back in the hotel. Some guys took some photos of what they could see, others went for a walk — something I didn't understand because from what I heard the things they saw had lasting effects on them. I had no interest in doing that at all — I was just happy to stay in the safety of the hotel. The first thing I did was pack my bags as quickly as I could so that at any time I was ready to go.

Some of us got together and had a card school during the afternoon. And it really was a very surreal environment. We talked about the different scenarios in the hotel which had glass everywhere, doors blown off hinges and shrapnel all over the place. We were just waiting around and passing time before we were able to leave at 5 pm. Time went so slowly. When we finally were able to go, the local authorities went out of their way to make sure we had as smooth a trip to the airport as possible. They cleared the roads for our trip to the airport and we had a large police escort.

Cherie McMillan: The thing I felt most nervous about was them getting to the airport and getting on the plane. Once you knew that the plane had left and was in the air, you felt OK. That whole time before they left was surreal; I just couldn't imagine what Craig and the other guys were going through.

It didn't take long before we started hearing different stories and theories about what happened and who was targeted. There was no doubt that foreigners were targeted. The bus that was blown up had European scientists on board. It was parked fairly close to our early bus — which was delayed and hadn't left by the time the bomb went off. I doubt that the suicide bomber would have known the two buses apart. It is still a freaky thing to consider whenever I think back to what happened.

Some of our guys could have been minutes away from losing their lives. Once we started talking and thinking about that, the magnitude of the incident really did sink in. We were bloody lucky. Everyone dealt with things differently. You only had to see Flem's reaction at the press conference when we got home to see how it affected him.

Bomb blast a 'haunting experience' for New Zealand players
Lynn McConnell
Cricinfo, 10 May 2002

New Zealand captain Stephen Fleming told a press conference after the team's arrival in Auckland today that he will be haunted forever by some of the sights he saw in the aftermath of Wednesday's bomb blast that ended the tour of Pakistan.

'I saw too much, I saw things people shouldn't have to see,' he said.

One horrifying moment was when he was running for safety in the car park of the team's hotel in company with the team's security advisor and saw a man walking from the area with a limb missing and making noises he said were quite distressing.

Fleming said people who commented that the team should have stayed longer before coming home had obviously not seen the carnage or they wouldn't be commenting like that.

'It puts a lot of things in perspective,' he said.

Fleming added that he expected the trauma of what the team had been through to hit players individually over the next few days as they broke away from the team unit and met loved ones on their own.

'Emotionally that will be taxing,' he said.

Fleming said there was an absolute feeling of relief when the team left Karachi and the mood of the side had lifted considerably.

He said he was at breakfast when the bomb blast occurred and was contemplating leaving on the early bus for the ground that morning.

That bus would have passed within 15 metres of the bombed bus, five minutes after the blast.

When the explosion occurred the blast had reverberated through his body several times, and the ceiling was flaking in the restaurant. The team security advisor Reg Dickason sent Fleming and other hotel patrons sprinting for the safety of the car park and Fleming said Dickason was required to move some people along very quickly.

His scariest moment was when he found eight of the team in the car park but didn't know where the other team members were.

It affected me badly too. I had no shortage of sleepless nights. When I did get to sleep I would more often than not wake up in a cold sweat. That is what I endured for six weeks after returning from the tour. I would be replaying in my mind what happened and what I saw that day. It was something I couldn't shake. Another thing that wouldn't leave me was the ringing in my ears. I would be semi-asleep and then I would just constantly hear this massive 'boom'. For at least two months afterwards it remained very vivid in my memory.

The Black Caps returned to Pakistan again in November 2003, but I wasn't on board for the tour. Players were given the choice whether they wanted to go back to Pakistan, a country which still had its fair share of problems. And Ian Butler, Lou Vincent, Scott Styris and I decided it wasn't worth it. Flem also missed the tour through injury.

We were told that we would have the choice. Certainly the players felt that the guys who had been through what happened should be able to make the decision on whether to be available or not. Trying to make guys go back there would have been irresponsible of New Zealand Cricket.

Heath Mills: Some of the players made it very clear to me that they couldn't put their families through them being in the subcontinent again while these security threats existed. We worked with Martin Snedden to get New Zealand Cricket to put a policy in place where if a player wanted to stand aside and not go on tour that NZC would not try to force the players to go on tour using their contracts. There were four or five players who made themselves unavailable for that tour — Craig was one of them. All those players had families and kids at home. While they hugely treasured playing for the Black Caps, they couldn't put their families through that situation again.

I had made my decision that I wasn't going to go back. I felt that cricket is just a game — that is all it is. I was in the process of getting married and I didn't want to be put in that situation again. Some guys felt that they had to go back, because of their position in the team. They thought maybe they wouldn't get selected again or their decision not to tour would be held against them down the track.

People might say that we also go to India and England and terrorism happens in those places — and that is true. But at that time, and it is still the case, Pakistan was a real hot-bed. When we first arrived in Karachi, Reg sat us down and talked about what we could and couldn't do in the city. He also told us Karachi, Johannesburg and Jamaica were the three most dangerous cities in the world, based on murders per capita. And they are three major cricketing cities!

Once I had got home and talked things over with Cherie, I made the decision that I didn't ever want to go back to Pakistan. At the time the bomb happened, it brought my life in front of my eyes. It made me sit back and realise that there was more to life than cricket. I didn't see the need to put myself back into that position, so I took the stance that I wouldn't tour Pakistan again, even if that decision could ultimately cost me my place in the side. I am sure it didn't help my situation, because it gave others an opportunity.

Once I had made up my mind, I was very strong at sticking to my decision. Going back, especially to a couple of those places, would conjure up a lot of the things that happened when we were over there. It took me a while to get through all of the stuff — I didn't want to have to go through it again. There are plenty of other places where you can play cricket without going to Pakistan.

> **Cherie McMillan:** I was quietly pleased when Craig decided that he was never going to go back to Pakistan. He never talked to me about what he saw or even how much he saw. I only knew what I'd heard through the media, and I never pushed Craig to talk about it. He knew I was there if he needed me. He, like all of them, dealt with it in his own way.

Don't get me wrong, I have nothing at all against Pakistan. One of my first tours overseas as a cricketer was with the New Zealand Youth team in 1994 — and we had a hell of a great time.

One morning the whole team went up to the Afghan border. On the way we drove through a multitude of little settlements and it seemed like everyone carried a gun, even the kids were running around with them. We took photos on the border with armed guards, things that today you wouldn't even consider. But back in 1994 it was obviously a much different time.

I have a lot of good memories of Pakistan. But unfortunately that bad experience in Karachi has clouded my mind. Because of it, I will never return there.

Fight for the right

There are times in your career when you have to stand up and be counted — even if it is an approach which doesn't impress everyone involved, including your employer. And that's just what happened in the lead-up to the 2002–03 season when New Zealand's leading players took on New Zealand Cricket in a bid to get a better deal and improved working conditions

Thoughts of forming a New Zealand Cricket Players' Association had been floated around the Black Caps' environment for several seasons. But by the time 2001 rolled around, nothing had been able to get off the ground. New Zealand Cricket had retainers for international players, a set-up which looked after a minority very well, while the majority were paid a far smaller figure.

This was all happening at a time when the money New Zealand Cricket was receiving from sponsorship and broadcasting deals was rapidly on the rise. I had always thought it would be great for the players to have an official voice. To have an independent spokesperson and organisation to express those ideas seemed like a fantastic and logical idea. We all knew there were other sports that had players' associations — it was something we had wanted for a while, in terms of our negotiations with New Zealand Cricket. But a lot of our recommendations were falling on deaf ears.

There's no getting away from the fact that some of the motivation for the push to create a players' association was financial. We were the shop window and generating a massive income for New Zealand Cricket. We wanted a bigger slice of the pie, which we believed was only fair. But it wasn't all about the high-profile guys in the national team — we also wanted to improve things for both the country's up and coming players and veterans who were struggling to earn a living in the domestic scene.

We wanted the wealth to be distributed fairly among not only the national side but the domestic players too.

It wasn't purely all about money. At the time we were training on substandard wickets around the country, including nets where the ball was seaming all over the place. Because you had spent your practice time preparing on a totally different sort of wicket, it affected the way you played on game day. If you don't have good practice facilities to work on, it makes it difficult for you to improve your game by upgrading your skills.

We thought we were being short-changed in a lot of areas. While some players had been unsuccessful in the past in getting a better deal, the arrival of Heath Mills and Rob Nichol on the scene in early 2001 certainly heralded a new era in New Zealand cricket — albeit one which was only secured after an emotion-charged period which left bitterness on both sides.

Heath Mills: I was director of sport for Mt Albert Grammar School and my brother Kyle had just made the Auckland team. One day Kyle and two of his team-mates, Chris Drum and Brooke Walker, approached me and asked if I could talk to Auckland Cricket about contracts. The players didn't have contracts, yet they were expected to do all this training over winter. I went to see Lindsay Crocker, then CEO of Auckland Cricket, and said: 'I see these three guys as being the key for Auckland in the next five or six years and you are not looking after them. They need to be on some sort of retainer if you want them to do all of this work for you in the off-season.'

We settled on Auckland Cricket paying them the princely sum of a $5000 retainer and all three signed up that day. The very next day I got phone calls from three other players in the Auckland team asking me to go and see Lindsay Crocker and cut them the same deal. I did and virtually all the players in the Auckland team got these $5000 retainers for the winter.

Two days later Dion Nash, who I had gone to university with, came and did a couple of days' relief teaching at MAGS. I said to him, 'It really disappointed me that Auckland Cricket wasn't looking after these young guys. It took me to go and strong-muscle the CEO to get these retainers.' He replied, 'Yeah, what we need in this country is a players' association.' He told me that Tim May in Australia had set one up and it had done wonders over there, and that their players were much better looked after. The next day I gave Tim a call, introduced myself and asked him all about it. Coincidently, at the same time, I had watched the News and seen another old friend of mine from university, Rob Nichol, fronting a story about the new rugby players' association that he was running. I gave Rob a call and told him what I was looking at doing. That effectively got us teamed up.

Three or four days later I ended up flying around the country with Dion Nash and had meetings with each of the six major associations under the cloak of darkness. We signed up every player to the players' association under the new constitution we had formed. We also spoke to seven or eight of the senior Black Caps in England, including the captain Stephen Fleming, and they all joined.

The meeting at Canterbury was held at Nathan Astle's house. He had organised about 14 of the Canterbury players to be there and that was my first meeting with Craig McMillan. They were particularly supportive of having a players' association formed and that something like this was long overdue. Craig certainly was one who felt very passionately about the concept.

The way things were explained by Heath and Rob made complete sense. It was also set out to us how important it was that things were kept in house — we weren't to talk to New Zealand Cricket or our provinces about what was going on. For this to work meant that when Heath eventually went to New Zealand Cricket for negotiations he was in a position of power. It was imperative that he had every single provincial player in New Zealand signed up and fully committed to the formation of the association. Past attempts had failed, so if we were to create a better environment and future for the players and New Zealand cricket then we needed to have everyone singing from the same sheet.

Heath did a great job selling it to the provincial players. The whole thing about it was that the provincial players were really the winners at that time. My goal was trying to sustain older players in the game for as long as possible. When I started out, I played against guys like Barry Cooper from Northern Districts, Justin Vaughan and Dipak Patel at the end of their careers for Auckland — people who had been around first-class cricket for a long time. To me, it was important that we had older guys like that passing on their knowledge to young blokes.

The association was formed in about two weeks, and a board was elected featuring one person nominated from each of the six major association teams. Then it was time for Heath to introduce himself to Martin Snedden, the new boss of New Zealand Cricket, shortly after his appointment in May 2001.

Heath Mills: I met him in his family law firm office in Auckland and it is fair to say Martin was rather quiet during the meeting — I certainly don't think he expected to be confronted with the formation of a players' association in basically his first week in the job. The timing was right for us. The players had seen New Zealand Cricket revenues grow significantly over a short period of time, yet it appeared to them that only the top four or five players in the country were being looked after. Everyone else was really playing for what I would describe as small contracts. There were New Zealand contracted players on $5000–$10,000 retainers, plus match payments.

And the domestic players weren't contracted at all. They were all playing for match fees apart from a few players at both Auckland and Wellington who were on retainers. You had a situation where unless you were in the top six or seven players in New Zealand, you had absolutely no security over your income. You had committed your life from the age of 14 or 15, entering academies and developing yourself into an international cricketer, yet once you entered the professional game you were playing for wages on a week-to-week basis. If players got injured, they simply didn't get paid.

You cannot have a situation where a player is worried about how he is going to put food on the table and how he is going to pay his rent. It was focused on taking that stress away, allowing players to concentrate on their cricket. We had got to the stage where it was fair to say the guys playing domestic cricket in New Zealand were university students or people who had come from backgrounds who could afford to play. The average age of the first-class cricketer in New Zealand had dropped considerably; it was in the low-20s. A player would get to 23 or 24 and if he hadn't made the Black Caps by then, he would effectively make the decision that 'I can't continue to devote six months of my life to cricket and only get $10,000 in match fees to do that. I need to get a career somewhere else and catch up to my peers who have been to varsity and are earning a solid income.'

We introduced ourselves to New Zealand Cricket and ended up having a meeting with all the six major associations and the New Zealand Cricket senior management team. We also sent New Zealand Cricket a notice saying we were wanting to bargain for a collective agreement on behalf of all domestic players in New Zealand. The New Zealand players who were on contract effectively came off contract around the end of April 2002.

We said from that point we wanted a new contract in place. We started negotiations with them at the start of 2002 and it was a long, drawn-out process. There is always a lot to get through when you establish a new collective agreement — they are fairly significant documents. And we had a feeling that New Zealand Cricket were happy to see the negotiations going on because they were almost testing the players to see how committed they were to this process.

The negotiations were going on alright in terms of the peripheral stuff within the agreement. But when we got to the numbers and the figures, we couldn't engage New Zealand Cricket on getting resolutions around that. All the players were off contract around 1 April and we were getting close to the 2002 tour of the West Indies. We didn't have a contract in place, so no player in the country was under contract. We didn't want to play hard ball with New Zealand Cricket. We wanted to do the right thing and get a deal done in good faith with them. We drafted an interim contract for New Zealand Cricket to sign 20 players up over the two or three-month period of the West Indies tour. We did that with remuneration levels which were pretty much close to where we wanted to get to in terms of the retainers and the match fees. But we were still quite a way away from finalising the collective agreement.

Despite the team going on tour, we couldn't get a commitment from New Zealand Cricket to get the deal done. So when the players came home from that West Indies tour they were pretty much off contract straight away. We were then coming under pressure from the players; they were asking us pretty fair questions, saying, 'What is happening here guys, are we getting the deal done, are we getting contracts?' You had to bear in mind that some had mortgages and kids to feed. And they weren't getting paid. We never seemed to get any commitment to really fleshing out the numbers.

As the months dragged on, the whole contract situation increasingly started being played out in the public. And that led to it being a very uncertain time for the players. We knew we were obviously taking on a pretty major challenge — but as time went on we increasingly found that we were being isolated. We were also being singled out for scathing comment in some areas.

There was no lack of emotion being used in the now-public battle. We were approaching a major season, including the 2003 Cricket World Cup to be held in South Africa. A lot of fear was put out into the public, including that the test and one-day international tour of New Zealand by India — our build-up to the World Cup — could be jeopardised if we were on strike. There was also the notion that those of us who were trying to be a driving force for the association would be missing when the national team was announced. But despite the scaremongering, it was time for us to step up our drive to get some resolution and satisfaction.

Health Mills: We needed to demonstrate to New Zealand Cricket that we were committed to getting a deal done. When you negotiate a contract for the first time, you have to have some heat. We had worked, quite naively, to avoid heat and do the right thing. And as pre-season camps to be held in Lincoln in October neared, it came time to change tack. The camps would mean the players would be taking four or five weeks off work to go down there. And straight after the camp in Lincoln, the Indians were arriving for their tour in November.

Our thinking at the time was: 'How can we send a message to New Zealand Cricket? We don't want to put any pressure on the Indian tour but they need to know that we can't go on like this.' So we thought as the players weren't contracted, we would advise New Zealand Cricket that they wouldn't be turning up to the camps. But we weren't going on strike — you have to be in an employed situation to go on strike. No one was under contract so there was no obligation on any of the players.

We were still a couple of weeks away from the camps and we thought if we advised New Zealand Cricket of our intentions it would speed things up — within a week or two we could flesh out a deal and everything would go fine. New Zealand Cricket obviously saw it a different way and virtually the next day they pulled the camps and said the players were on strike. We were very disappointed with that, we didn't want to impact on the coaching programme, the training of the guys and the camps. And then we entered into that awful phase where the negotiations were hammered out in the public domain — it made it so much more difficult for the deal to get done because you had the public pressures and the media pressures on you. It heightened the emotions of everyone involved.

The other thing that upset me was the fact that some of the younger provincial guys, who stood to earn a lot out of the association, couldn't see the long-term picture. Our guys signed up, but then three or four of them went back and played some of the pre-season games because they could see an opportunity for themselves to get a game for Canterbury. It was a by-product of New Zealand Cricket drawing things out — their approach certainly seemed to be testing our resolve and trying to weaken our stance by letting things drag on.

I can understand younger players struggling with the pressure that was increasingly coming on from New Zealand Cricket. But, at the same time, it was really disappointing that it was happening. While in the bigger picture it didn't alter things in the end, it probably affected those guys more when everything went through and they had to come back into the fold. It would have been difficult because they had let their mates down by jumping ship.

The pressure that was placed on the youngsters was nothing compared to the position the senior Black Caps were put in. We were the ones who had the most to lose — we were potentially putting international careers on the line to try to get everyone more money, better working conditions and a consistent competition. New Zealand Cricket seemed intent on isolating players and trying to pick them off one by one. And I suppose had they been able to pick off a couple of the major players, it would have created anxiety among the rest and the association could have fallen over. Guys like Cairns, Fleming, Nash, Astle and me were important. At the time we were the leading players in the New Zealand side. For something to be successful and work, they needed our support. As with a lot of things, the others followed the leaders.

As the debate raged on in public, it was spelt out to the Black Caps what they were potentially giving up by pushing for the association and its demands. And no more so than at the meeting we had at Nath's house where Martin Snedden pretty much said, 'You guys are ending your careers — if you don't take this deal, then you will be finding new careers.'

Some of us were still in our early to mid 20s, some were older, but being faced with that was pretty disconcerting. The meeting also included Flem, Cairnsy and Gary Stead; we were wanting to see how we could sort it out. But Snedden was almost saying to us, 'Your careers are gone.'

Heath Mills: We know that players were leant on and were presented with opportunities to break away from the players' association. And one of those players was Craig McMillan. The others were Nathan Astle, Stephen Fleming, Chris Cairns and Daniel Vettori. Those five players were the ones who were already very well looked after by New Zealand Cricket. But they decided that they didn't want to just look after themselves and they wanted to see a better environment for every domestic player in New Zealand. And they wanted to do this despite pressure from New Zealand Cricket and opportunities being offered to them to break away. They stuck together.

The really frustrating thing was the sensational headline that a lot of media went after, that the players were just 'money hungry' and 'greedy'. I have seen far less of that in the professional sports that I have worked in than in everyday business. It never ceases to amaze me that in the team sports we have in this country, and especially cricket, how caring the guys are about other people in the environment and how they want to make sure the right thing is done by everyone. To label these guys as money hungry quite frankly is irresponsible and a very narrow view to most of the issues we confront. But that's just what they had to put up with.

The arrival of November, a month before the Indians' arrival, still hadn't brought any resolution. Instead supporters from both parties were increasingly finding themselves in the media in what had become a very public wrangle. We had faith in the work that Heath Mills and Rob Nichol were doing. But those on the other side of the fence didn't, with Martin Crowe calling on the association to change tack and get Flem to handle negotiations. The frustrations boiled over in a press conference headed by Rob Nichol in Auckland on 5 November where he went on the front-foot, explaining why the NZCPA had rejected an earlier deadline to sign New Zealand Cricket's best offer. After explaining the reasons the deadline was not met, a decision that was made following a recommendation from the Federation of International Cricketers' Association, Rob went on the attack about some of the tactics adopted by NZC.

That included the release of NZC's payment offers and also the leaking of what some players were already being paid. That was playing dirty; it was a move to try to sway public opinion New Zealand Cricket's way. We had become so annoyed with the way we were battling the media full-stop — it seemed that the media were on New Zealand Cricket's side when it came to this saga. Really, from that point on, we were never going to win. Five days later a settlement was agreed upon.

Settlement reached between New Zealand Cricket and the NZCPA
New Zealand Cricket, 11 November 2002

The New Zealand Cricket and Major Association bargaining teams have reached an agreement with the New Zealand Cricket Players' Association, New Zealand Cricket chief executive Martin Snedden announced at a press conference today.

'We can now put in place a player contract system for a four-year period from 2002 to 2006,' he said. The terms of the agreement reached are largely in accordance with the settlement offer that we tabled on 1 November.

'Under the terms of the agreement the player payment pool has increased by $100,000, from that in the 1 November offer, to $5.1 m. There has also been some tweaking within the player payment pool including changes to the structure of player retainers. The number of players to be contracted by each Major Association has been increased from 10, in the previous offer, to 11.

'We have resolved the ICC sponsorship contract issue in a way which will satisfactorily protect New Zealand Cricket,' Mr Snedden said.

The agreement does not include funding of the New Zealand Cricket Players' Association by New Zealand Cricket or major associations.

'Both New Zealand Cricket and the Major Associations are happy to work with the New Zealand Cricket Players' Association in the future and we expect to develop a positive relationship with the players' association now that the contract issue is behind us,' Mr Snedden said. 'We can now look forward to the start of the domestic and international seasons.'

There was pain involved for both sides of the contract dispute. From a player's perspective, we had our character questioned — but I have to stress the whole process wasn't just driven by contracts and dollar signs. Far from it. Now our first-class grounds require a warrant of fitness. The agreement covers practice facilities and also has tackled the issue of pitches and players' facilities which weren't up to standard. Now there is a certain standard which all the grounds need to reach. If the grounds' management want to host first-class cricket, they are under no illusion as to what is required of them.

The ability to ensure guys were able to earn a sustainable living playing first-class cricket, as opposed to retiring early, and the competition becoming like an under-23 comp was a huge driving force during the whole process. It was my motivation. And now it is happening. The Black Caps also have a bit more say in terms of tours, the length of tours and all of those sorts of things. But it is not all about the current crop of players either — some of the stars of yesteryear have also been assisted by the association in regards to its Hardship Fund.

Heath Mills: I take my hat off to the senior players. Those few guys had the most to lose. And it is fair to say that one or two of them probably ended up getting paid less in the new collective than they were being paid individually prior to this point. Some of them made sacrifices to ensure that we got a professional contracting environment in place that was fair to everybody. I have huge admiration for those guys. It was a great thing, and a very honourable thing, that they did.

Everyone now who has benefited has a lot to thank those guys for. Quite frankly, if they had broken away and taken better contracts from New Zealand Cricket and looked after themselves, then the whole negotiations would have broken down. New Zealand Cricket could have built a team around those five guys and put pressure on other guys that if they didn't break away then effectively they wouldn't be playing for New Zealand again.

At that stage the top five or six players were getting paid big money — everyone else was getting paid peanuts. And this was from an organisation that was turning over $22 million a year. They had professional coaches in place who were demanding professional commitments from players; they were wanting the players to work seven days a week. Yet players, and this wasn't just in the cricket season, were being retained for contracts of $10,000 a year.

Although my first-class career in New Zealand is now over, I am still committed to the New Zealand Cricket Players' Association. In 2007 I was voted onto the board and over the next few years I want to be able to give a lot more to the association. I have pretty much gone full circle. I started out as the Black Caps team rep, the link man between the Black Caps and Heath. In many ways because I was the first team rep, I was tarnished a little. There was a bit of 'us and them' with New Zealand Cricket for quite a while, some real insecurity. I'm sure Flem was also tarnished. That was sad because if you look back at the bigger picture now, it was something that was long overdue and was certainly needed.

And while there was a degree of hurt which everyone went through to get to this point, looking back I can say it has been worth it. One of the things I am proudest of in my cricket career is the part I played in forming that organisation. It was only a small part, but to see the NZCPA now co-existing and having a good relationship with New Zealand Cricket is great.

Heath Mills: Craig has been one of the most supportive players of the association. He was significant in its establishment, one of the key guys early on. After we had got the contract environment in place, Craig was voted to be the player rep for the Black Caps. He was my conduit between the players' association and the team. And he was excellent in that role, always making sure that if there were any issues the players had that I was aware of them and working with him to address them in the team environment and with New Zealand Cricket.

In the last year he was elected onto the board and he is very keen to get experience in a governance role and contribute more to the association. And it is great to see that level of commitment from a player — he has been a great supporter, continues to be and always will be. A lot of players wouldn't realise how much support he has given the association, given me and given to other players behind the scenes.

He is a really whole-hearted guy, a guy who is very black and white in terms of right or wrong. And if he thinks someone is getting a raw deal, the rough end of the stick or that something is not fair, he will stand up and say it. And he will do that even if those issues don't impact on him or if he doesn't stand to gain anything from it. He would be the one who stands up for others.

World Cup agony in South Africa

One of the secrets to any successful campaign is the preparation that goes into it. There was certainly a lot of planning that went into our 2003 Cricket World Cup campaign in South Africa — including different tactical approaches — but unfortunately when it came to the crunch, a lot of it was totally unworkable.

Our planning for South Africa went into overdrive in November 2002, with a squad meeting where we discussed a range of issues including our game plan, specific player roles, the best way for us to move forward and even how the media and the public viewed us as a team following on from the messy contract wrangle. In the lead-up to the tournament we were also introduced to a convoluted piece of paperwork titled the 'Optimised Batting Resources' strategy — the brainchild of Black Caps' technical advisor Ashley Ross. Its goal was to give us the 'edge' in South Africa.

The basis was that while bowlers won test matches, it was the batsmen who won one-day internationals. Part of the theory included proposed lined-ups and who should be the next batsman in four different sections of the innings. There's nothing wrong with that; in fact it makes common sense to have people prepared to float up and down the order depending on the situation in a game. But what didn't make a lot of sense, and what essentially made it unworkable, was the information overload that was involved. It included not only changing the line-up depending on how we were going mid-game but also depending on the size of grounds. It was just way too complicated to work.

Being enmeshed in this piece of paperwork wasn't the only reason the lead-up to the 2003 World Cup wasn't the best time to be in the top or middle order of the Black Caps. We played India in a two-test series in New Zealand before the World Cup — a series which we won 2–0 but one in which I never really fired with the bat. The ball seamed around a lot and we knocked them over in both games pretty easily because we had pitches that were to our liking. There was no third test in the series, instead a series of seven one-dayers against India was scheduled as the last hit-out before we travelled to South Africa.

It's fair to say I struggled through this period, as most of the batters did. I didn't feel in great nick and with the pitches the way they were, it made it even worse. I wasn't in a great state mentally. The nature of the pitches, and the low scores, also meant it wasn't a great tour for the spectators. We bowled India out for totals of 108, 219, 108, 122 and 200 in the five matches in the series we won. They had to chase down just 169 and 200 in our two losses to them.

It was also in the series against India where one of the issues emerged that would see us come unstuck at the World Cup two months later — a real lack of stability in the batting line-up. I played only in the first four matches, posting scores of four, five, 22 and a duck in Queenstown before I was dropped. After I was dropped they played guys like Chris Harris at No. 3 and No. 4. They were batting him right out of position and he didn't score any runs.

So, to me, while we were listening to World Cup plan speeches, it actually seemed like no real planning had been done. I would have thought that you would have wanted your best and most stable side playing consistently right throughout the build-up to the World Cup. Yet I missed the last three games against India and then came back in for the first game of the World Cup. It just summed up the lack of structure we had during this period.

We went to South Africa, and my second World Cup, with a reasonable team. We had some experience blended with some exciting younger guys like Brendon McCullum. But there was also cause for unease early on, in particular with Richard Hadlee, the chairman of selectors, travelling on our bus a lot. There was a general nervousness among the team that he was so close to the team. As players, we certainly felt he wasn't keeping the distance that he should have.

It also didn't take us long to find out that some of the planning that Ashley Ross had done in the lead-up to the tournament might be a little wayward. Well before the start of the tournament he had travelled to South Africa for a pre-World Cup scouting mission, visiting the grounds we were to play in and checking on other facets of the tournament infrastructure. That included a scouting report of Bloemfontein's Goodyear Park where we were to play our first match of the tournament against Sri Lanka.

His feedback included that we needed to play pace bowlers as he believed the pitch would be wet in the morning and would do a bit. So our team saw André Adams play instead of Dan and we ended up getting stuffed by Sri Lanka. We won the toss and bowled first which we wanted to do with our seam attack. But the pitch didn't do anything at all — it was low and slow and the complete opposite to the information we had been given. So we were missing our star spinner, who in those conditions would have been a handful. Sri Lanka ended up making 272–7, a decent total which we couldn't chase down, even though Styris blasted 141 in a losing cause.

Another weakness also raised its head — just who would open the innings with Flem. Despite Nathan Astle's record being fashioned out of opening in the one-day arena, for the 2003 Cricket World Cup it was decided that his best position was actually No. 3. Ashley Ross had the theory that your best batter plays at No. 3. The brains trust also held the theory that if Nathan got through his first 15 or 20 balls then he scored well. And they felt that in South Africa, it might be better for him to slide down one place in the order and protect him from the new ball initially. That theory gained traction following Nathan's five-ball duck in our tournament-opening loss.

It was a policy which saw Daniel promoted up the order to open in our second match of the tournament against the West Indies at St George's Park, Port Elizabeth. Dan got 13 in our innings of 241, with me watching on from the sidelines after being dropped. Nathan also benefited from the move, top-scoring for us with 46 in our 20-run win. But that didn't change my view that, as he was our best one-day international batsman, he should be opening.

The plan continued for our third game, this time with me having to step into the breach at the top innings against hosts South Africa. It was an incredibly hot day when we took to the field at the Wanderers, Johannesburg, and we just copped sheep-shagging jokes all day from the South African fans who were pouring Castle lager down their necks. Herschelle Gibbs smashed us around all over the place on a very good wicket — he played out of his skin as South Africa posted a total of 306–6 for us to win.

Dan was initially meant to open again but he was under the weather during the interval between the innings and wasn't in a condition to bat. I was down to initially bat in the middle of the order and suddenly got thrown into opening with Flem during the break. I managed to score 25 in trying circumstances in an 89-run opening partnership. Flem went on to score a match-winning unbeaten 134 as we chased down 229 in a Duckworth-Lewis revised total. Opening certainly wasn't my best spot in the batting order — it was not something I felt overly comfortable with.

Denis Aberhart: At that stage Macca was on the fringe of getting into the side. He came in and opened against South Africa and he did a bloody good job, getting

25. People forget the contribution he made within that game — it was a hard ask: we were struggling at the top of the order, we didn't quite have people doing the job that we needed them to do. Fleming will be remembered for the fact that he got that wonderful century, but Macca actually got him the start there and did a really good job for us opening and getting things under way. His was a pretty important role for that game. And in the end he may have been under-used for what he could have provided us at that World Cup.

We were struggling at the top of the order. Mathew Sinclair was around the fringe and he wasn't doing the things. Stephen Fleming had come up to open. The discussion was that Nathan probably at that stage was getting out a lot at the top of the order, so perhaps we should put him in at No. 3. We were struggling to find someone to open at the top of the order.

It was probably really that people hadn't put their hand up in that opening position, and we are still struggling at that position in the order. It wasn't new then, and it isn't new now. We got to that World Cup and it was certainly a weakness in our side.

The chopping and changing of the batting order showed me that there was no rigid policy in place in terms of a batting order. The whole policy of Nathan being protected to bat at No. 3 was one that some of us didn't entirely understand. And if it was to be adopted, it was a decision which should clearly have been made before the tournament started and all of the guys should have been aware of what was about to come. There's no doubt that the problems at the top of the order certainly contributed to a less-than-successful tournament for the Black Caps — but it wasn't the reason for our eventual failure to make the semi-finals. Instead, that was due to off-field circumstances.

What ultimately killed off our World Cup hopes was the decision by New Zealand Cricket boss Martin Snedden for us to not travel to Nairobi for our group-phase international against Kenya due to safety reasons. And while playing for the Black Caps was something that I was prepared to, and did, make plenty of sacrifices for, the decision for us not to travel ultimately was the right one to make. It handed Kenya a walk-over win, but I was certainly in the camp that our safety should not have been compromised by sending us into what was a very unstable and unsafe environment.

Denis Aberhart: It was a difficult time for the players, but the point was that New Zealand Cricket made the decision. Martin Snedden had a meeting with us in Johannesburg and basically said that the information that New Zealand Cricket had was that there were two Al-Qaeda cells in Nairobi looking for Western targets. All the advice that New Zealand Cricket had been given was that it wasn't safe for us to travel to Kenya.

Sampling a beer during my formative years, something which my later diagnosis of diabetes meant was few and far between.

Only Kathryn (right) has remembered to smile as my mum Judith, dad Lindsay and I strike a pose.

About to blow out the candles while celebrating my seventh birthday with Kathryn and my nana.

My gran was a constant source of support and my official scorer. She never went to one of my matches without a notebook.

Caught here about to heave the ball upfield while playing age-grade soccer for Canterbury.

Second from left in the top row, pictured with my Canterbury under-13 team-mates.

Captured here sharing a smile with Sir Richard Hadlee, something that was rare between us in later years.

Taking time out with a soldier on the Pakistan/Afghanistan border during the 1994 New Zealand Youth team tour.

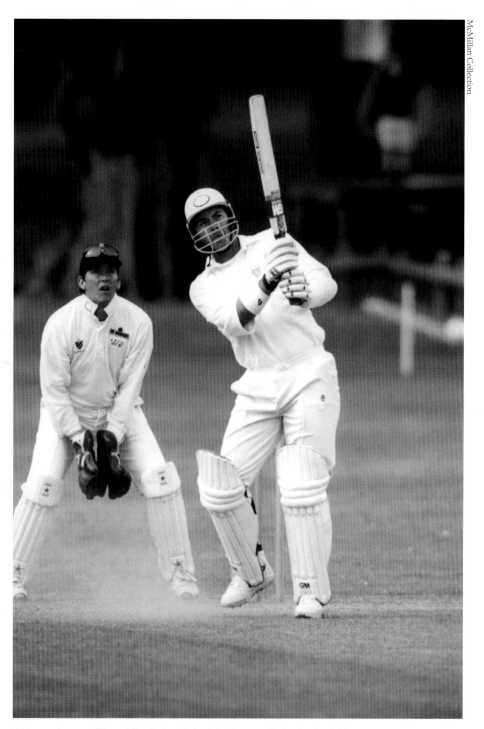

Taking to the opposition while playing club cricket for East Christchurch-Shirley.

I wanted to impress with the ball, even as far back as my early days with the Canterbury side.

No one was arrested for the fashion crimes the Black Caps committed during their 1997–98 tour of Australia.

The lights on the Gabba scoreboard highlight my half-century in my first-ever test innings.

The passion that Indians have for cricket was hammered home to me right from my first Black Cap tour in 1997.

Heath Mills: We were in constant dialogue with the team and New Zealand Cricket about the game in Kenya. We were very comfortable with the security advice we were receiving with New Zealand Cricket. In many respects it was the beginning of forging a very strong relationship with Martin Snedden. He was outstanding at that time. New Zealand Cricket were under enormous pressure for the Black Caps to go to Kenya. For South Africa, the 2003 Cricket World Cup was as much about showcasing Africa to the rest of the world as it was just about South Africa. They took it very personally that a team would not travel to another African country or even view it as insecure.

There was absolutely no doubt that the security reports that we saw and we received made it impossible to sit back and allow the team to go to Kenya at that time. Kenya was described as having the most porous border in the world — basically every terrorist group going had an operation of some sort in Nairobi and there were specific groups actively looking for Western targets. A number of the guys weren't comfortable about going and we worked very hard with the ICC to move the game to South Africa. But they were adamant, because of South Africa's position, that they would not move the game.

I was talking to Martin Snedden every night while he was in South Africa. Our position with New Zealand Cricket was that they could not afford to have another disastrous situation like they had in the early 1990s in Sri Lanka where they went to individual votes to decide whether the team stayed or not. New Zealand Cricket had to make the decision on behalf of the team on whether they went or not. Martin was strong in the belief that the players wouldn't be put at risk. And credit to him that he took on making that decision and pulled the team out of that match.

Everyone in the team had different thoughts; I personally wouldn't have gone. The information we were getting was pretty good about what was going on. There had been a terror threat. We had a team meeting and a letter was read out that we had received about what might happen to a team going to Kenya. It was chilling — it was a big deal. We sat there quietly and we couldn't believe what we were hearing. The management were trying to explain what it meant, where it had come from and it was hard to take in at the time.

We were there just trying to concentrate on playing cricket. And then we had this spanner being thrown into the works. You always have to look at the worst-case scenario. There is the approach that you should think: 'You will be alright; everything will be sweet.' But if you do go and something happens, how would New Zealand Cricket have lived with the responsibility of losing three or four players?

There was obviously so much on the line in regards to the match in Nairobi. Kenya might not have posed the biggest threat, even though they did beat Sri Lanka, but the competition points that were up for grabs were important. There were a lot of different scenarios being floated around the team — Cairnsy suggested we should fly in Nelson Mandela to keep the peace. It was also suggested that we fly in and out of Kenya on match day.

England had earlier voted not to travel to Harare to play Zimbabwe in what would have been their campaign-opening match. And that decision was made by a team vote. If our participation in Nairobi had gone to a similar vote, I am pretty sure we would have had 11 guys who would have gone. But without a doubt, if the match did go ahead a few of us wouldn't have travelled. I certainly wouldn't have gone. It was a decision which cost us a lot in the long run, but I fully backed the reasoning behind it. The fact was New Zealand Cricket's stance was about ensuring no fallout was directed at the players. For them to make such a big decision like that, not to send a team somewhere to play in a World Cup, just shows how serious the information was that they'd received. It was a big call to make. At the same time we were gutted — from a player's point of view, looking back we realise that it cost us a semi-final spot.

Daniel Vettori: Now reflecting on it, we were lucky to have Martin Snedden who made the decision based on the advice he had. First and foremost he had player safety at the front of his mind. And you are lucky when you have a CEO like that. It wasn't a case of 'There are a few bad things going on in Kenya, we can't go.' It was lot more detailed than that.

My personal view was that I was happy either way. I would have been happy to have gone to Kenya or happy if the team hadn't gone. But at the time I wasn't coming from the perspective of having a wife or a young family — Craig was in that situation and that made the decision a lot harder for guys who were in that position. There was probably a group of five or six of us who were comfortable with whatever went, then a group who were pretty pro going to Kenya and another group who didn't want to risk it.

But I would hate to put the position on us not making the semis just on the decision not to have played one game. We also didn't play as well as we could have. There were games in the Super Sixes that were there to win which we didn't. The responsibility was on us, not on missing that game.

Not only was the decision not to travel to Nairobi ultimately the turning point for our World Cup campaign, but the tournament itself was a turning point of sorts for my career. It was a period when I started to be in and out of the starting 11. Before that I was pretty much a fixture in the one-day side. You sort of take it for granted when you are in the team the whole time. When you're out of the team, life does get tough. Then when you are recalled, you tend to get only one chance — and if you don't succeed you are gone again. That aspect does affect a guy's performance.

When I started to go through that, I really started to appreciate the guys who weren't in the side. Quite often you take them for granted. You are in the playing 11 and that is all you think about. But it is bloody difficult for them too. If they get a call-up they are normally so intense because they know they have to make so much of the opportunity. Over the next two or three years that is what I went through. It was almost a case of you trying too hard when you did get the opportunity to prove you should be in the team.

I was given another chance in our next pool game against Bangladesh and again opened. That World Cup campaign was a first for me in any form of cricket where I was coming in at the top of the order. If it meant that was the way I was going to play in the team, I would have batted anywhere. But it certainly wasn't my best spot. I won the man of the match award after top-scoring with 75 in our win over Bangladesh in Kimberley — before backing that up with scores of 14 against Canada and eight in our first Super Sixes game against Zimbabwe. Then I was back on the sidelines again.

I was surplus to requirements for the Super Sixes clash against Australia at Port Elizabeth, with Daniel again promoted to open the innings with Flem. While I was gutted to be on the sidelines, there was certainly a fair bit to smile about in the way the guys started. Australia were left reeling at 84-7 in the 27th over after some stunning bowling from Shane Bond, knocking over Adam Gilchrist, Matthew Hayden, Ricky Ponting and Damien Martyn — eventually finishing with figures of 6–23. But then Michael Bevan, who has been our nemesis many times previously, and Andy Bichel somehow got Australia through to a total 208–9.

During the break in the innings there was a real sense of deflation in our changing room. After making such a great start to the game, there was just disbelief that we'd allowed Australia to add more than 120 runs with their last two partnerships of the innings. And that disappointment just increased when Brett Lee came out and knocked over our top order with a mix of pace and swing. We were dismissed for just 112 inside 31 overs, with only Flem offering some resistance.

It was a huge let-down, especially considering the fact Australia had done a similar thing just two games previously against England. Again it was Bichel and Bevan who had got them out of trouble. But that is why they are the best team in the world — no matter what situation they are in, they always have someone who will put their hand up and do the job for them. They are simply that talented.

The result meant we had to beat India at Centurion to progress through to the semi-finals. The good news for me was that I was back into the match

11, even if that meant having to open again. But I wasn't in the greatest of mind-sets, something that is probably recognised by my second-ball duck in the total of just 147 which we set India to win. Despite having them at 21-3 in the fifth over, with Bond picking up both Virender Sehwag and Sourav Ganguly, India eventually cruised to victory with seven wickets in hand.

The 2003 World Cup really was a campaign where we didn't play all that well. We scraped through a couple of matches, but we never bowled wonderfully as a unit — it really was only a couple of good batting performances that helped us get some of the wins on the board. Almost everything about that campaign seemed disjointed. Aside from the decision not to head to Kenya, which was the right thing to do, the biggest thing I remember about that campaign was that the team set-up was so destabilised. There was much chopping and changing in the batting order and rotations on who did and didn't play. We had lots of plans and talk about a vision and gaining an edge over the opposition. But, to be honest, I don't think too many could actually deliver on it.

A lot of it all sounded fine, but cricket matches are something you have to play as the situation arises. That is when you rely on your experience from both the number of games you have played and the different situations you have been in. We were tasked with trying to keep count of how many dot balls we bowled and the number of scoreless balls in a row we had faced when we were batting. It ended up that a lot of the guys had clouded thoughts when they were playing — it was information overload and it had an effect on us.

The loss to India didn't just end our World Cup hopes, it also spelt the beginning of the end for Denis Aberhart's Black Caps' coaching stint. Denis' departure four months later heralded the arrival of John Bracewell as Black Caps coach. And dark times lay ahead for both the Black Caps, especially in the test arena, and for me.

Bringing on Braces

The 2003 Cricket World Cup was to be the last time that I played under Denis Aberhart's coaching in the Black Caps. Just over a month after the failed campaign, he took a side to Sri Lanka. It was a tour that I missed out on. And it ended up doubling as Denis' swansong.

On the side's return, with Denis' contract up, New Zealand Cricket launched a contestable process to decide who would coach the Black Caps in a period that 12 months later would feature what is always a demanding tour of England. While I wasn't in Denis' equations for Sri Lanka, I had no doubt that he should have been rehired. Unfortunately, there were others within New Zealand Cricket who thought differently.

Denis was my first Canterbury coach and I really enjoyed my time with him, regardless of what team it was. He's probably also the cricket coach who really knows me the most. One of the things that Abo realised was that if players were happy off the field, they would perform on the field. A big thing for him was asking how your girlfriend or your wife was. He was in tune with those sorts of things — he realised if we were having any problems it could affect our performance. It's not as easy as just saying, 'Well you should just switch off and be able to concentrate on your cricket performance.' Family always played a big part in the set-ups of Denis' teams. Other coaches could learn from that!

Coaches also need to know and understand what works and doesn't work for different players. And Denis was certainly someone who realised that. If they get it wrong, it can lead to the wrong consequences. A classic example involves the actions leading up to Nathan Astle's premature retirement in 2007. The current set-up obviously got it wrong with Nath. They felt he needed a bit of a kick up the arse, a bit of a prod. But they went about it the wrong way. And the consequences were pretty dire, where he ended up retiring when he probably shouldn't have.

To me a good coach who had been around his players for a reasonable period, like a Denis Aberhart, would have realised that what worked for some players might not necessarily work for Nath. Recently, we have seen a lot of the decisions that have been made have been wrong ones. A good coach would have realised what Nathan really needed. And Abo had that trait — he had that man-management ability to get around players. If a player needed a kick in the arse, make no mistake he would do it. But he would do it on the side, do it quietly away from the rest of the players. Conversely, if someone needed a bit of nurturing, he would do that too.

When Denis became Black Caps coach, Flem took over things quite a bit. But Denis was prepared to sit in the background a little and let Flem assume more control. A lot of guys wouldn't have been comfortable doing that, but he saw it as perhaps something that would be for the betterment of the team and had no problem with it. During that period of time, Flem did all the interviews and the captain certainly was the face of the team. Abo was in the background doing his job and fashioning a pretty good record. It was a record that should have seen him being reappointed, without the process New Zealand Cricket instituted.

Unfortunately, I think there were senior members of the Black Caps who thought otherwise. What Abo was doing was certainly a change from past coaching set-ups. Make no mistake, though, he was very organised and did a bloody good job, especially in the way he allowed Flem to grow into the role and take new things on. The only reason I can give for the change was the fact that some senior players felt a change was needed — they thought they needed someone who had more of a public presence, even though the approach that Denis had taken was one which Flem, and the team in general, were thriving on.

Aberhart withdraws from process
New Zealand Cricket, 1 July 2003

Denis Aberhart has withdrawn from the selection process for the role of TelstraClear Black Caps coach to pursue other opportunities.

Aberhart, who has been coach of the TelstraClear Black Caps since August 2001, said he was looking forward to taking up a new position outside of cricket.

'I was not guaranteed a further term with New Zealand Cricket and another exciting opportunity presented itself and is likely to be confirmed later in the week,' he said.

New Zealand Cricket chief executive Martin Snedden wished Aberhart well.

'Denis has made a significant contribution to the TelstraClear Black Caps. The team is No. 3 in Test cricket and No. 7 in ODI cricket.

'The team has had some notable successes during Denis's two years as coach including excellent team performances in Australia during the 2001–02 tour, the

home ODI and Test series wins against India last season, our first ever Test series win in the West Indies and the recent tri-series win in Sri Lanka.

'The selection process for the coach's position is continuing and the successful candidate is likely to be announced next week,' Snedden said.

Denis was a great coach, but was undervalued and I definitely believe he got tossed aside way too early. I have no doubt that Abo's results were good enough for him to have been reselected — it was a no-brainer. Denis should have had at least another two years in the job and I don't think he got the recognition he deserves for the record we had under his coaching. He certainly made the job of his eventual replacement, John Bracewell, a lot easier when he came on board.

> **Denis Aberhart:** In the end it was my decision. I hadn't heard from New Zealand Cricket for a while; they were in a process. And probably I felt at the time it was the right thing for me to do for my family, for myself and the right thing also for the team at that stage to step aside. Of course, I would love to have carried on coaching. But I felt that it was right to withdraw from that process.
>
> The word was that John Bracewell would get the job — who knows? I don't know what would have happened in the end. But at that stage it felt that the right thing to do was to withdraw from the process, move on with my life and go to some other challenges that I was doing. And I haven't looked back and regretted that at all. I loved my time. It is a real honour to coach New Zealand and be involved in the dressing room. You do miss that, but in the end I never regretted that I did what I did.

It was just a matter of days between Denis pulling out of the race to be coach and John Bracewell being handed the job. It's fair to say there wasn't a huge amount of surprise when Braces was appointed coach. New Zealand Cricket CEO Martin Snedden had a close friendship with Bracewell and it was no secret that New Zealand Cricket had been after him for quite some time.

At times John and I have had a love-hate relationship. We started out together when I was captain of the New Zealand Youth team to England in 1996, a side he coached. I really enjoyed working with him and getting to know him on that trip. He worked us pretty hard, as he's a bit of a fitness freak and loves running. And it was on that trip that I got an insight into one part of his personality — he doesn't like to admit when he gets things wrong. During that tour he took us for a run which was supposed to last about half an hour. But he took us through a forest and we ended up getting lost and spending an hour and 15 minutes running. And he wouldn't admit that he had gone off track or got lost — but we all knew he had. He was still at the front trying to burn us off.

Hiring Braces as Black Caps coach was a decision which certainly would have an impact on my career over the coming seasons. In many ways it really was the start of a downward spiral in terms of my fortunes when it came to selection, particularly in the test arena.

John Bracewell: I thought he was a natural No. 6, but you had to get to that point. And in the modern style of the way tests were being played, where teams were scoring 300 runs in the day, and you have your No. 6 coming in for the second new ball, it set us up well. For a long time we averaged 450 for first innings scores, that was because we had reasonably solid starts with Richardson, the maturity of Fleming and then the style we were graduating to with Craig and Brendon McCullum.

But the emergence of Jacob Oram as an all-rounder was at the expense of Craig McMillan. We had moved away from that fiddler bowler, realising we had to get 20 wickets as well. You had Fleming, Styris, Astle and McMillan basically taking up three positions. Styris at that stage was bowling and bowling reasonably well. Astle was doing less and less bowling because of his knees. And Jacob was emerging. He was the more natural all-rounder that I felt we needed.

I didn't think Craig's health would allow him to be a genuine all-rounder, or his skill size. He had to concentrate on playing in the top five, rather than at No. 6 and No. 7. He was always going to struggle to beat Astle and Styris for those positions, and he certainly wasn't going to beat Fleming.

I always considered myself a No. 5. It was only when John came in that I found myself pushed down to No. 6. I found that frustrating because I thought I played reasonably well at No. 5. There was so much chopping and changing, with Flem going up and down the order, Mathew Sinclair being in and out of the team and then Hamish Marshall coming in.

I always saw myself as a No. 5 who could bowl a few overs if I was needed. I never saw myself as an all-rounder. While there was no doubt that he had big raps on Jacob, to be honest Jacob hadn't secured himself in the side in either form of the game at that time. A lot of that was obviously due to injury. I always thought my best spot was No. 5, and Jacob's was at No. 7.

Denis Aberhart: Whether it was John Bracewell or not, I don't know. But there were two players in Mathew Sinclair and Macca, that when things didn't go well they got the blame. Macca was often the scapegoat for things that were happening at the top of the order rather than in the middle of the order. It is pretty hard to perform in the middle order if the top order is not doing the job.

With Macca, you have to accept that you are going to have a player who is going to fail at times. But at other times he will win you a match and rip some people apart. Someone like him needs to be given the confidence to know that he is not playing for his place each time that he goes out to bat. I think that Macca is not someone who wants to have dwelling on his mind, 'Hell, if I get this wrong I could be finished.' He needs to be aggressive, he needs to think positively because his strength is taking people on.

If he is being negative in that way, then he is going to fail because he wouldn't be in the right frame of mind to do it. I felt that he didn't have the consistency that he needed for the confidence he needed to play his game. And that reflected in him being left out of the team.

Nobody, and I don't care how bullish Macca might be, can perform consistently when they are thinking that way. He was someone who should know 'when I go out to bat I have the support of everyone around me, I can get out there and play my game with responsibility'. But I don't think he could feel that because he wasn't sure when he was going to be in and when he wasn't going to be in.

Macca is someone who I often think of as your wee kid brother. He needs some encouragement, support, affirmation and kidding along. At times that might have been missing. People didn't quite give him the freedom to go out and play his cricket without too many constraints.

The hardest thing I always found with Braces was that he was always on an emotional roller-coaster. On his good days he was great. But on other days you were just waiting for a pin to drop and for him to explode. And the guys knew when it was going to happen. You would turn up for breakfast and you could tell by his demeanour when he was going to blow. It would take something like a simple fielding mistake in a warm-up drill and then he would explode and vent his anger. You were just waiting for it to happen so you could move on to the next thing. At times he was quite unapproachable because of this aspect of his personality.

It makes it difficult when your coach is on a roller-coaster because as a player that is what you are on during a game. You are on the roller-coaster through your performance within the team. So you need your coach to be very stable so you can talk to him about any issue — he has to be the constant. All the players will be different, depending on how they are going form-wise.

To me the coach has to be the one constant and stable person in the group. And if he is not, it just makes it very difficult, especially for the young guys. When they see the coach they want to feel like they can learn from him. But if they don't feel they can do that, because of fiery episodes and mood swings, it makes it bloody difficult.

His mood swings were probably the most disappointing thing for me on my last tour with the Black Caps, the 2007 ICC World Twenty20 tournament. On that tour there was a breakdown in the relationship between our manager Lindsay Crocker and Braces. There were squabbles which weren't hidden from the players. They would have heated arguments and it affected some of the younger guys in the side. Crocks had his hands full trying to handle Braces' changes in temperament in a diplomatic and non-confrontational way so that it did not impact on the team. After witnessing a couple of their discussions, I sympathised with Crocks.

On that tour, and for quite a while, Braces took pretty much everything on as a coach. When I came back into the side before the 2006–07 Sri Lankan one-day international series I noticed that there were a lot more management groups. He had off-loaded some of the workload and it had helped his demeanour. Assistant coach Bob Carter was on board and we had a fielding coach and a bowling coach. Braces had seemed to pull back and generally I found him to be more relaxed. It was almost as if he taken an about-turn from his former moody ways.

There were performances at the 2007 Cricket World Cup in the Caribbean when I thought he really should have ripped into us. After a couple of bad losses such as we had, a guy like Steve Rixon would have absolutely given it to us. But it never happened with Braces at the World Cup. You could see he was fuming at the time, but he held it in. It was definitely churning away in him and I have no idea what his release for it was. Bad performances were all of a sudden just cosied over at a time when we probably did need a rocket because we had played that badly. But it changed again for the worst at the Twenty20 World Cup.

> **Gilbert Enoka:** Macca got on really well with Stumper, he got on really well with Denis Aberhart, who was a good mate, and got on well with David Trist. He didn't get on as well with Braces. Braces was pretty straight with him, but it was never a disrespectful relationship. But he never entered the relationship with Bracewell to the same degree as he had with those others — it was mainly because Braces was in a position of 'Should we contract him or not? Is he going to make the team or not?' There were some challenges there, but Braces always wanted him to succeed. He was a big supporter of Macca even if that might not have appeared to be the case. Behind the scenes, he always wanted to do the right thing by him.

Throughout my time in the Black Caps under the coaching of John Bracewell it became really apparent to me that his handle on the one-day game was a lot better than on test cricket. When he was at Gloucester, his record in the one-day game was very good. I picked up that he felt a lot more comfortable coaching the Black Caps' one-day side, planning strategies for limited-overs cricket. And his record really shows that the same can't be said about him in the test arena.

Five years on, I wonder whether the senior players who wanted a change from Denis' style of coaching now regret that decision.

Nightmare on the road

In 2004 it was time to return for another lengthy tour of England, five years after our historic 1999 tour inspired by the 'Better than Before' mantra. And five years on, both that superb motivational tool and success were sorely missing for the majority of one of the most disjointed and unhappy tours I have ever been part of.

Just about anything that could go wrong in the build-up to the test series, and subsequent three tests against England, did. We were dogged by bad weather which seriously disrupted our build-up to the tests, the squad became bogged down by off-field distractions, camaraderie was at a low, our bowlers were again hamstrung by untimely injuries, communication was very poor and our coach John Bracewell was certainly finding the going tough.

Braces was quite highly strung on the trip because he was returning to England with a real point to prove, having left Gloucester to coach the Black Caps. There was no mistaking that this was an important trip for him. It seemed to me that whenever we played either England or Australia, Braces was at his most volatile. I suppose the fact he coached in England for a number of years contributed to that, and his history with Australia went back to his playing days.

Volatile was certainly an apt word to sum up his behaviour at times on tour, and the more responsibility he took on the worse he got. In some ways I suppose I didn't help the issue when I accidentally injured our manager Lindsay Crocker early on in the tour, in the process hospitalising him for a couple of days.

We used to play this little warm-up game called 'Shit-kicker' with a soccer ball before we went on the field to practise. We would be in a circle and you would start with the ball and you could pass the ball to anyone else apart from the person who had passed it to you. And you only had one touch to move it on. So if you took two touches, basically you had to get on the ground on all fours and everyone in the group came up and gave you a wee punch in the guts or the leg. It wasn't anything too hard — just a wee tap. It was one of those silly little warm-up games that we played for five minutes before we got into our serious fielding. It became quite an event and we would generally try to pick on one or two guys so they got dead legs.

Crocks ended up playing one day and was forced to get on the ground. I gave him a wee tap but unfortunately it must have hit him right in the kidneys. He went down for a while and ended up having to spend a couple of nights in hospital.

Crocks' situation meant that Braces had to take over as coach/manager. Now when Braces gets too much on his plate, his head explodes. And that is just what he did on tour when it came to enforcing an old rule that was brought in when Steve Rixon took over as coach and John Graham took over as manager in late 1996 — a rule which made us shave for matches.

The pair had taken over during a pretty turbulent time with the team and the need for discipline and rules was quite high. They brought in a lot of new things which the team adhered to brilliantly and over time some of the rules were relaxed a bit. And one of the things that we felt could be added to that list was the shaving rule. It was certainly something that I was very hot on.

The rule stated that you had to be clean shaven for a one-day international and each day of a test match. You couldn't have any stubble on your face. Bryan Young was one guy who had a superstition that he never used to shave during a test match. But he had to change his ways when John Graham came onto the scene and he felt pretty uncomfortable about doing so. But because of what had had happened with individuals in the team previously, it was something that we, as a team, signed off on collectively.

By the time the 2004 tour to England had rolled around, we were all seven years older and were trying to say that we had all moved on from that stage and would like to have the option of whether to shave or not. A lot of guys would have kept on shaving, others certainly wouldn't have. I was in the latter group, I don't like shaving for a game — I like having a bit of stubble, especially when you are playing in the hot Asian countries where you are always sweating. You need something on your face, like stubble, to hold the sunscreen on.

During the England tour we had a lot of talks and arguments about trying to get the rule relaxed. It got to the point where I felt we, as a team, were spending so much time on little things that wouldn't affect our performance at all — like the shaving rule and the haircuts. It seemed the management was more worried about whether we were clean shaven than actually how we were playing. As a team we were spending our energies on things that shouldn't have been consuming our time. There was talk about the perception of the team being lowered if a certain guy had a beard.

We thought we should all have been given the option of whether we had to shave or not. It all came to a head when we were bussing to our hotel in Kensington. Braces was wearing his managerial hat and came down to the back of the bus and told us that we had a head and shoulders photo shoot ahead of the test series. And he made it clear that everyone had to be clean shaven. I questioned him on it, saying, 'Surely we don't have to because it is not a match day. Why do we need to be clean shaven for a photo?' Cairnsy pretty much said the same thing.

With that, Braces lost it. He launched into a tirade and had steam coming out of his ears — he absolutely lost the plot. Eventually, Daniel, Cairnsy, Nathan and I thought, 'Stuff it, we are not going to shave. This is bullshit, we are old enough to decide whether or not to have a shave.'

Ten minutes after we'd arrived at the hotel, we had to turn up for the photo shoot. Cairnsy and I were unshaven, Dan had trimmed his beard and Nath had done a U-turn and was completely shaven.

That, in itself, highlighted one of the many minor, peripheral things that were dividing and worrying the team. You shouldn't be thinking about whether a guy has had a shave, whether his hair is too long or whether he has an earring. It was a bone of contention among quite a few of us for two or three years. And I know my attitude towards it got me offside at times with some of the management.

John Bracewell: That sort of thing is a red herring that mature people should just deal with. In all societies there are rules. My understanding is that rule was put in place in India, before I came on board, and had always been a bone of contention for two or three players. So therefore it became almost the main event which I thought was the immaturity of our particular group. They thought it was more important over whether you shaved or not, rather than whether you should be batting or bowling. That is not a coaching issue; it is a management issue. I found those sorts of things frustrating.

What we were saying to them was that the increased maturity of the group meant that we could get past the stage where we were told when we could and couldn't shave. That rule, along with others, was brought in during 1997 when there were issues within the New Zealand side which were well documented. It was a rule that was brought in three terms previously and needed to be revisited. And at least half the team felt that way. We were saying, 'Hey, we are seven or eight years further down the track, we have guys who are married with kids, we have other guys who have been in the workforce. Surely, if someone doesn't want to have a shave during a test match then that is OK.'

It was one of those things that I believed the management felt was there and was easier just to leave it there. But it became a bone of contention for at least half of the guys.

The thing they kept saying was that it reflected badly on the image of New Zealand cricket if we weren't shaven. We couldn't get our heads around that. What we believed the most important thing to be was how we performed on the field, as opposed to being worried about whether we were clean shaven.

It was one of many issues that played a bigger part than they should have off the field, and I have no doubt that they dragged onto the field as well. Braces might call it immaturity, but I don't see it like that at all. It was more about blokes wanting to take ownership. We were saying, 'We will run the team ourselves.' If someone was looking scruffy and untidy, we wanted it to be left up to the senior guys to sort out. If it remained a problem, we would discuss it with management.

Unfortunately, it wasn't the only distraction which affected us off the field during a very unhappy time in the lead-up and during the three-test series against England. And while the continuation of the shaving rule may not have been one that directly impacted on our performance, initiatives brought in to help our injury-plagued bowlers certainly did.

There were certainly a lot of side issues going on in the camp, especially surrounding our bowling stocks. For a start, the bowlers were put on a managed bowling load when we arrived in England. It was the first time it had been instituted on tour and meant that they could only bowl a certain number of hours in the nets at a certain percentage of their range. They weren't always bowling flat out; they might bowl three overs at 70 per cent and then two overs and 100 per cent. And believe it or not, that might be their session.

The policy was meant to try to get our bowlers through the tour. History shows that not even this policy worked in achieving that. And unfortunately for those that did last the distance, when we needed them to bowl for long spells at good pace they couldn't produce the goods.

One of the bowlers on tour was my former Canterbury team-mate Chris Martin. He is one guy who I have always thought just needs to bowl; he is a player that will just continue running in for you. He needs a workload, and the same goes for Daryl Tuffey. The more he bowls, the better he gets — if he is undercooked and underdone, he is not quite the same bowler.

While the policy might have lightened the load for our bowlers during preparation for the warm-ups against County opposition and the test series, it made life as a specialist batsman a disaster. It meant that we hardly ever got to face our bowlers in the nets as they were just bowling such minimal and restricted loads. And we batsmen found that come game time, it was us who struggled.

Instead of facing test-quality bowlers during practice, our net sessions were against bowlers who weren't that quick and they lacked the intensity required. They were second and third 11 County bowlers. Then we were thrust into the tests and had to go out into the middle to face guys like Steve Harmison, Andrew Flintoff and Matthew Hoggard — guys who were at the top of their game. And we all came up a little bit short.

It's fair to say there was a bit of a divide on that tour between the batters and the bowlers over our fortunes in the subsequent test series, which we lost 3–0 to England. There was blame being assigned by both parties. The bowlers felt the batters weren't scoring the runs that they should have made. We batsmen felt the bowlers weren't doing the work, so we were undercooked when it was time to go into the tests.

The crazy thing about the workload some of us had was that we had just come off a home season — we hadn't gone away on tour without having a decent workload behind us. Everyone was ready to go and we should have just continued on what we were doing in the home series.

It wasn't the only side issue involving our bowlers. Wellington coach Vaughn Johnson accompanied us on that tour as an assistant coach looking after the bowlers. The decision for him to come meant that we had a 14-man squad — had he not gone we would have travelled with 15 players. It was a poor decision. A lot of the team wanted that extra player on board, especially with the bowlers not being able to bowl a lot in the nets.

We thought it was a great opportunity for a young promising bowler to come on tour and be able to bowl a lot in the nets and learn about the team environment. Taking that extra player seemed to be a better long-term benefit than travelling with an assistant coach. That view was even more relevant considering the majority of our bowling attack went away under some injury cloud — it was also a tour which Shane Bond failed to last.

In fact it's arguable whether three of the bowlers were even fit enough to be on tour. They were trying to be managed through the tour, rather than actually being fit enough to go hard and complete a game. They were just trying to last a game — that is a big difference.

There were other issues which should never have arisen on what was a major tour, issues which management had a key role in. Some of them concerned communication, or a lack of it, during the first half of the tour. For example, we didn't know that Ian Butler had been selected to replace the injured Bond until a couple of guys read it on the internet.

That just wasn't good enough. You would have thought something as major as a mid-tour replacement would have been announced to the team before, if not at least at the same time as, it was broken to the media.

Another heavily debated point was the management's decision for us to travel at the end of a match. Whenever a player did well, we thought it was important to celebrate. It would have been good to have gone back to the team hotel and have a few quiet drinks. Doing that every now and again on tour helps with team spirit and camaraderie. But instead we all jumped on a bus after each game and went off to the next place. It was kind of like groundhog day — it was a really short-sighted decision.

All the side issues, combined with some shocking early-tour weather, compounded to make for a hellish build-up for our first test at Lord's. Rain meant our scheduled three-day tour-opening match against British Universities in Cambridge was restricted to just 35 overs of action on the final day. The weather also mucked up our next clash, a five-day match against Worcestershire at Worcester. But what action we did get gave me the chance to grab 86 in my first innings of the tour. We managed to get a bit more action during our final warm-up to the test series against Kent, even though we went on to lose by nine wickets.

With that we travelled to Lord's, the spiritual home of cricket. My previous visit to that very special place was certainly a happy one: the second test that we won during the historic 1999 tour. Sadly, it wasn't a case of a happy return five years down the track.

We lost first up to England by seven wickets. It wasn't a great test for me personally with the bat, scoring six and then a two-ball duck. We set England a total of 281 to win, which they did pretty comfortably with just the loss of three wickets.

The loss didn't have any impact on the miserly workloads our bowlers were set at training time. But it did in other areas when it came to preparation for the next County game against Leicestershire in Leicester. In fact, we had some of the longest training runs we had ever had. The attitude from up top was, 'Well, we are not putting the work in, so we have to train harder and longer.' It really was like a naughty schoolboy reaction — if you lose you go and spend time in the nets.

It's fair to say there wasn't a lot of trust between the players and the management on that tour. In hindsight, I think that was behind the decision from management for us to travel straight after games. They probably thought we would be on the piss, drinking too much and doing that sort of thing. But I have to say in terms of the international teams I have seen on the circuit, New Zealand would probably be the smallest drinkers around.

When you compare the Black Caps to some other teams, our guys are very well disciplined and controlled. Yes, occasionally when the guys get the chance they will have a night out. But I see some of the other touring sides are straight onto it after a match, even to the point where they are probably affecting their performances for the games to come. And our team at the time certainly drank a lot less even from when I joined the team in 1997. So drinking, for us, was a real non-issue. But for the management it was. They had a perception that things might get out of control off the field.

That feeling was hammered across to us very clearly as we were going through our warm-ups before the start of the four-day match against Leicestershire. The night before the match a couple of guys, including one who wasn't even playing, went out and had a couple of drinks. They didn't get pissed; they just had a couple of quiet ales.

Braces got wind of it and on the day of the game he sat us down on the ground and gave us the biggest lecture you have ever heard about our professionalism and a whole lot of other issues. Many of us had partners on tour and had spent the night with them, so we didn't know what the hell was going on, what it was all about. It was just way over the top and it wasn't until later that I realised what it was all about. The whole performance stemmed from a lack of trust in the team set-up.

Four days later and it was proven that the duo enjoying a quiet drink the night before the game didn't have any impact on the result. We recorded a 328-run win, with Dan bowling great to take nine wickets, including spells of 4–60 and 5–92. After failing in the first test at Lord's I had a far better time with the bat, scoring 43 and 68. But the latter innings was cut short when I was struck on the hand, suffering a broken finger that kept me out of the second test at Headingley.

There was obviously a lot of determination to right the ship in the second test and we started well, posting a total of 409 in our first innings after losing the toss and being put in to bat. But the wind was taken out of the side's sails when England responded with a massive 526. The Black Caps could just post 161 in the final innings and England chased down the 45 runs needed to win with the loss of just one wicket. It sure made for frustrating viewing from our team room.

Two-down in the series and it wasn't just Braces who was feeling the pressure. So too was our off-field leadership. But even that was becoming an issue in itself. By the time we headed to England the senior players' group had been born. It was something we had meetings on, debating just who should be part of it. I have to say that since that tour in 2004, that leadership has been disbanded, started again, numbers cut down, numbers enlarged about a dozen. So, to me, that says it is not working. It is almost like the team has been clutching at straws in the search for an answer.

The senior players' group on that tour had nine players in it. That's a pretty top-heavy group when you consider we only had 14 players on tour; we pretty much had the whole team involved. Before the tour we had many discussions trying to decide who should be on it — should it be done on how many matches you have played and seniority? But we all had discussions and some of the guys wanted Bondy involved in it, even though at that stage he had only played 10 tests and 27 one-day internationals.

To me it should have been four or five players tops, and for guys who had played for eight or nine years — Fleming, Cairns, Astle, maybe me and Dan. We were the senior players, guys the others should have expected to look up to and follow. So it really lost all its momentum having nine guys. The other five guys on tour were asking, 'Well, should we form our own group for coffees, etc?' While the intentions of the senior players group were good, it had splintered the team.

There was also debate within the camp about the issue of players' partners going on tour. Half the group had their partners on tour, half didn't. At times there seemed to be talk that the team was split because some of us were spending more time with our partners. To me, that is a non-event because when you partner does come on tour it is only for a specific time that is allowed by team management. It might only be two weeks out of a seven-week tour. So obviously you are going to want to spend more time with them — that is why they are there after all.

You have spent all the time on the field, in the changing room and on the team bus with your team-mates so when you get back to your hotel surely you don't have to spend more time around the team. It was an issue again with some, including management. But I think the idea that having partners on tour affected our performance was just bollocks. You are clutching at straws if you believe that theory.

We had one last chance to redeem ourselves in the series with the final test at Trent Bridge, Nottingham. Again we got off to a good start in our first innings, with the top three of Mark Richardson, Stephen Fleming and Scott Styris scoring 73, 117 and 108 respectively. Unfortunately, we lost our final seven wickets for just 112. I was back from my finger injury but wasn't able to trouble the scorers, recording my second duck in the series.

But we still had a lead of 69 going into our second innings. Again our openers got off to a great start, with Richardson and Flem putting on 94 for the first wicket before we lost our last nine wickets for just 124 runs. My contribution was 30. On the fourth day, England polished off the 284 needed to win, losing only six wickets. And with that we lost 3–0, a result which also brought down the curtain on Chris Cairns' test career.

We didn't play badly in the three tests. The difference was that Steve Harmison and Andrew Flintoff were at the top of their game. They were both bowling at 90 kph and were at the peak of their powers. We had chances to win all three tests but when it came to the crunch a couple of their guys stood up.

John Bracewell: We had only a couple of days of cricket leading into the test matches and then we basically played back to back. We played the Lord's test and we'd only had a few days of cricket. The warm-up games were affected by bad weather and Bond had broken down. If you look at those test matches, we competed really well. We just got beaten.

The difficulty of touring England is that at that time a lot of our guys were negotiating winter contracts. You had Chris Cairns who was on his farewell tour, so it was like a benefit trip. And trying to get guys to meetings was difficult; they were having meetings with agents in the lobby. It was quite a frustrating tour administratively because it was at a stage when the New Zealand side had a number of guys who were being touted to County cricket, given that there was an Ashes series the next year. Because Australians wouldn't be there, New Zealanders became the next target.

A lot of our guys were being distracted; the pound was at three to one at that stage. I am surprised at how we competed in that series. The Poms knocked off 270 in the first test; we had three guys break down in the second test and we hardly had a bowling attack. It was just one of those tours when you think, 'Shit, it looks like we got hammered but in fact we were bloody lucky to have competed the way we did given the losses we incurred.'

Daniel Vettori: I reflect on those as being three very hard-fought tests. And all three of them could have gone either way. We had positions of dominance where we were never able to put them into place — that was generally in our third innings and fourth. We would bat and bowl really well in the first two innings of a game and then we were pretty poor in the last two. I have never been able to find an answer for that.

The 3–0 test loss wasn't the end of the tour. We had the one-day international NatWest Series against England and the West Indies. At that stage the tour could easily have gone right off the rails — but it didn't. And I credit one person for that, and he wasn't one of the 14 players on tour.

If it wasn't for Gilbert Enoka's input, the one-day leg of the tour could also have been a disaster. He was always meant to go over to the UK for that stage of the tour, but when his tickets were booked he probably didn't expect to arrive in the role of mediator between the players and team management.

We had one meeting at a hotel where pretty much everything was put out there. Gilbert was very good; he was able to facilitate things and do it in a way that didn't cause any rifts. Everyone came to a general consensus — he worked with the players and management alike.

Gilbert Enoka: I went over there and the team unit was just a mess. It was certainly an interesting time. Sporting environments can become really dysfunctional really quickly if the culture isn't nourished, if the system is not right, if the leadership isn't working in the right direction. And they had just got themselves into a hole.

We went into the room at 8 am and came out about 3 pm — the object of this meeting was just to go right at all the issues. And I had to really take my hat off to Braces; he was really keen for me to do that, to do that warts and all. We worked through the issues, put all of the things on the table and used some pretty straight talking. We restructured the leadership and by the time we walked back through the door we made a commitment to leave what had happened in the past.

There were issues with everybody. There were things coming from all directions. But everyone was still committed and wanted to get it right. In all the times I have worked with John Bracewell, he has always wanted success. He is driven hard by that and will do anything to achieve success.

My role was to facilitate some free and frank discussion. We reconstructed the leadership, got them working on things they needed to do to make the unit function and make them accountable. As we lived those day by day, we began to gather some momentum.

Daniel Vettori: It took a little bit of an honesty session with Gilbert Enoka to tell us what the hell we were doing. We were a better team than we were proving to be. A lot of things went on, there was a bit of forceful language and we got to a position where we thought through what we needed to do.

Our one-day series was impeccable after that. Our results in the one-day tournament made us see just how poor we were in the first part of the tour, seeing that we could get together and could play together as a team. Probably in the first part of the tour, it felt like we were 15 individuals and that made it tough to come together at game time and get things to happen.

You get that on tour sometimes, where it is not feeling as good as it can. You can never quite put your finger on it. You just need one thing to set you off again and it was that session. It was the realisation that we weren't acting as a team and we probably weren't acting as a group of mates — there were too many distractions and too many other things going on. It was a bit of a different environment. Touring England is always good fun. There are always lots of friends to catch up with and maybe we were disjointed during that time.

The fact we went on to win the NatWest Series had a lot to do with Gilbert. He changed the mood in the team; we seemed a lot happier and actually started to feel the taste of victory in one-day internationals against England and the West Indies.

We played some good one-day cricket on that tour, beating the West Indies in the final at Lord's. To win a final on that ground's hallowed turf is something very special in any cricketer's career. We all chipped in during the final, and I scored 52 in our total of 266. The match also marked Chris Harris taking his 200th one-day international wicket for New Zealand and Dan ended with impressive figures of 5–30, including the wicket of Shivnarine Chanderpaul who I caught at long-on to win the game.

What we did in the NatWest Series final was a good all-round team performance. It was nice in a one-off game like that to win a series overseas, something at which we haven't been that good. But our winning ways in that tri-series didn't make up for what was an otherwise forgettable tour, especially for those of us who had enjoyed the success of 1999.

John Bracewell: Did Gilbert help? It is yes and no, really. There needed to be some order put back into what we were doing, to refocus on what we were doing. So I think he facilitated a fairly good meeting in that regard.

But most of the players had made their winter signings. And with the mentality of the team, sometimes you just get a tipping point that gives you some rhythm and some momentum. James Franklin bowled particularly well in Durham, picked up five wickets against the English, and we picked up some momentum. Therefore confidence blossomed. We haven't lost that many one-day series at all over the last five years. We have lost in South Africa and we have lost in Australia. The rest of the time we have been pretty successful.

I think they were quite a detached team, mainly because I thought they were a selfish team in regards that they spent most of the time touting for County contracts the next year, knowing there was an Ashes series. I have looked at that 1999 series, and if you looked at that England side they weren't great. The England side in 2004 were a very good side; they had some pretty classy players. And Flintoff makes a huge difference to their test side. Harmison had hit his straps. If you look at that 1999 side, they had some pretty ordinary cricketers playing for England. And you had a New Zealand side that was at their physical pomp with Nash and Cairns, in particular. That is a timing issue.

My understanding is that they were a pretty loose unit in 1999, but they seemed to have a lot of fun. Everyone has a lot of fun when you are winning. And I think they tried to replicate that same amount of fun in the following tour and lost. So therefore it wasn't a great time.

I disagree with Bracewell's take on the tour. In many ways the England team of 1999 was actually a stronger team, with all of the experience they had. The England team in 1999 had some very useful players in Alec Stewart,

Andrew Caddick, Nasser Hussain, Mike Atherton, Mark Ramprakash, Phil Tufnell and Graham Thorpe — they had some stalwarts of English cricket to be brutally honest.

I think we hit the 2004 English team at a bad time — there were two or three players at the top of their game, in Andrew Flintoff and Stephen Harmison. And that was really the difference, a lot of the time it just came down to a single performance from one of those guys. Generally, it was Harmison with the ball who knocked us over or someone like Thorpe using all of his experience to get them home as on the fourth day at Trent Bridge.

Any tour of England is a huge tour, and many mistakes were made leading up to and on that tour in 2004. One was not taking any advice in terms of travelling. And the decision not to try to find out what was successful from the 1999 tour was a massive mistake. We had created New Zealand cricket history on that tour, done it the hard way and so to ignore that, and not even try to use some of the good things from it, was just crazy. Maybe a lot of it came from Braces and was based on his thinking after he had coached in England. And I don't agree that the 1999 team were a loose unit. In face we were a cohesive group which the management had nurtured, that was quite a bit different from Bracewell's team of 2004 which was detached from the management group.

It was a tour where we just didn't bond. In those tough situations we really needed guys to stick their hands up and take the game by the scruff of the neck. But that never happened. It wasn't an enjoyable tour to be on — there was just so much going on in the background and niggles here and there.

Suggesting that the problem was that our minds were on County deals is just crazy — that is real paranoia. If that was the case, it could really have been only one or two guys. The tour was a bit of a parade for Cairnsy in that it was his final tour of England with the Black Caps, every game was a send-off and after half a season of it, it had taken its toll. But to say our minds were on County cricket is just wrong — there is no substance to that at all.

Braces seemed to suffer from real paranoia that whole tour. Losing Crocks for a while wasn't ideal and everything just got on top of Braces. He had a lot on his plate and it showed.

In the spotlight

From a young age I have always been someone who has read newspapers, whether the stories about me have been good or bad, and listened to the radio. I like to know what was being said about me, even though I might not necessarily like what I read or hear. And the best thing about that is the balance I had about it — I read the good and the bad. You will find other guys read only the good stuff; others won't touch a newspaper at all.

Despite what some of the scribes out there might think, I never had a problem with criticism if it was about my game and it was valid. But once things went over the top and got a bit personal, that is when I started to have a problem. I really struggled to deal with that. And it's fair to say that was quite often the case with sections of the media's treatment towards me over the years.

To me, taking in what is in the media is something that I have never been able to get away from. It is not an obsession; rather it is purely human nature to know first-hand what people write or say about you. And I sure wasn't prepared to be one of the other athletes who use the throwaway line that they ignore what's in the media, when they definitely do read what is being written.

Gilbert Enoka: One of the things I think is really important is that a professional athlete normally doesn't read the paper. A journalist has a job to do for a newspaper, they have to create a readership otherwise they don't have a job. We used to talk about that as a team. But if there was one person who would always have a paper, and have it open, it would be Macca. He just wanted to read and hear what was being written and said about him. He was open, honest, free and frank about that.

Did it have a toll on him? I would say it definitely did. I don't know any person for whom criticism doesn't take a toll. Those who say it doesn't are just pretty good at keeping it under the surface. He knew everything that was being said about him. Part of his nature was that he always read it because he wanted to stay in touch with it. He would be sitting there at breakfast and the papers would be around. He would yell out to a team-mate, 'Hey, see what they are writing about you.'

Tony Veitch: At least he is honest about the fact that he does listen to the radio and read the newspapers. How many sportsmen say they never do that? And that is just absolute bollocks. If you know you are the centre of attention on the back of a rugby or cricket test, you are going to listen to the media or switch on and listen to the radio — that is just human nature, you want to know what people are saying. A lot of sportsmen who want to have a crack at you, about something you have said or written or people have heard you say, are coming from second or third hand because they try to play the whole game where they don't listen.

I think I've got pretty thick skin — I've had to have that over a number of years. Criticism is just something that I have had to put up with. At times people have said that the criticism and the chance to prove people wrong has been my motivation. That has never been my motivation. There is no doubt that at certain times I have taken delight in proving some of the media and the punters wrong — that even goes back to the 2007 Chappell-Hadlee Trophy series. But it was never my ultimate driving force.

One of things that I have never been able to understand is why I have been deemed a so-called 'controversial figure'. Maybe the people who have watched me, and said certain things about me, could answer that better than I can. I have never understood why I have polarised people's opinion, or just why people have either liked me as a cricketer or disliked me. At times I have heard myself being compared to someone like a Carlos Spencer, in terms of how diverse people's opinions are about me.

At times with the media you have to wonder if the reporter was actually at the same ground as the game. It was like that at times with Richard Boock who used to work for the *New Zealand Herald*. He would write these articles and you really had to question whether the bloke was actually at the ground, or whether he was writing his report from the sanctuary of his hotel room. Some of his reports on our games were just theatrical.

Another guy who has written a fair bit about me is the *Dominion Post*'s Jonathan Millmow. It seemed to me that over a period of time, about two and a half years, he just wanted me out of the Black Caps. It seemed he decided I wasn't up to it and that is pretty much the angle he took in quite a few of his articles. Millmow had come down to Canterbury and we had played club cricket together at East Shirley for a couple of years and I got on well with him. My record at the time was pretty good, especially in the test arena. When he started writing some of this stuff I just couldn't understand where he was coming from and I found it quite frustrating.

It got to the point where I confronted him in Hamilton. We were there to play a test against Pakistan and as I got out of the lift to head to my hotel room he was standing there. I said, 'Jonathan, what is going on? You have been killing me for about three years. Have you got an issue? What is the problem?' He said there was no issue. But some of the personal nature of his articles suggested that there was a problem. One of them likened watching me trying to score runs to watching a clown at a circus. It was shit like that! There was no explanation from a cricketing perspective; it was just a personal attack that I found cheap and unnecessary.

Steve Rixon: I thought some of the coverage was unfair and very naïve — those critics had no idea what was actually going on and what we were trying to achieve. I did speak to media at different stages about what I was prepared to live with from Macca. Unfortunately, they took it for what it was worth and wrote their stories anyway.

I always used to try to analyse what we would get from Macca. And in doing so, you have to rob from Peter to pay Paul. I saw Macca as a match-winner. Dougie Walters was a match-winner and he would go out and get three ducks in a row. But when he peeled off his hundred, not only had he put you in a good position, he had normally won the game for you. I saw that in Macca.

Whereas a lot of the scribes, the cynics and the critics didn't like the insecurity of Macca going out there and missing out two or three times, I lived with it to a degree because I knew he was going to produce a performance on his day that was going to win us a test match. And I was about winning test matches.

Craig is thick-skinned; there is no doubt about that. But he is also not a man who is just going to sit there and cop criticism — he will rebound and defend himself at all costs as people with a bit of character do. I think there were quite a few times when it did affect him. There was a bit of a facade there on occasions; he would say they wouldn't get on top of him but the only thing I could hear him talk about was such-and-such a story. So that meant they were getting at him, whether he liked it or not. His game did deteriorate on occasions, and there were times when he decided, 'Well, I will show you blokes.'

Daniel Vettori: We always used to laugh when he had his transistor on before he went out to bat, listening to Radio Sport. For me, I have always tried to avoid what the media have said. I don't think embrace is the right word, but Craig was always part of it by reading or listening to it.

In some ways I admire guys like him and Chris Cairns who never took a backward step, a lot of guys would sit back and think, 'This is the way the media goes, I will play the game and hopefully not cause too much of a ruckus and get on with it'. I think Craig was right to question people about things that were either written or said about him — it is only human to be affected by it at times.

Whether it got to him from a performance angle, I don't think it ever got to that stage. But it probably consumed a bit more of his time than it should have. But I always sat back and thought, 'This guy is being true to himself, this is how he feels about a certain situation, so why shouldn't he talk about it or confront someone about it?'

The hardest thing I have had to endure is what impact the media coverage has actually had on my family, not what it may have had on me. The worst instance of that happened leading up to the 2007 Chappell-Hadlee Trophy series. Soon after John Bracewell named the squad for the World Cup and the subsequent series against Australia, Radio Sport breakfast host Tony Veitch and his producer Goran Paladin created a limerick involving me, Braces and Daryl Tuffey.

I'm not going to repeat exactly what was said in the jingle — because it was defamatory. The first I heard about it was when Cherie rang me. My mum had heard it on the radio while she was driving to work. She was brought to tears and was so upset she had to pull over.

I have always wondered why my family even listened to talkback or read some of the stories. Generally, if people are talking about me it is either really good or really bad. There rarely was any middle ground when it comes to people debating me. Unfortunately, in the case of the skit, they were tuned in for the sports news when it came on — there was nowhere to hide. I'd be lying if I said it didn't hurt me a little bit, but I can deal with it and shut it off. But for my family it is different.

I couldn't understand where Veitchy and his producer were coming from. Tony had been a critic of mine for a number of years. They got carried away, thought it was funny, when it certainly wasn't. It was in really poor taste.

Tony Veitch: It was pretty dumb, but at the time it summed up where I was with Craig McMillan. I couldn't understand the guy. I couldn't understand how this guy who had an incredible amount of talent would just do some dumb things on the cricket field. I looked at so many other players, for example Mathew Sinclair, and I wondered why that guy was bumped out of the team and Macca seemed to survive.

I look back now and I admit that it was a big learning curve for me — at the time I had been perceived as being always the nice guy on radio and I wouldn't have a crack at anyone. And I was also in between these so-called radio personalities. I thought, 'Well, let's have a crack and be hard and do it.' And that is something I really regret.

It was meant to be something where we were having a little bit of fun with the audience and trying to get something across, and that was: it was about time this guy fronted more for New Zealand. In the end it got personal, something which I didn't want to do — I had fallen into the trap a lot of other media did. You can have a go about someone's batting, but leave all the other crap out of it.

It wasn't just me or my family who were unimpressed. New Zealand Cricket, who had a business arrangement with Radio Sport, certainly didn't see the funny side of the gag either. The extent of what went on was never made public at the time, but lawyers were involved, New Zealand Cricket asked John, Daryl and me how far we wanted to take it and there was talk of court action.

In the end I thought the biggest thing for me to do was to accept an apology from Veitch. I could have said, 'No, that was out of order, I am not going to accept your apology', and take legal action. But who would the winner be in that situation? He would have continued to have had a shit attitude towards me, so I would be getting bagged regardless of how well I was doing. And as much as I wanted to do that, because it was bullshit what he had said and done, I tried to look at the bigger picture.

The repercussions meant that the breakfast show had no access to the Black Caps during the Chappell-Hadlee Trophy series, The Radio Network admitted there was a breach of the Radio Code of Broadcasting Practice, Tony Veitch apologised personally to me, the breakfast team was reprimanded and sent off to a seminar with a top Auckland defamation lawyer and an on-air apology was issued.

Tony Veitch: New Zealand Cricket were well pissed off about it, and rightly so. Craig was obviously upset and pissed off and John was pissed off. I went to my boss Bill Francis at the Radio Network, and said: 'I fess up, it was a dumb thing to do, I made a mistake — how can I deal with this?' I was told by my bosses that New Zealand Cricket had said that under no circumstances was I to contact Craig, that they were possibly going to take legal action. It was getting ridiculous — it was dumb, it was a one-off, but it was fixable.

But in the end, it was Macca's call to say how he wanted to deal with it. The day before they were leaving for the Chappell-Hadlee Trophy series he got on the phone and we chewed the fat. Macca was honest; he said: 'I was pissed off, my family was pissed off, my wife was pissed off and it upset me.' I let him vent it, go through it and then he asked me a question, saying: 'What is it that you have got against me? You have always seemed to have had a crack at me.'

It wasn't meant to be a personal crack at him. It was merely coming from me, a guy who likes cricket, wondering why Craig had never fulfilled the promise. It was about why Craig would play the reverse sweep when New Zealand were 180-4 and probably needed to be a bit more conservative. It was about why his test average was so fantastic in the early years, but he never managed to go on a lot of times. That is where it came from. As a cricket fan I had watched the Black Caps probably underperform, and I think Craig was seen publicly as the face of that. If there was one guy who would cop it if the Black Caps failed, it would be Craig McMillan.

We had a long conversation. At the end of it a lot got sorted. Without sounding all very nancy about it, in some ways our situations were very similar. I am in the career where I have copped a lot of grief, it gets personal and it is horrible. The thing that frustrated me the most about it was that I had fallen into the same trap of going down a line that I had always sworn I wouldn't — I know how much it had previously affected me.

Personally, I was stoked with his approach. He could have tried and followed it through to the letter of the law, and things could have got quite nasty. I guess he was trying to work out where I was coming from. It was interesting the way the different people and organisations handled it. New Zealand Cricket went to ground; we couldn't get anything out of them. Bracewell went into hibernation, which is what John does, with the attitude: 'There is no way on earth I am going to talk to that person ever again.' And he still refuses to go on the show. And I think in the end, John is a terrible interview so it has been no great loss as far as we are concerned. All the other bridges were healed except for John Bracewell.

It was interesting after the Auckland and Hamilton one-dayers when Tony put his hand up on air, saying that he was a critic of mine but then said I had played pretty well and he took his hat off to me for my performances. As I said, the whole incident was pretty distressing for my family. But probably the most pleasing aspect about it for me was my own reaction. I was able to put it to the back of my mind and just concentrate on playing cricket.

Almost a year on from that limerick and things turned almost full circle with me and Tony Veitch, getting a weekly spot on his breakfast show to talk cricket. By taking the longer view of accepting the apology and moving on, it has created a work opportunity which in February 2007 would have seemed highly unlikely.

Tony Veitch: We first discussed it when we spoke after the limerick. It was like a little light switch went on. I just thought he would be a great correspondent — he is opinionated and he knows his sport. The thing about Macca is that he lives, breathes and eats sport and listens to Radio Sport all the time. Trying to find voices out there who can comment on a lot of different sports is not easy. It's hard in New Zealand, as there aren't many sportsmen in New Zealand who fundamentally have the knowledge, the passion and desire to talk about other stuff.

It is always a risk when you try out someone new on air. And this was a risk. I knew Craig was nervous and apprehensive about whether he would be any good. But the first day we had him on we got an incredible amount of feedback, a lot of it was good. I have been incredibly proud of the fact that we have gone from a situation where we were possibly at war, to a situation where I think he is one of my favourite people to talk to. And this is a guy who says he hates public speaking, has never been the greatest fan of the media, but he is great on the radio. And I think, long term, if Macca decided it was something he wanted to do, he could be good in a media career. And I think he is learning that. It is definitely something he could now consider.

The biggest frustration I always felt with the media was that there was normally no recourse or action from New Zealand Cricket against those guys who spread mistruths. If they wrote something that was hugely unfair we still always had to front up to them. They could pretty much write whatever they wanted, even if it wasn't close to the truth, and we would have to keep giving them our time. They would say 'Jump' and New Zealand Cricket would say, 'How high?' The only time I have seen them actually confront the media was after the Radio Sport incident.

As players, we get frustrated with the media because we don't think there is enough onus put back onto them as to what is being written at times. The key to me is how accurate the information is and how balanced any story is. A lot of the time it is unbalanced. And at times that sort of stuff has got my back up and I felt like I didn't have to give these guys my time when a lot of it, I felt, was unfair and unbalanced. I thought, 'Bugger you. I am not going to do an interview.' That probably got their backs up as well, adding to the problem.

It made me very wary of who I talked to, what I said and what I did through that period. I certainly felt that there were other guys in the team who were struggling and who weren't being touched by the media. The constant focus was on me. Maybe I was a good topic. I don't know.

Some of the coverage in New Zealand on the rival ICL and IPL set-ups has reinforced to me the lack of balance and lack of accountability in the media. There has been a lot of hysteria about the signings, most notably written by Richard Boock. A lot of the things that have been reported are nowhere near correct, but they make good stories. I also find it amazing that New Zealand Cricket came out at the time and said we wouldn't be selected for the Black Caps when in fact the majority of us had retired from international and domestic cricket. That was a beat-up article by Boock, someone who seems to be very fond of writing positive stories about the rival IPL. Boock appears to be someone who is trumpeting loudly the IPL in New Zealand, and at the same time slamming the ICL.

When I read some of that stuff I couldn't help thinking back to the 2007 Cricket World Cup when New Zealand Cricket helped contribute to the cost of his trip to the West Indies. From New Zealand Cricket's point of view, it was money well spent.

One of my other frustrations with the media is that the good things about us rarely get reported. I suppose that comes down to cynical journalism, in terms of selling a story and selling a newspaper. Some of the treatment that Shane Warne has received from the media is a classic example of that. They would rather write about some of his non-cricket activities. But they don't report the other side of him. In Hampshire, for example, the dying wish for a couple of kids who were very sick with cancer was to meet Shane. We were in the thick of the County championship, but he went out of his way to invite the kids into our changing room, spend some time with him and introduce them to the rest of the players. Just to see their faces was amazing — to meet and speak with Shane Warne was the biggest thrill of their life. He went out of his way to help a lot of those causes but you don't read anything about that.

There are certain guys in the media I do respect. One is Bryan Waddle, the voice of New Zealand cricket on the radio for a number of years. Generally, I found his feedback was well balanced and well thought out. He is one of the few guys in the media who I have enjoyed talking to.

And sitting back now, I do realise that we cricketers can be pretty precious. There is no doubt that we don't always respond that well to criticism. But I still think at times our media are over the top. We do very well as a cricketing nation. Everyone expects us to be No. 1 or No. 2 in the world — but that is unrealistic. We are up against India and Pakistan, countries with populations of 1.2 billion and 161 million respectively, where kids play cricket non-stop through the streets. They have the biggest talent pool and their infrastructures are just so incredible.

Barring Eden Park and Seddon Park, you struggle to get decent training facilities in New Zealand. We are a rugby nation, with rugby grounds that you play cricket on. If we had the facilities that they have in countries like Australia or England then I have no doubt we would be a better cricketing nation.

For the resources and infrastructure we have, some of the criticism we cop is unwarranted. Making the semi-finals of the 2007 Cricket World Cup was no mean achievement, especially when other teams like Pakistan, India and South Africa missed out. How can making the semi-finals of the World Cup be a failure? It's not a failed campaign. We box above our weight in terms of the population we have, the player depth we have, our facilities and weather. And it would be good sometimes if the media would appreciate that.

In trouble with the law

The face of cricket has changed significantly since I first played for the Black Caps in 1997. When I came onto the international scene, sledging played a big part in the game. Some of it was quite clever — some of it was also pretty basic in terms of just blatant abuse. But, like it or not, it was part and parcel of the international scene. And especially during my early years in international cricket, I wasn't immune to dishing it out.

But things have changed. And as more of what is said on the field is picked up by pitch-side microphones, cricket's officialdom have progressively clamped down on what can and can't be said on the cricket pitch. Step out of line and you face a date with the ICC match referee, the risk of a substantial fine and possibly even suspension. Over the years it is something which has hit me in the pocket.

It is a process which has gone too far one way and has taken a lot of the character and emotion out of the game. I realise that, as role models, you don't want to see players over-reacting and using profane language. But there are times when you want to see some emotion, some heat in the battle. And from my own experience, once charges are laid against you, generally the ICC match referee has made up his mind before you even walk into the hearing.

You are up against it. They really are waiting there to hang you out to dry. If you get off a charge of any nature, you're doing well for yourself. The fact that the umpires are in the room to give evidence against you makes it doubly difficult. A match referee is naturally going to stay close to umpires. If he is seen to be taking a player's word over an umpire's word, that will create problems in itself.

Over the last five or six years the ICC match referees have really clamped down on the players. And a lot of the players are ending up robotic. It's sad that you're not seeing the real personalities coming through. If they do show their emotions, some players aren't going to spend a lot of time out on the field. In many ways the issue of on-field conduct has gone from one extreme to another. Cricket is known as a gentleman's game — but that is now nothing but a throwaway line. That might have applied in W.G. Grace's era, but it certainly doesn't apply now. And as history will tell you, W.G. Grace certainly wasn't the finest of cricket's gentlemen.

The clamping down on conduct hasn't totally removed sledging from the game. Instead some players simply got a lot smarter in the way they say things which could get them in trouble if they said them out in the open. Glenn McGrath was a classic example — he used to mutter and swear under his breath, but he would always hold his hand up to his mouth as he did it as he was turning away from the batsman. If you were the batsman you could hear it as plain as day, but the umpire could never hear it.

I've been ordered to front ICC match referees three times in my international career. Perhaps the time that summed up how comical it is was my second instance, in just my third season of test cricket, in 2000 during our five-wicket loss to South Africa at Bloemfontein's Goodyear Park. I was batting with Flem at the time and was certainly riding my luck, nicking a few deliveries off Shaun Pollock wide of the slips. Needless to say, Pollock certainly wasn't seeing the funny side of the luck I was having.

I ran two runs off one ball I nicked off him, only to be welcomed by a verbal barrage from Pollock, telling me how useless I was. There was a bit of a joke among the guys when it comes to Shaun Pollock that he was a dead ringer for Richie off *Happy Days*. That entered my head and I simply responded by saying: 'F… off Richie Cunningham.'

He just lost the plot and it was pretty clear he wasn't happy at all. Off his next ball I got a single and trotted down the other end. He came over to me, grabbed the grill of my helmet and started going off his head in Afrikaans at me. Obviously, I couldn't understand a word he was saying, but it was pretty plain the type of sentiments he was trying to get across. He kept a grip of my grill, gave it a shake and then patted me on the head.

To my mind, that was out of order and I told him in clear terms where to go. The umpire told him to move and that was the end of that. But at the end of the day's play I found out that I was required to see the ICC match referee because I had been reported. It just seemed crazy — Pollock had manhandled me, yet I had been reported.

We had a hearing with Pakistani match referee Naushad Ali — who was officiating in his first test — and it was seriously like being in a circus. The arguments were put before the referee, and Pollock admitted that he'd manhandled me. I made it clear that I never touched him; I just said a few things to him.

It seemed like Ali wanted to make a bit of a statement. So Pollock was fined 50 per cent of his match fee — I went for 30 per cent. I got done for swearing because I had used the 'F' word. Even though we'd had words on the field, Pollock and I both walked out of the room shaking our heads at how inept it was. We were looking at each other laughing, it was just unbelievable.

Pollock, McMillan fined by match referee
Cricinfo, 21 November 2000

South African captain Shaun Pollock and New Zealand batsman Craig McMillan were both fined portions of their match fees by match referee Col. Naushad Ali at the conclusion of the first Castle Lager/MTN Test match in Bloemfontein on Tuesday.

The pair were involved in a verbal exchange on Monday afternoon during which, according to the match referee, 'unparliamentary language' was used.

Pollock was fined 50 per cent of his match fee for being in violation of clauses 1 and 2 of the ICC Code of Conduct while McMillan was fined 30 per cent for being in violation of clause 2.

It was the first time I had copped a fine under the system, but it wasn't the first time I had been made to go through the officiating charade. Two years earlier I was introduced to the system during the ICC Knockout tournament in Bangladesh. During our five-wicket win over Zimbabwe at Dhaka I was given out caught behind off the bowling of Paul Strang. The only issue was that I didn't hit the ball. I went to play a shot, missed the ball totally and could feel that I was in the process of lifting my back foot, so I quickly put it back down. Their players went off, appealing after their wicket-keeper Andy Flower had taken the bails off. I knew I hadn't hit the ball, I didn't even come close to it, so looked out to square leg to make sure I wasn't going to be given out stumped. Square leg umpire Peter Willey hadn't given me out so I got on with starting to prepare for the next ball.

The next thing I know is that Steve Bucknor, the umpire at the bowler's end, is re-raising his finger. I could not believe that he had given me out caught behind so I took a bit of time leaving the crease and walked off dejectedly back to the changing room. For my trouble I found myself in front of the match referee who said that upon an umpire's decision, you had to leave the crease immediately. My defence was that there was a real state of confusion because I thought they were appealing for the stumping, so I was looking at square leg and I didn't see Bucknor raise his finger the first time. Then when I eventually saw him raise his finger, I was slow to leave because I was taken by complete surprise as I hadn't edged the ball.

McMillan escapes severe penalty
ICC release, 25 October 1998

New Zealand batsman Craig McMillan narrowly escaped penalty today after an ICC Official Hearing here in Dhaka this morning. McMillan was accused of dissent after being given out caught at the wicket by Match Umpire Steve Bucknor in yesterday's Wills International Cup match against Zimbabwe

Match Referee Raman Subba Row decided that although there were mitigating factors relating to whether the appeal was for a stumping or a catch at the wicket, there had been some degree of unacceptable dissent. However, the only penalty imposed was a severe reprimand, and a warning as to future conduct, and McMillan will not face any suspension.

It must have been something about Bangladesh, because when I returned six years later I again found myself up in front of the dreaded ICC match officialdom. Again I felt I had been the victim of a pretty poor umpiring decision in a one-day international against Bangladesh on our 2004 tour. All I could do was shake my head in disbelief as I saw the dreaded finger come out — and from where I was coming from, what I did was just a very natural decision.

But the Australian ICC match referee Alan Hurst didn't quite see it that way, deciding that my actions amounted to dissent. I wasn't the only Black Cap to be summonsed by Hurst, with Scott Styris also charged with swearing. We all fronted up to the match referee's hearing afterwards and the feeling was that I had a pretty strong case and should be OK. But it wasn't so rosy for Scott; he appeared to be gone for all money. Ross Dykes, who was our tour manager, said I would be fine but didn't hold out too much hope for Scott. Again Hurst was new to his role. It was just his first one-day international series, and it seemed that he too wanted to make a statement as to how players should be acting. And with that attitude, my hopes of getting off with just a telling off went right out of the window.

McMillan and Styris incur match referee's wrath
Cricinfo, 9 November 2004

New Zealand's victorious tour of Bangladesh ended on a slightly sour note as both Craig McMillan and Scott Styris were brought to book by Alan Hurst, the ICC match referee, after the third and final one-day international in Dhaka.

McMillan was fined 25 per cent of his match fee after a show of dissent and swearing at the umpire on being given out leg before, while Styris — who was Man of the Series — was given a severe reprimand for giving Mohammad Ashraful a tasteless send-off after dismissing him.

Interestingly, New Zealand were the recipients of the Spirit of Cricket award at a ceremony organised by the ICC just two months ago.

The fact that Scotty had got off just showed how much of a joke the whole process was. His actions were seen on TV, but good on him for getting off a far more serious charge. All I could do was shake my head after the meeting. Even Ross was laughing at the different outcomes reached.

In many ways I had no chance of winning because as soon as I walked into the room, Hurst pretty much said that I was guilty. I told him that may be so, but it all came from a very bad umpiring decision, so what was the recourse against the umpire? That probably didn't go down too well. I just wanted to point out that the umpire had made the mistake, he gets off scot-free and because I show a little bit of emotion I end up copping a fine.

While I had my fair share of run-ins with the process, there certainly are some very good match referees out there, including Sri Lanka's Ranjan Madugalle. He is probably regarded as the best. The fact that he has played at the highest level helps, but in saying that it doesn't help all of them. At times it can be jobs for the boys — a lot of former test cricketers are doing it. A match official is a position which needs common sense, diplomacy and also an understanding of how things work on the field.

One of my biggest frustrations about being summoned before the ICC match referees, and I am sure it is a view shared by other cricketers, is that often it is due to a reaction following a poor umpiring decision. Yet while players are left to count the cost of their frustration-inspired actions, too often the umpires who make the on-field blunders are back the next game as if nothing has happened.

I don't think the expectations on international umpires are yet tough enough that if someone does have a couple of bad games, they get the same treatment as a player receives and they get stood down. But I would love to see what happens in the NRL, when refs are stood down if they have a shocker, replicated by the ICC. The only time I can really say I have seen an umpire being stood down after an error-ridden showing was Bucknor after the Australia–India test at the SCG in early 2008. I would like to see a lot more of that — it would inject a lot more credibility into the disciplinary process.

It concerns me that guys like Bucknor and Rudi Koertzen keep going when they appear to be past their used-by date. Every one of their blundering decisions is creating huge conflict among cricket nations. And it is no surprise to me that the best umpires in the world are the younger ones, guys like Simon Taufel — someone who is not only fit in body and mind, but also has good man-management skills with the players. I don't see much respect aimed for someone like Bucknor now. Most of the players think he is past it.

In fact Bucknor has been guilty of some terrible calls for some seasons now. In the 2004 test against Australia at the Gabba when Gilly and I had words, there was a classic example of a shocking umpiring decision. A ball from Jason Gillespie to Brendon McCullum seamed off a crack, missed the bat by a foot and yet Brendon was given out caught behind. It showed me again just how poor an umpire Bucknor is. He gave it out and yet you saw it seconds later on the big screen — it was just embarrassing.

When I think back to my time in international cricket, I think of good umpires being David Shepherd from England and a younger Koertzen from South Africa. But I qualify my comments on both by saying the ICC generally let umpires go on too long, two or three years past their use-by date. And that is definitely the case with Rudi. Because they have been such good umpires for a long time, the ICC just believe they will keep on like that.

Billy Bowden is a good umpire. He is obviously quite eccentric and not your typical international umpire. But to his credit he has toned a lot of that down. His mannerisms are now a lot less over the top compared to what they used to be — it is not so much about Billy in the middle, it is about Billy doing his job and being part of the whole game. Whenever I have played games he has controlled, he has pretty much got all the decisions right. He has confidence in his ability and is one of the best umpires New Zealand has produced.

I don't think there is any doubt these days that, with developments in technology, umpires are under more scrutiny than they have ever been. The technology has helped the umpires, but it has hindered them as well. One factor I have noticed in recent years is that batsmen have gradually lost the benefit of the doubt since the introduction of technology. Before the third umpire came into play, the batsman always used to get the benefit of the doubt, especially with run outs and stumpings. Nowadays when things are referred upstairs, the decision is out more often than not.

I would like to see more use of technology. But I don't want to see robots having to stand out there and having to refer everything upstairs. There are situations such as the possible inside edge onto the pad for certain lbw appeals — that is a contentious one that I see an umpire get wrong in almost every test I watch. It would be a simple task for the third official to look at it on TV once: if it hasn't hit the bat the batsman is out, if it has hit the bat he is not out. At a fast pace, those decisions are the hardest ones to see.

But I don't know whether technology is good enough yet to be used when it comes to making a decisive call on some low catches. Generally, there are shadows involved. It comes back to the umpire's call. And I don't think you should be relying on players to make the call. You saw what happened in the early 2008 Australian–India series where that fell to pieces. So the umpires, who have the best view, should make the call. And if there is any doubt, the batsman has to be given not out.

One of the good things I see umpires doing now is them coming to team practices, standing and watching in the nets for a period of time. They are watching the batters and bowlers, gaining more information on the players they are going to officiate. It also increases their interaction with the players and means we can get to know them a little away from the serious business on the field. It means if a bad decision is made down the track, a bit more forgiveness will be offered from the players. That can only help with relationships between players and umpires.

Getting in the zone

I've always been quite nervous when I've been waiting to go into bat, especially during test matches when your wait to go out into the middle can be quite long. A constant battle for me throughout my career has been trying to get into a state where I feel comfortable and, all-importantly, relaxed when it is time to go out. For some time, when I went out to bat it felt like I'd already played my innings; I was mentally drained from the anxiety. It was something I struggled with for a long time, having the freedom to get myself into a comfortable state from where I could perform.

Cricket is the toughest team sport I know — it's very much an individual's game within a team sport. As a batter, I can't rely on anyone else to score my runs. And that is why I believe it's imperative that you have freedom to prepare in the way that best suits you as an individual, as long as it is something that doesn't impact on your team-mates.

For a long time in the Black Caps, however, I found a series of archaic rules really impacted on the way that I could best prepare myself for what was to follow. These included the banning of listening to iPods or personal radios in the team enclosure, or bringing any reading material into the room. The rules were originally instituted in a fairly lax way under the coaching of Steve Rixon, and even then some guys would read newspapers and the odd book. But they were fully enforced as Flem first started calling the shots under the coaching of Denis Aberhart, and later on when Bracewell took over the team.

I never understood the argument that Flem and then Bracewell put up. Their view was that you weren't watching and taking in what was happening out in the middle and that you could miss a team-mate's achievement, such as someone scoring a 50 or a century. That is just nonsense. With all the guys I know, if you are reading a book you read a few lines, look up and watch the ball being bowled and then put your head back down. And, of course, if something does happen, you clap for your team-mate.

But there was just a blanket attitude that if you were listening to or reading something, you weren't showing support to your team-mates. They wanted you to watch every ball for the whole day. Flem was the big one on no reading during a game. I argued with him a number of times about the ban on reading and listening to music on a personal stereo. As captain, he was obviously in agreement with the protocols which were put in place. I couldn't see any harm in reading — one eye would be on your book, the other on the game. You never missed someone reaching a significant milestone, you were still aware of what was going on out in the middle — but half your mind was relaxing and able to focus on something other than cricket. The other thing was the perception of people seeing us reading in the enclosure; Flem believed they might think we were more interested in a book than we were in the game. I don't agree with that either.

I had a real problem with the policy, especially in the test arena. A five-day test is mentally tiring; it is a tough sport and you need your break. You need to be able to have some time to sit down when you aren't batting, bowling or fielding and chill out. And I felt that being made to watch every ball of a game certainly wasn't a great way to get that mental break. For me, having to watch every ball in a day's play could be incredibly mentally fatiguing. I had always liked to try to switch off when I wasn't involved. But unfortunately that was really difficult to do with these policies.

John Bracewell: There was a period of time when the players said they weren't going to listen to things. That was when Craig went and bought a radio and stuck it on his head. He would be sitting there, moving his head around as if he was listening to music but he was actually listening to the commentary.

We often talked in the dressing room about it. If they are rubbishing you the whole time on the TV and radio, why would you listen to it? If he had one weakness, he was almost obsessive in listening to criticism and then got quite upset by it. His reaction would be, 'Well, stuff you. I am going to belt the shit out of it.' It was one of hostility. I am sure that affected his form loops as well.

A lot of guys listened to music, whereas Craig listened to the radio. He wouldn't have a Walkman on; he would have a radio on and would be listening to the commentary. You could see him getting fired up. He would march out into the middle, not to show the opposition but to show the person who was making the comment — that was the impression I got. I reckon that ate away at him more than he is willing to admit. It certainly wasn't a healthy thing for the environment.

I never remember the team backing a blanket ban on listening to music and so on in the team room. It is an individual thing that shouldn't be covered by an all-consuming team policy. And the only time I generally listened to Radio Sport was when I was already out. Before I batted, I would listen to an iPod or radio. There were a couple of times where I did lie there, waiting to bat and listened to the cricket commentary — but it certainly wasn't very often. It was all about my ways of trying to relax and compose myself before I went out to bat. I found it quite soothing. I didn't enjoy watching the game as it made me mentally tired and I struggled with that. I found listening to something a lot more relaxing. But as far as using the commentary and getting fired up, that never happened.

The management was inflexible about the team protocol for a long time and it certainly annoyed me. I know it annoyed some of the other guys too. Management just couldn't see the value in allowing guys to listen to some music or the radio or read a book or a paper. It came down to me saying, 'Everyone is different, everyone is a different specimen — what relaxes me might not relax you. And if I need to get in this state to perform, that is what I have to do.' Anyone who has played the game knows that it is virtually impossible to watch every ball in a day's play. For some guys, it is fine. But everyone is different. Some guys need to go and have a power-nap for 30 minutes or read a magazine to recharge their batteries.

The issue of preparation is something that I brought up at a number of meetings. But you really felt like you were asking for the earth. After numerous debates there was a bit of leeway allowed. I had made it very clear that I needed to listen to my music before I batted. So a compromise was made in the lead-up to the 2003 tour of India where I could try a couple of different things, including listening to music, to calm my nerves.

I felt that listening to music was one thing that would work for me. So, in India, through Gilbert and Ashley Ross, we decided to do it. I had to get it ticked off by team management and I still had an issue that we had to sit in a team enclosure and watch ball after ball. It was a compromise by the team management and they eventually allowed me to listen to a set limit of a dozen songs. That included a bit of John Farnham, Jimmy Barnes, Britney Spears and Westlife — needless to say the boys weren't real big on my music catalogue.

I also wanted to lie down on the physio bed. I would watch the first five or 10 minutes of the innings and then go and lie down in the dressing room and visualise. It meant I could relax. The results showed that the approach worked for me. I would be woken by the noise of the crowd following a dismissal, but I would wake up totally clear and I felt all energised when I walked out into the middle.

The first test was played at Sardar Patel Stadium, Ahmedabad, in a match where batsmen from both sides cashed in on the conditions. It was a good test for me, scoring 54 in the first innings — with Nathan chiming in with 103 — and then backing it up with an unbeaten 83 in the second innings.

A week later, following the draw at Ahmedabad, we arrived at Mohali for the second test at the Punjab Cricket Association Stadium. Flem won the toss and put us into bat in ideal conditions — what followed was a record-equalling effort with Mark Richardson, Lou Vincent, Scott Styris and then me all scoring centuries in our total of 630–6 declared. It was only the second time four New Zealanders have scored centuries in the same innings, one short of the all-time world record set by Australia in 1955 against the West Indies and Pakistan against Bangladesh in 2001.

There were other times when I went and sat by myself, away from the changing room, just to have my own time. A lot of shit is often talked about in the changing room during a day, and generally not a lot of it is about cricket. As a batter waiting to go into bat, sometimes you can be caught up in it. There is a fine line between being relaxed, knowing what is going on in a game and being apart from it. I had my best tour for years in India in 2003, where I averaged 237, and wondered what might have been if some degree of sense had prevailed through earlier years.

Denis Aberhart: The important thing is that there are 11 equal players in a cricket team. Everyone needs to be given a fair suck of the sauce bottle so everyone gets a go. You have to treat everyone differently, everyone has a different personality.

People prepare in different ways. And I think too often in the set-up at times there is an expectation from the senior leadership that 'Hey this is how you should prepare, this is how I prepare. This is how I work at the game, so this is what you should do as well'. But not everyone is like that. It is counter-productive; you need people in their right frame of mind.

People like Macca know how to get the best out of themselves. And if they don't, then give them a kick up the backside. But they know what they need to do to prepare — as a coach you need to support them in that and provide the resources they need. In the end, it is the players who need to take responsibility in making sure they have signed off on their preparation and what they need to do. Players need to take individual responsibility for that.

I used to be able to pick when he would have a good day. And I used to give him a kick up the arse when he wasn't in that right frame of mind. When he was going to have a good day he focused very early on. If he was walking around the dressing room or talking to people, I knew that he wasn't switched on.

When he played his best innings he would go away and sit on his own, have his helmet and gloves on all ready, and be focusing on what was needed. It was just an attitude and a look in the eyes, I knew that: 'Hey, he is really in the zone. He is really switched on today.' We talked a few times about the fact he needed to remember what he did before that innings, because he was in the zone and wanted to do well. It was a body language thing and a look in the eyes.

While I was able to get a bit of latitude for my preparations in India, some things weren't up for debate. That included the ban on reading papers and novels in the team enclosure during our turn at bat. But a couple of guys managed to get around that one a little by bringing the *Cricket Almanac* into the changing room. Team management deemed that OK because it was a cricket book. Guys would be reading the *Almanac* and someone like Styris or Vettori would ask a question and the rest of the guys would be trying to answer it — it would be a general cricketing question, sometimes involving one of the guys in the room. Then it got to the point where the *Almanac* was regarded as being OK because it wasn't regarded as reading material. That attitude was just crazy; it summed things up for me in terms of how far we had gone downhill.

I wondered sometimes if all the rules and regulations regarding our off-field build-up corresponded with how we performed in the third innings of a game. It was so often the worst innings of our test matches. I wondered whether if it was due to us being mentally tired; we were having lapses that would kill the rest of the game because of the desire by some to ensure that players stayed 'switched on' at all times.

On borrowed time

It only took one test series with Bracewell as coach to make me feel that my time in the national side had become more turbulent. After the 2004 test series in England, he sat me down at breakfast and told me that the selectors were going to leave me out for the upcoming test tour of Bangladesh. I found this surprising and very disappointing as in the previous overseas test tour against India, in India, I had averaged 237. I was flown over for the subsequent three-match one-day international series against Bangladesh, but that really was only a small consolation.

Next up was the two-test tour of Australia in late 2004, and again my name was missing when the test squad was revealed by New Zealand Cricket. I had played 52 tests up to that point, but it was starting to look very uncertain whether I would add to that number in the near future.

As it turned out I didn't have too long to ponder my latest exclusion, getting called up as cover while Flem's ongoing fitness issues surfaced and Nathan Astle battled a back injury. I landed in Sydney the night before the warm-up clash against New South Wales and was basically told I wouldn't be playing, that I was just there for cover. With that in mind I did all the warm-ups on match day and was told just before the toss that Nathan's back was no good and I would be playing.

We played a very strong New South Wales squad whose attack included Brett Lee and Stuart MacGill. We played pretty averagely and started the tour poorly by neither batting nor bowling well. I scored 14 in the first innings, being given out caught behind off MacGill even though I didn't nick it. I had an old favourite bat I was using and it had a squeaky handle. I played and missed a delivery, but the handle made a noise and I was given out. I looked at the replay later on and there was a decent-sized gap between the bat and the ball. So that was the last innings that bat was used in.

It was bloody frustrating because I was in the process of playing myself in, I had struck three boundaries and I was trying to get a score on the board so I might be a chance for the test. In the second innings we got knocked over for just 201 and lost by nine wickets. But after the match I was told by management that I was staying on tour and we headed up to Brisbane to prepare for the first test. Even more surprising than that was news a couple of days later that I would in fact be playing in the first test at the Gabba — the strangest thing about the selection was that I was picked ahead of Hamish Marshall, who was an initial selection in the tour squad.

I was really nervous going into bat in the first innings of the test and the Australians brought Shane Warne on early to bowl to me. I hit him for a couple of boundaries and a six and was just starting to feel comfortable, reaching 23. But then I decided to come down the wicket, continuing my aggressive approach, and hit him over the top, but I missed the ball and got stumped. It was one of those dismissals that looked really bad — it certainly wasn't great. In fact not many of us played well in that first innings. It was only an outstanding unbeaten 126 from Jacob Oram and 69 from Mathew Sinclair that helped us post a total of 353.

By the time I went out to bat in the second innings we were in dire straits. We were under huge pressure just to stay in the game — the Aussies were at their aggressive best, they were letting us know the situation of the game. They had attacking fields and their bowlers were on top of things. To me, it felt like my international career was on the line. Part of that was down to the way I had got out in the first innings. I could hear the vultures starting to circle again. I knew I needed something substantial to keep my place in the side. And I walked out to the wicket with that in mind.

Trust me, they certainly aren't the best emotions to be running through your head when you go out to face the might of the Aussies. To make things worse I got an inside edge off the bowling of Jason Gillespie which was gladly caught by Adam Gilchrist. I clearly hit the ball, but given what was on the line I stood my ground and waited for umpire Steve Bucknor to raise his finger. But for some reason he didn't; he must have thought it came off my thigh.

After it was clear Bucknor wasn't going to give me, Gilchrist yelled out: 'Come on Macca. That is a massive edge.' I was pretty fired up at the time — I was under no illusion that I was batting for my career and as such I was pretty intense about the whole situation. So I snapped at him, saying: 'F... off Gilly, we are not all walkers like you.' All I could see was Shane Warne, who was at first slip, laughing behind his hands. Gilly wasn't going to let it rest and fired back with something else.

Shane Warne: The thing with Gilly is good on him if that is the way he wants to play his cricket and walk. But everyone is entitled to do what they want. I just thought it was quite ironic that he was trying to preach to Macca. I just found that hilarious. I would have just said, 'Great mate, go and preach to somebody else.' It was funny seeing him and Macca just going for it. I was just laughing; I enjoyed it.

I have always been a firm believer that no matter whether you know you are out or not, you don't walk. They have umpires for a reason, to decide whether you are out or not. Cricket has taught me what goes around, comes around — it all evens out. I have never walked. As frustrating as it is when you are in the field and you know someone is out, but has been given not out, it just goes with the territory. You just learn to accept it.

I was lucky to survive, but I certainly didn't help my cause when I was out lbw for just nine off the next ball. The worst possible thing to do is get out the next ball after having such a massive confrontation. I felt really low. In fact I was shattered and thought that was it as far as my test spot was concerned. We ended up being bowled out for 76, losing by an innings and 156 runs.

But it wasn't the end of things as far as debate over whether I should have walked was concerned. After the match when both sides shook hands I came across Gilly. We had a chat on the boundary — he wanted to state his case, I wanted to state my case. We probably should have done it away from the public viewing, because it inflamed things again. The next morning I woke up and was welcomed by a picture in the local paper of Gilchrist and me pointing at each other. They also had a transcript of what was said out in the middle, thanks to the stump-cam microphone. It played out for a couple of days — there was quite a bit of heat flying around in the media.

Fleming accuses Gilchrist of walking 'crusade'
Wisden Cricinfo staff, 22 November 2004

The ramifications of the on-field spat between Craig McMillan and Adam Gilchrist rumbled on as Gilchrist cancelled a planned press conference after the game and McMillan was made unavailable by the New Zealand management.

The pair clashed on the fourth afternoon at Brisbane as New Zealand slid towards defeat. McMillan appeared to get an inside edge off Jason Gillespie which was well taken down the leg side by a sprawling Gilchrist. The confident appeal was turned down by Steve Bucknor — who minutes earlier had given Brendon McCullum out caught behind off a ball he missed by inches.

The stump microphones caught the moment when McMillan turned to Gilchrist — who accepted the decision with a wry grin — and told him that 'not everyone is walking Gilly . . . not everyone has to walk, mate'. The exchange continued and Bucknor ambled down the pitch to ensure that it didn't get out of hand. McMillan was out lbw to the next ball.

At the end of the match, the pair continued their conversation on the boundary edge, as McMillan told Gilchrist that he thought he was 'being a little bit righteous'. Gilchrist countered by saying that he had no issues with him not walking, but added that 'if you nick it you expect to cop it'.

Stephen Fleming then waded into the debate by accusing Gilchrist, who has a reputation as being a genuine walker, of trying to pressurise opponents. 'When you've got one or two players on a crusade, it places pressure on people in terms of whether they choose to walk or not,' he told reporters. 'We all like to see the game played in the best spirit but if some individuals choose not to, which is their right, then so be it. We have to respect that. Whether you're placing pressure on players for walking or not walking, it's the same scenario. You do have to be very careful.'

Ricky Ponting looked to play down the situation. 'I think this whole walking thing has been blown completely out of proportion,' he explained. 'He (Gilchrist) doesn't expect anyone in our team to walk either, so he can't expect that of any opposition players. What can happen is that if there's one we think might be out and you're a batsman who stands there quite often you are going to receive some words from the opposition. It happened in our batting innings as well if you have a look at one of Justin Langer's early in the game. There's been no big deal made of that.'

And the idea that Gilchrist was on a crusade was rubbished by Gillespie. 'He (Gilchrist) doesn't instil his beliefs on his team-mates or the opposition. There wasn't anything to do with "you should walk". What everyone saw yesterday was a bit of gamesmanship out in the middle and a batsman reacted to it.

'A lot of people don't realise how much we do cop it in return from opposition teams but we don't make a song and dance about it,' he continued. 'We don't go and flay our arms and say we get sledged, we just get on with it.'

There was a lighter side to it. Both the New Zealand and Australian teams were on the same flight to Adelaide to prepare for the second test. Cherie and our little boy Mitchell were with me on the flight, about 20 rows behind where the Aussies were sitting.

I saw this note being passed down the back of the plane. It ended up in my hands and was from Gilly. It said: 'Mac, would love to catch up for a chat. Sorry to see that your boy got your looks and not your wife's.' We went for a family walk in Adelaide and bumped into Adam, who was also with his family, and had an impromptu catch-up on the street and both apologised, agreed we should probably have done it better and said there were no hard feelings. We had a laugh about it and decided to move on.

I've always admired Gilchrist, even though he has often made our life hell with his power hitting. Gilchrist has been accused of double standards by walking when he hits the ball, but appealing for some dismissals which TV replays have shown aren't out. The thing I would say about that is that at the time of appealing he probably thought the batsman was out. Now with technology, and the power of five or six replays, viewers can see that maybe some dismissals are incorrect. But he doesn't get the chance to go through those and then decide if he wants to appeal or not. He appeals for whatever he thinks is out and I would never doubt his intentions.

My efforts in the first test weren't deemed enough to warrant selection for the second match at the Adelaide Oval. Instead I watched on as we were beaten by 213 runs, with the match being wrapped up just after lunch on the final day. And that was my game-time on tour, with Bracewell not requiring my services for the Chappell-Hadlee Trophy one-day series which was to follow.

I was now well and truly on the selection merry-go-round, recalled for the one-day and test series against the Australians back on home soil in early 2005. I was then overlooked for the two-test tour of Zimbabwe, although I was included in the one-day squad for the following tri-series also involving Zimbabwe and India. It was great to be back in the side, but it wasn't a great time returning to one of the first countries I had visited with the Black Caps in 1997.

Back then Zimbabwe was a great country. There were a lot of British ex-pats over there, mainly involved in the farming industry. And Harare seemed no different from any other major city — there was the odd pub, the odd sports café and restaurants. The Zimbabwe dollar was strong and we certainly had a good time, on and off the field. We would go out for an occasional drink and meal, and you could certainly move around freely. Heath Streak owned a farm and a few of the guys went out and shot wildebeest and other game on his farm.

And it was obvious right from my first tour to Zimbabwe how much cricket, and the Zimbabwe national team, meant to the nation's president Robert Mugabe. We met Mugabe during one of the one-day internationals against Zimbabwe in 1997. He was supposed to fly into the Harare Sports Club for the lunch break and there was a short ceremony planned when he would meet both the teams. But he was late so we started the match again. Mugabe lived in a massive place right next door to the cricket ground and he eventually flew in. So we had to stop play and shake his hand, then he flew off to his house next door and we continued playing.

I had toured Zimbabwe for a second time in 2000 and again it was an enjoyable experience. But to return in 2005 was a case of going to a place that I didn't recognise at all. For a start, their currency was in disarray. It cost ZIM$1 million just for a can of Coca-Cola and each meal was costing us between ZIM$5 million and $6 million. Each day we would get our daily allowance and it came in wads of cash that were several inches thick and stapled together. The worst thing was walking around the hotel with all this money in your pocket which you needed to pay for a couple of cans of Coke or a lunch. You felt really unsafe.

We had absolutely no freedom in Zimbabwe during the 2005 tour. We stuck to the hotel and played a lot of cards. It was totally different from 1997 when I remember walking out of the hotel in Harare and having a look around the streets. There were a lot of people around but I never felt unsafe. Eight years later, the mood of the country had changed a lot. This time around none of us ventured out of the hotel because of the things we were hearing and reading. It certainly wasn't the safest place to be around. And when it came to doing media interviews, we were told to stick to cricketing issues and not go into any other areas. We had standard answers for everything.

It was massively disappointing. In 1997 Zimbabwe was a really nice country, a really great tourist destination with lots of things to see and do. Now the country was a skeleton of what it was. It was a real shame. It was the same with its national cricket team. Eight years previously they were very good by world standards and had the likes of the Flower brothers, Heath Streak, Henry Olonga, Dave Houghton, Guy Whittall and the Strangs. But now the side is a shadow of its former self.

The triangular series was at a time when the ICC had its super-sub rule in place — and Braces had designated me as being the sub. He thought I could go up and down the order to bash the ball around if I needed to.

But the problem with being the super-sub was that in some games you got a go, and in others you were pretty much made redundant on the strength of the coin toss. And as Flem didn't have the best win/loss ratio with the coin toss, it wasn't great for my position as the super-sub. At times we effectively didn't get to play with the super-sub. In one game against India as soon as we lost the toss, my game was over. We were going to bowl first and then at the end of the 50 overs I would come in for one of the bowlers, slot into the middle order and go from there. But with us losing the toss and being made to bat first, they couldn't risk playing me and then being a bowler short.

It was frustrating. But again, it was one of those things I had to deal with. And as I was soon to find out, far bigger struggles were to follow.

Steve Rixon had a profound impact on both me
and the Black Caps as a team during his coaching
tenure.

Acknowledging the Gabba crowd after bringing up my debut test half-century, with Ian Healy joining
the applause.

A special moment for the McMillan family, with nana Noeline and mother Judith on hand at the Gabba.

Blazing away against Australia at the
Basin Reserve.

Lining up at the Basin Reserve during one of the rare times the New Zealand national anthem was
played before a one-day international.

A truly special moment for me after scoring my maiden test century against Zimbabwe at the Basin Reserve in 1998.

The 1999 World Cup wasn't always the happiest time for me with the bat.

At full stretch as I manage to regain my ground on my way to a century at Old Trafford against England in 1999.

I responded with 142 against Zimbabwe at the Basin Reserve in 2000 after being put on notice by Sir Richard Hadlee.

Back in action at the bowling crease during
the 1998 one-day international series against
Zimbabwe.

In the wickets again against Zimbabwe at Eden Park in 2001.

The emotions say it all as I leap for joy after securing my first-ever one-day international century, against Pakistan at Jade Stadium in 2001.

Celebrating scoring 26 runs off an over against Younis Khan in Hamilton, 2001. At the time I didn't know it was a world record number of runs in an over in a test match.

The hardest cut of all

My cricketing existence was changed by a phone call to the McMillan household in mid-2006. On the other end of the line was Black Caps manager Lindsay Crocker — and he certainly wasn't the bearer of good news. Instead Crocks, as part of his role in the national set-up, had been charged with telling me that I had missed the cut for one of the New Zealand Cricket central contracts offered to the country's top 20 cricketers as deemed by the selection panel.

There is no such thing as good timing when you find out that you have been dumped from the contract list. And the timing of the call from Crocks couldn't have been worse. It was a busy time in our household when I lost my New Zealand Cricket contract. The news came just a week and a half before Cherie gave birth to our daughter Lucie. It's a big enough change in anyone's life to have a new baby to care for, let alone being told that you are effectively out of a job.

Cricket had been my job since I left high school early in my seventh form year. Yet all of a sudden it looked like it had been ripped away from me, leaving me with some serious decision-making to go through. That included the possibility of battling on and trying to get my Black Caps spot back or probably opting for the much-easier decision, quitting cricket and getting a day job. And with all that was going on in my life at the time, combined with the shock of the news I was handed, it's fair to say it took me a week or two to really digest what I'd been told.

What I really struggled with in the early days was the apparent magnitude of my drop in the eyes of the selection panel. Twelve months earlier when the 2005–06 contracts were handed out, I was awarded contract No. 11. In 12 months time I had been bumped down to No. 21 in the rankings list, one spot out of the magic Top 20. Needless to say, it was something which I struggled with. In my mind, to drop down 10 places on the contract list in such a short space of time was a huge jump backwards. And I had never known anyone else who has gone close to being shunted down like that in a similar time-frame.

Craig McMillan lashes out — 'I am totally gutted'
Sunday News, 4 June 2006

A bitterly disappointed Craig McMillan is set to dust off his CV.

His international career is now in limbo after he was axed from New Zealand's top 20 contracted players.

McMillan said he was 'gutted and bitterly disappointed'.

The veteran of 55 tests and 175 one-day internationals lashed out at the Black Caps selectors, saying he had a better record than some of the youngsters selected. And this week he will enter the job market.

'First and foremost this week, I am going to look at some job opportunities,' McMillan told Sunday News.

'I have got six months of no income coming up with two kids and a family to feed. I can't sit here and look that far ahead to the domestic season. I have to travel down a road that is going to be new to me.

'I have had 11 years of first-class cricket and nine years of international cricket. Now I am going to have to be proactive in getting my name out there and getting some job opportunities and offers. I have to pay the bills over the next six months.'

McMillan, Chris Harris, Craig Cumming, Daryl Tuffey, James Marshall and Paul Wiseman were the casualties of the list of contracted players released on Friday.

André Adams, Mathew Sinclair, Jamie How, Peter Fulton, Ross Taylor and Michael Mason were additions. Sinclair was still yet to accept his deal.

McMillan, 29, said it could be the death knell to his hopes of playing at the 2007 World Cup and he warned the selectors could rue their decision to axe so much experience from the 'Top 20'.

'One of the things I thought I had in my favour was being pretty experienced. One of the lines I have heard from a lot of people was experience, and not youth, wins a World Cup.'

Shortly before being cut from the contracted list I went through the annual review with the Black Caps' brains trust, headed by coach John Bracewell, Lindsay Crocker, medical advisor Warren Frost and mental skills expert Gilbert Enoka. The meeting was held at Gilbert's house. I sat down and we all talked through the season and they raised areas that needed improvement and other work-ons. Crocks ran all the meetings as manager. After Braces had had his say, they would then seek your views on how you went and give their thoughts, and also what you thought moving forward to the next season.

John Bracewell: We do a case management review at the end of each contractual year. We sit down with a number of the coaches and management; the meetings were often facilitated by Gilbert. And we had a number of pretty deep discussions with Craig in Gilbert's front lounge about what he needed to do with his physical condition as well as his cricket.

I know in Craig's particular case, Gilbert was pretty heavily involved in those programmes. We attached a physical trainer personally to Craig as he was getting heavier and heavier and the demands of touring were becoming more and more. We were going into a cycle of continual travel, play, travel, play. And unless Craig actually addressed some of the physical issues, he was going to struggle. And I know a lot of those discussions were about the 2007 World Cup and the importance of his role that he could play in the World Cup.

We needed to get more consistency. My feeling was that if we got him fitter, mentally he would be stronger to deal with the demands of touring and the lifestyle of it. The mental fitness comes from the fact that physically you are getting tired and worn down. And with his particular health issues, Warren Frost was constantly on it.

I'd be lying if I said I had been in great form in the months leading up to contract time. I had been dropped after the Chappell-Hadlee Trophy one-day series and I hadn't played a lot of test cricket. But I felt that I had had an OK season for the Black Caps, especially in the one-day arena, leading up to that series against Australia. Unfortunately, the 2005–06 domestic season became a complete write-off for me once I was dropped from the Black Caps. I was doing everything I could to get back into the Black Caps so that I lost focus on playing for Canterbury and doing it well.

That said, I still believed I was among New Zealand's top 20 cricketers. I left the meeting at Gilbert's feeling that I was getting a bit borderline though, thinking that I was probably going to sneak in at No. 19 or 20 on the contract list. Nothing could prepare me for what was to come. Looking back, it's hard to miss the irony that I became a victim of the contract system that I had been such a supporter of getting introduced back in 2002. When it comes to ranking points, those handed out for test ratings are weighted more heavily than those for one-day cricket.

My biggest problem was that I was seen as a one-day international player. You would think that would be a good way to be viewed in the season leading up to the 2007 Cricket World Cup in the West Indies — a season which would see the Black Caps play just two tests. I had played 13 one-day internationals during the 2005–06 season and thought I would still gather a reasonable amount of ranking points despite not getting a look-in in the test arena. But under the contract system, it counted for very little.

I found it a fundamentally flawed system — here we were under 12 months out from the World Cup, yet guys who were viewed as one-day international specialists were being disadvantaged when it came to the ratings. There were other guys who earnt contracts for the 2006–07 season who featured solely in two tests for the Black Caps. In World Cup year, that was wrong. And for someone who was feeling the pain at missing the cut in those circumstances, it was terribly frustrating.

> **John Bracewell:** Craig got very few test points, which left him outside the numbers. It often depends on the cricket you have played, not necessarily the cricket you are going to play. In my opinion, it is not one of the world's perfect systems. For instance, if we were going into the World Cup season as we did last year, when we only played two test matches, we were giving a 1.5 grading for test matches on your contracts, yet you are going to be playing 30-odd one-dayers. It didn't quite make sense. But it is set up by the CPA and we just submit our numbers to a formula. Craig didn't make the numbers which is an anomaly with the amount of one-day cricket we played.
>
> It is an anomaly if you are in the one-day side and not in the test side. That can cost you — as it did with Craig, it cost him a contract. He was always touring in the one-day side. He was always in the top 14 which means that is at least 14 points from each selector. But it wasn't enough points for him to get a contract because he wasn't scoring enough test points. I will get that surprise every year. The balance is so tight that it only takes one selector to pick two or three guys from outside the square and rate them for someone to drop off the other end.

The start of the Bracewell era was probably the start of the period when my position in the Black Caps certainly became less stable. There is no doubting that John and I have had our moments during my time in the Black Caps under his coaching. And the way he handled, or should I say mishandled, my exclusion from the 20-strong contract list really did leave a sour taste in my mouth. Aside from the obvious of actually missing the cut, the thing that disappointed me the most was that he didn't ring me to tell me why. It was Lindsay Crocker who had the job of calling me.

Instead John took the easy option and pushed it onto Crocks, the manager, and I didn't think he should have been asked to do that. To my mind, if the coach thinks you are not good enough to be in the team, he should be ringing to say, 'This is what you should work on. This is what you should do.' That just appears to be common sense to me. Let someone know why they missed out, give them some tangible reasons and let them know what they need to do to get back. That was all I wanted to hear. But I initially never got any of that. And as the season was played out, it proved to be not the only case of questionable communication from Bracewell.

Leanne McGoldrick: When he didn't get his contract I think he was stunned. I know I was, and I think a lot of other people were. It is a harsh reality and it took time for that to hit him. I don't think the communication was great and, to be fair, I think the whole thing could have been handled better.

Heath Mills: We questioned his omission from the 20 and I got back quite a detailed response. I put that in front of Macca and he was obviously deeply hurt at missing a contract, as it had severe implications for him. While he certainly disagreed with the selectors' logic, as you would expect, he held his dignity at all times during that period. No system is perfect in any contracting environment, but we do have one and it is a pretty good one by world standards. Unfortunately, some guys miss out, that is part and parcel of professional sport and that is the profession they choose to be a part of.

And it was tough on Macca. The worst time for us is when contracts are announced and guys miss out. You feel every bit of pain with them and you want to do everything you can to help them. You know it is going to have a financial impact on them and affect the people around them. It is the toughest time in cricket without a doubt for us. I am not over-dramatising it, but I have had very emotional guys on the phone. I have had other people close to them upset on the phone; trying to work it through with them is hard.

A lot of different theories were floated around, one which stated my exclusion was meant to act as a wake-up call, to try to get me to focus on what I needed to do to be at the top of my game again. It makes me laugh when it has been said that the players need to be kept on edge. Everyone in the side is always on edge — the reality is that if you don't perform you are going to be dropped. It doesn't matter whether you are a senior player or a new boy. I was always on edge because I knew if I had one bad series then I might be dropped.

I didn't need someone telling me that. It was a tactic which Bracewell has employed with other senior players — most notably Chris Cairns and my brother-in-law Nathan Astle. I don't understand that whole thing of putting the senior players on notice. If he wanted to get rid of all the senior players from our group, which he pretty much has done now, he has got that. And the different theories being debated provided no comfort for me. The reality that I had to live with was that in one short phone call my life was practically turned upside down.

Gilbert Enoka: One of the hardest things in the role is when you know the guillotine has already swung. You are having to interact on a day-to-day basis, understanding that decisions have been made that impact on him in a way that he is not yet aware of. To look at it from his viewpoint, he burst onto the scene ever since he was the young cricketer that Bill Duncan saw down at East Shirley. He was smacking the ball all over East Shirley; he was always the cream of the crop, the top of the group and ear-marked as being a supremely talented person. He went through all the age-grades, through the academy and into the Black Caps. But all of a sudden the summer was going to end — and that would be frightening.

It forces you to have a look and ask yourself, 'Well, what else have I got? What else can I do?' My role in the whole place was to assist him to see the reality and to manage the transition into what life was going to be beyond the contract. It was bloody hard, especially when some of the reasons given may not have been what he agreed with. That became a challenge. It is a part of a job that I know was hard for Braces. But he wanted to be honest and tell him straight, and he believed he did. My role was to support Macca. When you are given some feedback and all of a sudden the road you are on has ended, you lose a high degree of certainty and it becomes a very scary place.

Losing my New Zealand Cricket contract was a double blow for me financially. Shortly before the contract list was revealed I had been offered a contract to play County cricket for Glamorgan. It was a great offer and would have been fantastic to have played two and a half months of County cricket, something which I believed would benefit me when called on for national service again. But the trouble was that the County stint overlapped the dual New Zealand A tours of Australia, one of the sides of which I had been named as captain.

Glamorgan presented me a lucrative offer. But deep down I felt that had I chosen to go and play in the County scene, in the process overlooking the New Zealand A tour, I would face the very real risk of sliding down the New Zealand Cricket pecking order and possibly missing out on a contract. Instead, I thought it was better to show my commitment to New Zealand Cricket, turn down the County offer and go on the A tour. A week after making that decision I found out I wasn't among the Black Caps' selectors top 20.

Despite the fact my cricketing existence had pretty much been turned upside down, I had very little time to feel sorry for myself. The A tour beckoned, by which stage it was the last thing I wanted to go on after losing my contract. For the first three or four weeks after receiving Crocks' news I really did nothing fitness wise — I wasn't in a mental state to do anything. I had been told I wasn't among the country's top 20 cricketers, with the reality of the contract snub meaning I was now a massive outsider in my hopes of making it to a third Cricket World Cup. I was hurting and, to be honest, playing cricket was the least of my priorities. And that probably showed when I fronted up for fitness tests before both New

Zealand A sides went on tour. Probably my numbers weren't as good as they should have been. And it was something which Bracewell didn't miss out on reminding me, and the public, a month down the track.

All the while I was trying to get my head around what was next for Craig McMillan. Was it time to pull the pin on my international ambitions, including my dream of making it to the 2007 Cricket World Cup? Or was I going to fight to get my spot back? The latter certainly seemed like a world away from the predicament I found myself in.

Leanne McGoldrick: In my early discussions with him, I thought that he wouldn't come back. After he didn't get a contract, that was very much the direction that our conversations were heading. It was like it was over, that he couldn't or wouldn't come back. But I think as reality of life without cricket hit home, his resolve began to harden. He became more and more determined to come back. He went full circle in a relatively short space of time. You could never have foreseen where he was going to be.

Gilbert Enoka: He looked around and asked, 'How am I going to feed the family? What is life after this?' He was now looking at getting a CV together which he had never done before. But I think it was good for him, everything had previously fallen on Craig's plate. Things had just presented themselves to him because of his talent.

I probably thought he would get a day job; I wasn't sure if he would get back. My job wasn't to predetermine anything, but to assist him in the process of coming to some sort of decision. I like not to give people advice, but to expose them to the options. He was told he needed to perform on the domestic scene, get runs under his belt. When he peered into the other world I think he realised how important it was to get back into his cricket. I think he probably went back and realised he had to make something of it.

The reality of my situation, namely the fact there were bills to be paid and I had a family to feed, meant I had to investigate what options were out there in the workforce. With that in mind, the first job I applied for was to be adidas' South Island sales manager. It was a pretty major role, with the applicant servicing 90-odd portfolios, and to be fair it was a long-shot option given my lack of work experience away from the cricket pitch. It would have been a massive first-up fulltime job to have.

But I still got through to the last seven or eight contenders, gaining a face-to-face interview with adidas New Zealand's sales manager and their human resources manager. It was a great experience but it was bloody daunting, certainly going into the unknown. Going for a job interview was something I had never had to do before. There were a lot of things I fell back on in terms of things I had learnt in cricket, things such as it being a big company and the need for teamwork.

One of the things I didn't have in my favour was that I had no sales experience on my CV. At one stage they brought out a shoe from a bag and I was told, 'We are going to go out of the room. You have two minutes and then we are coming back and you can tell us why this shoe is so good.' I had no idea. It was just a shoe and the specifics of it are what you get taught once you come on board. They went out of the room and the two minutes seemed to last like 15 seconds. They came back and I was charged with trying to sell one of them the shoe as if they were a store manager. I went with what I knew and rattled off about how it was the favourite shoe of one of the All Blacks, I said Tana Umaga used it as his core running shoe because it gave him stability and all this sort of stuff.

I did manage to get through it and they had a good-natured chuckle — I think they thought it was quite funny. The whole thing about it was that it put me right out of my comfort zone. I don't enjoy those sorts of situations where I am thrust in front of people I don't know. So it was good that it extended me and made me think about things that I certainly will need to think about in a couple of years' time.

I also signed up with an employment agency and they were looking for prospective jobs for me — at the time getting a day job was deadly serious. I even got a proper CV done for the first time in my life. If I had been offered the job, I would have taken it. And that would have meant that I wouldn't be playing cricket — it would certainly have been the end of my cricket career.

The road to redemption

With my international career seemingly in tatters, we boarded a plane to England and a stint playing in the Lancashire Leagues. In many ways, it was a case of perfect timing and allowed me to get away from what had become a pretty dark place for me. It was a chance to go away with Cherie and our kids Mitchell and Lucie, enjoy some great family time with them and also do some pretty serious, and very necessary, thinking about my future. The priority was to reflect on just what I wanted to do — and at that stage it really could have gone either way.

With that in mind, we pretty much hibernated north of Manchester, with me thinking about the road ahead. And the setting couldn't have been better: I was out of the spotlight and had the opportunity to talk to a range of different people about my next plan of attack. Throughout it all, Cherie was just outstanding. This just wasn't a decision that was going to impact on me as a cricketer; it was a decision which would have a major impact on the McMillan family.

As the weeks went by, I realised that deep down I felt I still had a lot more to offer and more to do in the international arena. I would have been gutted looking back on my career if it had all ended by me not getting a contract. I would have felt that my talents were unfulfilled and there certainly would have been some regrets. And Cherie played a big part in me coming to that stage of my thinking — she knew that I still wanted to play for New Zealand and had more to give. She was very supportive in saying, 'Well, this is obviously what you have to do and want to do. You have to try and go out on your terms.' Once I got that support from Cherie, it was a pretty easy decision to make that I hadn't finished and wanted to make my way back into the Black Caps.

Cherie certainly wasn't the only person who helped drive me on. It's amazing when times get tough how you find out who your real mates are.

That includes former Black Caps coach Steve Rixon, a guy I rate as a good mate, a real friend. He has always had a lot of belief in my ability, even at times when maybe others didn't share that faith. And during the aftermath of my non-contracting a note he gave me during the 2002–03 season, when I was going through a lean patch, certainly lifted my spirits. It was a short note, telling me I was a good cricketer, things don't change, back yourself and believe in your ability. That note meant a lot to me and I always kept it in my cricket bag.

> **Steve Rixon:** I just wanted him to understand that no matter what happens that he should never forget what made him successful. The note was meant as a reinforcement of how good a player he can be and if he let the peripheral issues take over, he would be taking his eyes off the ball. I wrote, 'Mate, you must remember what we went through, how you got there, how good you were when you were there and how good it felt. At the moment I can only feel that you're feeling that everyone is on your back and things aren't going to plan. You are better than that Macca. You get your head around it and you will get a second chance.'
>
> I would ring Macca if I ever saw anything wrong, just as I would do for many of the boys. That is part of a special relationship I have with some of the guys, obviously including Macca. He's like a relative. He obviously got quite distressed with his omission and his place in the side. I think they took away the one thing that I first saw in Macca, that flair. In trying to change that, you change the character of a bloke who has been playing that way for quite a while and been very successful. I just think they lost a major asset when they tried to change Macca's style.

It was great to be getting the support I needed, allowing me to make a clear decision. I was enjoying my cricket in England and starting to look forward to doing myself justice in the domestic scene with Canterbury when I returned to New Zealand. But the positive head-space I was in was sorely tested when, first, I found out I had missed the cut for an initial 30-man Black Caps squad to prepare for the upcoming 2006 ICC Champions Trophy, then came across a news report from back home featuring quotes from Bracewell explaining my omission. If it wasn't bad enough to miss out on a contract, now I wasn't even rated in the top 30.

Craig McMillan dropped from New Zealand squad
AFP, 16 August 2006

Craig McMillan has been left out of the 30-man squad for the Champions Trophy to be played in India from October.

John Bracewell, the New Zealand coach, said that the 29-year-old McMillan, who has played 55 tests and 175 one day internationals, was dropped because of a lack of fitness.

*'Craig McMillan was omitted from the 30 because of concerns about his fitness,'
Bracewell said. 'This does not mean Craig has been ruled out of contention for next
year's World Cup but he will need to focus his efforts if he is to be selected for the
Black Caps over the summer.'*

*McMillan's international form has been poor in recent seasons but he scored
a century for New Zealand A against India A in Darwin last month. The squad
includes seven players yet to represent New Zealand in seamer Mark Gillespie,
Otago off-spinner Nathan McCullum — brother of test wicketkeeper Brendon,
wicketkeeper Peter McGlashan, seamer Warren McSkimming, all-rounder Mark
Orchard, batsman Jesse Ryder and seamer Bradley Scott.*

The squad will be reduced to 14 next month ahead of the tournament.

I was pissed off when I read that report. He was pretty much saying that
I had turned up for the New Zealand A tour unfit, and now I was going
to pay the price by missing out on being considered for selection for the
Champions Trophy. With everything that had gone on leading up to that
tour, the fact that my cricketing career had been turned upside down, I
felt it was totally unfair. Sure, it was a trip I didn't want to go on — I was
between a rock and a hard place. I didn't turn up so much out of shape in
body, probably more out of shape in mind.

And it wasn't as if I had had a terrible tour either, scoring a century
in our first-class clash against India A in Darwin. I batted for about five
hours, in pretty fierce heat. So if I was that badly out of condition I don't
think I would have had the concentration or ability to bat for that period
in the heat against a quality attack. There have been a lot of rubbish stories
written over the years, and this one was right up there.

While I realised Bracewell's comments were a sign of just how big a
battle I faced to try to regain my spot, I still felt I returned to New Zealand
from the stint in England in a great frame of mind. The hunger to get back
on the international stage was there, but so too was a different mindset
— I knew I had to concentrate on the things that I could control. And
that meant first and foremost performing consistently for Canterbury. I
had made the mistake previously of taking my eye off the ball — and look
where it had left me. I now had an attitude which meant I didn't worry
about the little things. And even if I did get knocked over for a duck, I
knew that Cherie and the kids would be there for me when I came home.
The kids would still need a nappy change, a hug or a kiss no matter if I got
a duck or scored a century. I had balance and I realised that cricket wasn't
the end of the world.

Cherie McMillan: To go back to play for Canterbury, where they were focused on
his 'so-called' fitness problem, Craig did talk about the intensive trainings and the

schedules. It seemed so much more intense than I had ever known at that level, but I am sure it played a big part in him getting back into the Black Caps. And at the end of the day he had to have the motivation to do it. I think Canterbury coach Dave Nosworthy really gave him the encouragement and belief that he could get through it and return to the Black Caps. He just had to put the work in and he did it with the conviction and determination that made him a Black Cap in the beginning. For me to see him put that sort of work in I knew he had a passion and desire to get back into the team. The anger of the loss of a contract had been pushed to the back and the drive to be a Black Cap again was there.

Throughout it all, I always believed in him, and that he would get back into the Black Caps. It just wasn't right or fair that his long-standing career would end like that and he wasn't about to let it. Craig never really understood why he didn't get a contract. And to be honest, I don't think any of us did! We had obviously talked about a possible retirement, but we were both determined for him to get into the World Cup squad. He was also determined to go to the Twenty20 World Cup and after that is perhaps where we saw the retirement happening. It was really tough when he started getting dropped, picked again and then dropped again — your emotions are all over the place. I think about the guys who are on the fringe of team selection now, and their life is just so inconsistent and until you go through it you don't realise what it takes for those people to stick at it. No one likes to live a life of such uncertainty and it is very unsettling.

With the pressure off to a certain extent, I started really well in my return to the local domestic scene. I was scoring hundreds again, but if I was being honest there was still a nagging doubt whether I would wear the silver fern again under the coaching of Bracewell. I must have been about fifth in the queue to get a spot in the middle order. He was batting guys like Hamish Marshall at No. 7, finding spots for other guys who hadn't played in those positions before. And while my concentration was on Canterbury, part of me did think that I mightn't be able to force my way back in, regardless of how many runs I scored domestically.

John did surprise me, however, when he came down to see me play for Canterbury against Northern Districts in Rangiora early in the 2006–07 season. His arrival followed a call to him from Dave Nosworthy. John simply told me, 'You have made a good start to the season, but I want to see you back that up by scoring hundreds.'

John Bracewell: Did I think he would have quit? No, not at all. I went down and watched him in Rangiora. Generally, he likes to show a persona of anger at times, but not necessarily as angry as the shell portrays. I approached him and asked how he thought he was going. He had gone through the job interview thing and I just started to get the feeling that it was the best thing in the world that had ever happened.

Unlike a lot of people in international sport, he had to taste a bit of reality and his value to us was probably enhanced because he had touched reality. The real world is quite tough and cricket has actually been a privilege, rather than something that you own. The real world is that I have to go and find a job. None of these guys have worked. And with the advent of the IPL and the ICL, they may never have to. I think the fact that Craig had to go to a job interview was the catalyst for his form — it was like, 'I have been given a chance to do this as a job. And I am going to make the most of it this time?'

I did just what John said in my next game, but still missed out on selection for the initial Black Caps Twenty20 and one-day international squads to take on Sri Lanka in their November–January New Zealand tour. After the runs I had scored, and Bracewell's comments, I felt that I had a good shot at least of being picked in the Twenty20 side; I couldn't see how I wasn't one of the best sloggers in the country. To find out I hadn't made the cut was certainly gutting. But there was no point moaning about it, at least Bracewell had come to talk to me face to face and I knew I just had to keep scoring runs, making it impossible to be overlooked.

Surprisingly, my communication with Bracewell just continued to increase. After we met in Rangiora, I fielded about four phone calls from him over the next two weeks — it was the most communication I had ever had with him. It was weird, I still wasn't in the team but he was ringing up to see how I was going, checking on my form and telling me to keep working with Warren Frost on my fitness. That strangest thing was that this all came after a period of no communication at all.

Then came the call I had been waiting for since last playing for the Black Caps in a one-day international against Australia on 10 December 2005. In a belated Christmas present, I finally earnt my recall for the second one-day international against the touring Sri Lankans for the New Year's Eve clash at Queenstown. It followed an injury to Nathan Astle, struggling after being hit three times on the thigh by Chaminda Vaas in the series opener in Napier. I don't know what I felt — ecstatic about being recalled or just relief.

Heath Mills: When Craig missed out on the contract, in the past he may well have walked away from cricket. But under our system we have contracts in place for domestic cricket and they certainly pay the bills for a six-month period. This contracting environment kept him in the game. He was able to go away to England for a couple of months, clear his head and work on his game. He came back and he was very determined to get out there and play, and play well.

He got into a great head space, he played well and scored runs and he got called back into the Black Caps side. In the months ahead we were about to see how good Craig McMillan really was and it was really rewarding to see. You feel good about a guy who has gone away after taking a big knock, who stays in the game and comes back to fight another day.

I was certainly happy to be back, feelings which were ultimately dampened by my showing in Queenstown, scoring just two before being undone by Murali in our one-run victory. I wasn't required for the third match of the series in Christchurch, but again featured in Auckland in the fourth ODI. In one of the worst performances I have seen, we were dismissed for just 73 chasing 263 to win, the second-lowest total ever by a New Zealand team in a one-day international. If there was any bright spot for me it was that I top-scored with an unbeaten 29. Brendon McCullum, with 17, was our only other batsman to record double figures.

It was great to be back in the team. Even better was when my name was read out in the squad to head to Australia for the Commonwealth Bank Series, a sign to me that I was now becoming a contender for the upcoming Cricket World Cup in the West Indies. But I wasn't stupid enough to be taking things for granted; I knew I was still walking a fine line. I had been given another opportunity — I now had to take it while it existed. It was something I was unable to do in our first-up losses to Australia and England in Hobart, scoring two and 22 respectively. And as we prepared to head to Sydney for match three against Australia, I started feeling the pressures again after the two failures I'd experienced in Hobart — I knew I was no longer a certain selection.

We arrived at the Sydney Cricket Ground on 21 January 2007, on a 40-degree day, batting first on a pitch that looked like it would be quick. Brett Lee was right up there in terms of his speed, knocking the top off our order and I found myself walking out to bat reasonably early with our score at just 4–53 in the 18th over. Aside from a bit of anxiety about where my career was heading, I went out feeling that I had to go and play my natural game. I was there for a good time, not a long time.

Early on I edged a short, wide delivery off Glenn McGrath and it went through to Adam Gilchrist. Everyone went up, but Asad Rauf for some reason didn't raise his finger. When I looked up I couldn't help but have a smirk on my face. McGrath was right in front of my face and I waited for the usual expletives to come from him. He simply asked, 'Macca, you hit that didn't you?' I told him I had done and he replied, 'Fair enough, I wouldn't walk either.' I definitely did play my natural game after that and went on to score 89. I was finally given out caught, but it was a waist-high full toss that the umpire didn't call. But after what happened at the start of my innings I didn't really have a lot to complain about.

I honestly think if I had failed there, I would have got the chop. Getting away with that decision off McGrath could have decided whether I fulfilled my dream of making it to the upcoming World Cup or not. That innings was a key moment for me. And there was no better place to do it than at the SCG against Australia. The thing I really liked about that innings is that it was my natural game. I charged Clarke and hit him back over his head for six and also hit Lee for a six. It was a real confidence booster. But it still wasn't enough for us as a team, as we crashed to a two-wicket loss.

Daniel Vettori: His innings in Sydney was probably one of the best innings I have seen him play. It made us stand up and say, 'If Craig can bat like this, he will be a big part of our success.' He moved into that role of No. 6 and No. 7, closing off innings or coming in when we were in trouble. It seemed to be a role he could thrive in. To his credit he made a comeback. In the final months of his career I think we saw the best of Craig McMillan. No one can maintain a 10-year spell of form. Unfortunately, he had a dip in form and lost his place. But near the end of it he was back to his best.

We had played together for such a period of time and he had been crucial to a lot of our success over a number of years. So to see a guy who you had played so much with not around anymore made it tough. In the first six months to a year of it, it hit him pretty hard. I don't think he understood the rationale and maybe even the fact that he perceived some guys were getting more a chance than him. Whether that is right or not, I am not sure.

He was pretty frustrated and was hurting, so he questioned whether he would get back. I think he really wanted to, but maybe in his mind he thought it would be too hard; he had burnt some bridges and he wouldn't be able to make it back. But the whole way through, the selectors have always picked people who have performed. Craig did perform in the domestic level and got his spot back. I always thought he was hurting there, but once he got on with it he decided to give it one last shot and go from there.

Two days later we finally got a win on the board, beating England by 90 runs at the Adelaide Oval. After the game there was a great feeling in the camp, but little did we know that it would be the last match Nathan Astle would play for New Zealand, with him announcing his retirement shortly after we arrived for a two-day stretch of matches in Perth. He had been struggling and I don't think he ever really recovered from being dropped from the team in 2005. While Nathan managed to fight his way back into the team, I don't think it was ever the same for him. He struggled to get over the mixed communication between the selectors and Bracewell — finally he got to the point where he felt it was time to move on.

While I wasn't overly surprised at Nathan retiring, what did surprise me was the timing of it. I seriously thought he might have tried to go through to the World Cup. But desire is a big part of international cricket. And once you lose that spark, it can be the difference between being successful or not. Once it is gone, it is gone — you don't just get it back. It was a brave decision for him to make. And there is no doubt that down the track at the World Cup we did miss his experience. He had been to three tournaments before — I had already been to two. We both had a pretty average time in 1999 and he did pretty well in 2003. I thought that 2007 could have been the World Cup where he really was going to be successful.

We were only to win one of our remaining four matches in the Commonwealth Bank Series, returning to New Zealand in time to watch England beat Australia 2–0 in the finals series. And as the tournament dragged on we started to get particularly sloppy in the field, dropping a succession of chances which we would normally expect to take. It was frustrating because fielding was one area we had long prided ourselves on and it was a facet of our game which had won us many games in the past.

But exciting times were just around the corner, both for the Black Caps and me.

Three great days

Any win over Australia should be celebrated — so winning three straight one-day internationals against the most dominant side in world cricket certainly is something to savour.

We didn't have long to prepare for the 2007 Chappell-Hadlee Trophy series after returning from our less-than-successful campaign in the Commonwealth Bank Series across the Tasman.

Within two weeks of returning from Australia I had been confirmed in the 13-man squad for the Chappell-Hadlee Trophy matches against Australia in Wellington, Auckland and Hamilton and the 15-man team who would head to the West Indies for the Cricket World Cup beginning in March.

All the hard work I had done, the pain and the dedication, had been worth it. But, that said, I was in for a bit of a rude shock when we were briefed before we played Australia in the first of the Chappell-Hadlee Trophy series at Wellington's Westpac Stadium on 16 February.

I remember being told I was originally supposed to be be batting at No. 7 for the duration of that series — that is where I batted in Australia, with Brendon McCullum batting at No. 6. It really disappointed me. I felt that No. 6 was my better slot; I didn't quite understand the mechanics and the reasons for it. It wasn't explained to me — that was just the way it was going to be.

But at least I was in the team and we headed to Wellington intent on continuing to build towards the upcoming World Cup. Australia were without the likes of Ricky Ponting, Adam Gilchrist and Andrew Symonds. Brett Lee was then ruled out of the series on the eve of the first match after injuring his ankle during a training session at the Basin Reserve.

A pace bowler still dominated at Westpac Stadium, with Bondy bowling really well for us — his stunning caught and bowled to dismiss

Cameron White is what a lot of people remember that game for. And quite rightly so.

I came on and dismissed Michael Hussey. I was surprised to be bowling at all, but Flem obviously had a 'feel' and went with it. Australia never got going in their innings, mainly because all of our bowlers were doing pretty well on an OK pitch. Australia always try to set their dominance on you from an early stage. But they weren't able to do that in Wellington, through good bowling and fielding.

They set us a total of 149 to win, which was about 60 runs light. But whenever you play Australia it doesn't matter what they have scored, you never feel like the game is won. There is always a nervousness around the changing room because you are playing Australia and you know how good they are. And that was how we felt between innings at Westpac Stadium.

Our run chase was all a bit surreal, watching the way that Flem and Lou Vincent batted. Both of them played so well and we were sitting there shocked, watching them knock the runs off without a loss. It is something that no New Zealand side had done before against the world champions. We certainly hadn't expected to win in that fashion. However, the celebrations were tempered afterwards, guys were ecstatic but it was all low-key.

We then moved onto Auckland with just a one-day turnaround between matches. And we certainly saw the 'real' Australia with Hussey, Hodge and Hayden bullying our attack around Eden Park. They asserted the dominance they hadn't been able to show in Wellington, with Hayden in particular walking down the pitch to Tuffey and hammering him. Bondy also came in for some carnage after his initial spell where he swung the ball and got rid of Phil Jaques.

Hussey played beautifully. Eden Park really is a left-hander's ground and the short boundary means that you can easily get a six just from a mishit. Whenever I played there I wished I was a left-hander because of the angles of the ground. If you are a left-hander, you can score very quickly just by using them.

We managed to hang in there with some good fielding, including a great catch from Ross Taylor to dismiss Hussey for 105 off my bowling. The heads never dropped, even though we were hit around for 336. We were pretty quiet at lunchtime, but at no time was there a feeling that we were out of the match. The reality is that you will probably only win one match in 10 when you are chasing a total of 300 plus. And Australia had Glenn McGrath and Shaun Tait.

Ross Taylor played brilliantly. Batting at No. 3 Rosco played as he can, and will for a number of years, to get us into a position where we could challenge Australia. The other good thing was that we kept wickets in hand — we had a bit of strength down the order.

Again I was down to come in and bat at No. 7, but was promoted one place up the order when Ross was dismissed when we were 4–228 in the 39th over. Both Brendon and I were padded up but I was promoted up the order. We needed 9.5 runs an over when I went into bat, with 11 overs remaining.

Not only was I pleased with the promotion up the batting order, I also liked the instructions handed my way. I was given a licence to attack from the first ball and I certainly didn't need a second offering when that was said — that is how I like to play.

It really was a situation where it was hit or miss. If I had missed out I am sure I would have copped criticism for playing loosely — whatever shot I played wouldn't have been right in some sections. But as I went out to bat in front of an incredible crowd, I felt if I could get a couple in the middle of the bat then anything could happen.

Early on I nicked one for four from an inside edge and thought, 'Maybe this might be my day.' And in that sense, the omens were right from the start that maybe I was going to be onto something at Eden Park. Although I had already been named in the World Cup team, the pressure was still on to perform. I hadn't batted in Wellington and felt that my place in the starting 11 was still under threat.

Spinner Brad Hogg was one bowler who we had to milk some runs from. And early on I decided that I could get runs by employing the sweep. I did just that when I was on five, but the ball had a lot of spin on it and headed on the full out to Jaques who was on the boundary. I thought, 'Oh great, I have blown another one. This is not meant to be.'

Jaques ended up dropping it, in fact he was lucky to get a hand on it. And that was the turning point for the final six months of my international career. After that one dropped catch, I hit everything in the middle of the bat and blazed it. Then Tait came on and I hit him for a few boundaries. The same with Bracken: I was moving around the crease and managed to pick up a few off him.

I was then caught off a no-ball which I hit straight to McGrath at mid-off but was given not out. I did the same thing with the next ball, hitting it to Hussey. But I had done my job, to go and bring the run rate to something that was sustainable. When I left, having scored 52, it was at about six runs an over.

It was a nice feeling walking off Eden Park and soaking up one of the loudest crowds I have ever played in front of in New Zealand. They were just loving it. They had obviously enjoyed the way that we had won in Wellington but this was a bit more special — our backs were against the wall, we weren't the favourites and we were chasing 337 which you aren't supposed to be able to do against the might of Australia.

Even being out in the middle, I remember a couple of times when I hit one in the middle of the bat and the whole adrenalin rush got to me. I punched the air as if to say to my team-mates: 'Come on!' I don't know where it came from but I got caught up in the whole thing of 'Yes, we can win this'. The adrenalin, intensity, noise and support from the crowd fuelled that.

I walked off thinking that I was pretty happy with my part. I just hoped that the guys would continue on and finish the game off. And that's just what they did. Peter Fulton batted beautifully to carry us home, ending unbeaten on 76. He was a great help to me; he gave me the luxury to be able to come straight out and play my shots. He knew that was going to be my role.

The win gave us the series. And, needless to say, the boys were really stoked in the changing room that night, it was just so special.

Next up was Hamilton and the talk had gone from winning the series, which we had done, to claiming a clean sweep. We hadn't done that well in games in the past that hadn't really mattered. Generally, we are a side that does well when our backs are against the wall. With the series won, we rested key players — the likes of Vettori, Oram and Bond. I wasn't sure how we were going to go in that game and things only got worse when they won the toss and batted.

Matty Hayden played one of the great innings, blazing us for an unbeaten 181. I dropped him midway through his innings. He hit it back so hard at me that it hit my hand and bounced straight down. He then deposited my next couple of balls for six. Near the end I dropped him again; it was a routine catch off Mark Gillespie. I just wanted somewhere to hide. It wasn't a nice feeling to know you'd dropped him twice. Gillespie broke his toe with a sharp yorker but that didn't stop him. While he wasn't able to run anymore, he just kept hitting the ball further and further. Seddon Park doesn't have the longest boundaries, but Hayden's innings was unbelievable.

Back in the changing rooms it quickly dawned on us that instead of chasing 337 to win, we now had to get 347 to earn the clean sweep in Hamilton. But because of what had happened at Eden Park, there wasn't any sense of deflation. We were disappointed that Australia had scored so many, but everyone realised that if we played as well as we had in the last game we could win. We needed someone in the top five to score a hundred and then get some others to chip in with cameos near the end.

But it didn't quite work out that way. We were 41–4 after just 9.1 overs.

One of the things I like about playing cricket is that at halftime you get your lunch, sit down and batting at No. 5 or 6 you get to watch in your jandals and shorts hoping that other guys can bat for an hour or so. But in Hamilton we kept losing key wickets. I hadn't even made it up to the viewing area; I was in the room sorting my gear out, when the wickets started falling.

By the time I had got upstairs we had lost two wickets. So I ended up going back down the stairs and getting my kit on. By the time I was fully kitted up I was in — I was walking out to bat without sitting down and watching any of the cricket.

But when I got out I was seeing the ball so vividly and so clearly — I remember hitting Mitchell Johnson over cover and the ball almost went for six. I thought, 'Crikey, that has gone a long way. I didn't mean to do that.' Fults was also going at that stage; we were both chipping in. He was in that mood where he couldn't really pull back, eventually holing out for 51.

Brendon came in next and we were still a long, long way out. The first thing I said to him was that I felt I was in some sort of zone and that I needed to keep playing positive and hitting the ball hard. Brendon decided he would feed me the strike and work around me — that was unusual for Brendon because he is such a clean hitter of the ball himself.

For a lot of our partnership we were going at more runs an over than the required run rate. It is probably the only time in my career that I remember being in that zone in terms of hitting — it didn't matter if it was Tait bowling at 150 kph or Johnson or Hogg, everyone got hit.

Then Australia brought Adam Voges on. I said to Brendon, 'He has got to go.' He was bowling to the shorter boundary and he was a spinner — my lack of respect for spinners kicked in, especially someone like Voges, which meant I was always going to go after him. Brendon and I got a single each of the first two balls. Then I thought, 'Right, let's go.'

We took 10 runs off his first over. Brendon told me at the end of the over, 'Well, you have killed him. He won't get another over.' I couldn't believe it when Hussey threw him the ball for a second over and I realised this was an opportunity to take another 14 or 16 runs.

John R. Reid: I went to Hamilton with one of my golf mates from Taupo. I got us some tickets and shouted him some lunch. We were chasing 347 and we lost those quick early wickets, so I thought we should just get in the car and get back to Taupo. I had the radio on in the car and then Craig came to the wicket. By the time Craig got in I thought the match was lost. And then we heard this commentary and I thought, 'What the hell are we doing in the car?' So we pulled into the nearest pub in Putaruru and they had the cricket on. We got there when Craig was on about 30 and ended up watching one hell of an innings. And I kicked myself for leaving early. I think that certainly is his signature innings, although sadly I didn't see it from the very start.

We took nine runs off Voges' second over, thinking that surely that would be the end of the spinner's time at the bowling crease. But, for whatever reason, Hussey persisted with him and gave him a third over — it really was time to cash in. And that's just what we did, plundering 14 runs off what was his third and final over in the match.

Cricinfo, Live Scoring, 20 February 2007

30.1 Voges to McMillan, no run, fired in on middle and leg, he drives back to Voges.

30.2 Voges to McMillan, SIX, I'm counting each one for you, and that's 23 sixes today! What a hit on this small ground! McMillan sashays down the track and clubs that over long-on for a big six!

30.3 Voges to McMillan, SIX, HOLY CRAP, that's out of the stadium! Superb hitting, it's like a baseball home run derby! McMillan dances down and lifts Voges miles over the sight screen . . . 24 sixes in the game and McMillan celebrates his 100 with a feisty pump of the fist . . . immense innings!

30.4 Voges to McMillan, 1 run, tossed up, McMillan comes on the front foot and drives it to cover.

30.5 Voges to McCullum, 1 run, looped down the leg side, McCullum goes to the back foot and glances it to short fine leg.

30.6 Voges to McMillan, no run, full outside off-stump, he leans forward and drives to White at cover.

End of over 31 (14 runs) — New Zealand 226/5 (121 runs required from 19 overs, RR: 7.29, RRR: 6.36)

CD McMillan 101 not out (69 balls, 12 x 4, 5 x 6)

BB McCullum 27 not out (35 balls, 1 x 4)

I brought my hundred up in that over but I wasn't aware of my score or how many balls I had faced. The scoreboard was behind me, and I thought I was on only 88 and the six I hit took me to 94. But I was actually on 94. I hit the ball into the stand for six and the first I knew I had actually brought up my century was when the crowd started screaming and yelling. Baz came up to me and gave me a hug. I said to him, 'Is that my hundred?', and he said, 'Yeah.' Then came the emotion. If I had known I was actually on 94 I wouldn't have been that stupid and tried to hit it for six. It had been a while between one-day centuries for me and I would have just noodled the ball around. It certainly was a great moment for me, as anyone who was at the ground or watching at home on TV would have seen.

After I'd reached my milestone I pulled back a bit and tried rotating the strike. My next 17 runs took about 30 balls, a lot slower than the previous 100 runs I'd scored. We were still chipping away at the target and Brendon was starting to come to the party and hit out.

Eventually, I was dismissed for 117. Prior to that I had had the jelly beans run out to me because I was feeling a bit low. It had been a really hot day in Hamilton and it had taken a lot out of me. A few people afterwards told me they'd seen me on TV and I looked stuffed. I was low and the mental exertion towards the end of the innings started to wear on me. Unfortunately, I chopped an inside edge onto my stumps when there was still a lot of work for us to do.

> **John Bracewell:** If there was ever a game set up for Craig it was that night in Hamilton — playing on good wickets, small boundaries and fearless chasing. The bigger the score, the bigger the opportunity for him — there is less thinking and more doing. He is a proactive thinker; it made him hit forward of the wicket.
>
> It was about giving him a defined role. And that role was to hit the ball without fear. We had people who could play around him. He was the point of difference for us because he had that power. And we gave him the right to use that power.
>
> There are dynamics and there is importance. In terms of an entertaining spectacle, chasing down that many, the execution was as good as I have seen. He played a shot through the covers early on and you thought, 'Man, that is something special.' Then he just got on a roll. In terms of purity, probably Hayden's innings was a majestic brutal innings, whereas Craig's was just brutal, that was the way he played. It was as brutal an innings as I have ever seen — he just smashed the ball.
>
> That carried through to the World Cup and onto the Twenty20 World Cup. Singlehandedly, and I say this without any hesitation, Craig got us to the semi-final of the Twenty20 World Cup. Unfortunately, we didn't have enough guys in form to back him up.

It just seemed one of those games where it was meant to be. Mark Gillespie went out to bat with Baz, and Dizz isn't one of the bravest guys around with the bat. I remember playing for Canterbury against Wellington and he got hit in the face by Hamish Bennett and had his nose splattered — it was an awful injury. The thing about Dizz is that he can bat; he can play shots. He backed away a couple of times against Tait and got inside edges for four — he got 28 off just 15 balls, which was pretty crucial. It was like he was using half the bat and just taking the piss — but every time he moved away from the stumps he never missed the ball.

That partnership of 36 runs was vital. And they did it off just 24 balls, which was also important. The other key was Brendon's finishing at the end — he'd done it before and he showed just what a skilful guy he is at the end of the innings. I think he felt comfortable in that position, he knew what his job was and he backed himself. He was outstanding to see us home.

McMillan rides high to World Cup
Cricinfo staff, 21 February 2007

After completing his transformation from out-of-favour all-rounder to national hero with a match-winning century, Craig McMillan said New Zealand could go to the World Cup without fearing any target.

McMillan was a crucial figure in the final two Chappell-Hadlee Trophy matches as New Zealand overhauled scores of 336 at Eden Park and 346 at Hamilton to secure the country's first clean sweep over Australia.

Back-to-back performances of 52 off 30 balls and 117 off 96 were also hugely satisfying for McMillan, who was dropped from the squad in 2005 and not offered a New Zealand contract.

'Hopefully, I've shown people I can still bat and I've still got something to offer this side,' McMillan said in the Dominion Post.

'I've always had the ability but at times that belief gets knocked when you are not going as well as what you want. But I suppose the key for me was the knock in Sydney (last month) when I got 89, that gave me the belief that I can foot it.'

New Zealand were in severe trouble at 4 for 41 at Hamilton when McMillan walked out to perform a brilliant rescue and collect the fastest century in the country's history. Partnerships of 75 with Peter Fulton (51) and 165 with Brendon McCullum (86 not out) pushed them towards their aim before McCullum finished the match with one wicket and three balls to go. The series result and the manner in which New Zealand achieved the whitewash will give them extreme confidence heading into next month's World Cup.

'From 40 for four we didn't have a lot to lose and sometimes teams can be dangerous from those situations,' McMillan said. 'We got a couple of partnerships going. It's special and the icing on the cake was winning the game. Now we can head to the World Cup believing we can chase down anything.'

My innings in Hamilton was my third one-day century. My innings of 105 against Pakistan in 2002 against a bowling line-up of Wasim Akram, Waqar Younis, Shoaib Akhtar and Saqlain Mushtaq was always going to take some beating. That was a special innings because it was against a great bowling attack and was scored in Rawalpindi, Akhtar's home ground.

But in terms of what the innings meant to me, I could never go past my innings against Australia in Hamilton. It meant pretty much everything after what I'd gone through in the past 12 to 18 months. That one innings made all that hard work, pain and angst feel worthwhile. It was so nice to actually get a reward, to get something positive out of what had happened in that period of time.

Gilbert Enoka: It was wonderful. It was like karma in a way. He had been through this path of despair, because it was despair. And it wasn't only for him, it was also for Cherie and the family as well. They all felt it. And then all of a sudden he got another opportunity and boy did he take it. He was the best player by miles in the Chappell-Hadlee Trophy series — he was playing the best team in the world and dealt to them in a way no other batsman in the history of our country has done. All he needed after going back to Canterbury and performing was one opportunity. He got that opportunity and away he went.

It was seriously the only time in my international career where I really felt in the zone. From ball one, I was seeing the ball so well. There are other times when you bat and you are thinking about your feet, your back-lift, how quick the bowler is, how much the ball is turning or the fact you need eight runs an over to win. But there was none of that during that night in Hamilton, even though we were 41–4 when I went into bat. It felt that I was just out there batting against Australia; there was no other pressure.

Part of my success during that special week against Australia was that I went back to trying to hit the ball as far as I could — to dominate and do those things that I did earlier in my career. There was a period of time, especially during the 2005 Chappell-Hadlee Trophy series, when I was only using half the bat. I went away from my power hitting game, something that was always my number one strength.

When I did come back into the team I decided I was going to use my power. And to be fair to John Bracewell, he did encourage that.

It was a perfect finish to an amazing series for everyone in the Black Caps — in your wildest dreams you probably don't ever think you can really clean sweep Australia. I know a lot was said in certain quarters that it was a 3–0 clean sweep against an under-strength Aussie side. Lee and Andrew Symonds missed the series through injury — they'd only left Ricky Ponting and Adam Gilchrist behind to rest. Even if those two had been playing, Australia wouldn't have scored higher totals than they posted in Auckland and Hamilton.

Some of that talk was frustrating. OK, they had two of their best batsmen back at home, but the batters who came in did just as good a job as the other two would have. It was not like they scored poor totals — they still put on 336 and 346 in the final two games.

And something people who try to downplay the result should also consider is that we also left three of our key players out in that last game.

Crazy times in the Caribbean

My whole motivation for coming back after missing out on a New Zealand Cricket contract was to try to make the 2007 World Cup in the West Indies. I had already been to two previous tournaments; they are a special thing to go to. I really felt that this time around we had a side that could go a long way. My motivation levels to get to the Caribbean in 2007 were increased even further because of the way both the 1999 and 2003 campaigns had ended.

Every effort throughout the season leading up to the World Cup was to make it into that squad. At the start of the season, when I wasn't in the reckoning and didn't even make it into the 30-man squad to prepare for the ICC Champions Trophy, it was pretty obvious I was going to have to come from a long way back. I didn't have a New Zealand Cricket contract at the start of the season, but I had determination.

When I missed out on the contract I know there would have been very few people who would have truly backed me to win World Cup selection. And there were obviously times when I questioned that myself, especially during the time when I was figuring out how to put a CV together and reading job advertisements.

Needless to say I was absolutely stoked and over the moon to be named in the World Cup squad. A lot of hard work had been done to get to that point — but it had all now been worth it. Cherie had been great too. She knew how much I wanted to get to another World Cup and she said all along that she was prepared to do anything, including looking after our kids at home, so I could do everything needed to get to the West Indies.

I had another reason to be excited about heading to the Caribbean, having played my part in our 3–0 series clean sweep over World Cup favourites Australia in the Chappell-Hadlee Trophy series. The timing of my innings at Eden Park and Seddon Park couldn't have been better.

John Bracewell: To win the World Cup, we had to develop a point of difference. We knew we were going to be playing against some dobby bowlers; we knew we were going to be playing on some slow wickets. That was one of the reasons we started developing Jeetan Patel two years out. It was also one of the reasons we fast-tracked Ross Taylor.

We knew that our style of play had to be more dynamic. We knew we couldn't just try to graft our way to certain points — we had to have people who could take a game away from the opposition in the correct positions.

Craig McMillan was always in the back of my mind as one of the guys who could do that. But Craig had to get his shit together. He had to last the tournament of eight and a half weeks. He had to be fitter, he had to face the reality that he wasn't invincible — that he couldn't eat shit food and go and play in an eight and a half week tournament. He had to get to a certain standard of fitness.

While it might not have been comfortable for him, I think it was the best route we took. He got a shake-up, he got a taste of the real world, realised it wasn't that shit-hot and realised there was more he could give in world cricket.

The West Indies has changed a lot over the years — it is not what it used to be. With touring sides that went there in the late 1980s and early 1990s there was a real fear factor that isn't there anymore. But it is a nice place to tour: they love their cricket, and it is a different experience with a lot of singing and dancing at the grounds. The fans are drinking plenty of rum and generally having a lot of fun. And at each island location, they have their own form of music and costumes.

I had toured the West Indies in 2002 and was certainly looking forward to playing in front of some of those incredible crowds again. But, unfortunately, I returned five years later for the World Cup and found that so much about playing in the Caribbean was missing — and all through some very poor decisions made by the ICC.

The most disappointing thing about the whole Cricket World Cup was just how the tournament was effectively taken away from a decent section of the cricket-mad fan base in the Caribbean. The ticket prices were just way too high. The ICC, in their efforts to make as much money as possible from the tournament, had clearly overlooked the financial plight of many in the region that was hosting the World Cup.

It was crazy that they were charging massive prices for tickets, considering all the money was actually being made in TV rights. The high costs of the tickets meant that most of the people at the grounds were tourists — lots of Poms and Aussies. And I am sure many of them had travelled over there expecting real party atmospheres at the grounds.

They got anything but that, again due to a short-sighted decision from tournament organisers. For whatever reason, they also decided to ban fans from taking musical instruments into the match venues. So a lot of locals just decided not to go to the games — they either couldn't afford to go or were turned off by the rules and regulations surrounding alcohol and instruments. It wasn't until halfway through the tournament that the World Cup organisers relaxed some of those rules. But it was too late — the damage had already been done.

We were also to find that the scheduling was a mess, including times when we had a week between games. Whether we played poorly or well, you only wanted two or three days between games. If you had played poorly, that would give you a chance to get back on track. If you were playing well, it would also allow you to maintain the momentum. But we never had that because of the way the itinerary was set.

That, at times, was cause for a bad case of cabin fever. We did a lot of gym work and spent a lot of time in the nets even to the point of overkill — we were training for the sake of training because it filled in time during the day. From that point of view, it just wasn't enjoyable at all.

We opened our campaign against England at Beausejour Stadium, St Lucia, and we had been looking forward to this game for quite a while. In terms of our group, we needed to win this game to go through to the next stage.

We have always felt that England looked down on us slightly. We've always been a better team — they may have had better individuals, but we've had a better collective team, which quite often has got us across the line against them. We were also further motivated after England had knocked us out of the Commonwealth Bank series in Australia just a couple of months previously.

We won the toss and put England into bat. And it was a decision which paid dividends from the start, with James Franklin dismissing England opener Ed Joyce with the first ball of the match. England found themselves 52–3 inside the 16th over, but then they launched a fight-back through Paul Collingwood and Kevin Pietersen. Styris broke the partnership when he dismissed Collingwood, before Shane nabbed both Pietersen and Flintoff with a superb second spell. He did exactly the job Flem had asked him to do. After those two dismissals the wind got taken out of their sails. Paul Nixon put on a few in the end to get them through to an OK total of 209–7.

Again we lost early wickets: Lou lasted just four balls without scoring, Rosco had an identical fate and then Flem went for seven, leaving us reeling at 19–3. Styris and I set about rebuilding things and we both played pretty freely and got the run rate back up.

And we did just that, sitting at 72–3 before I took on Monty Panesar in the 16th over. It was a case of showing no respect to another spinner.

I played a horrible shot and was caught at deep cover. I came down the pitch and tried to go over long-off. It was a poor shot in Panesar's first over.

As I tended to do, I went back to my youth, and from the first couple of balls I was just charging down the wicket. It didn't put us in a good position — all of a sudden we were four down. But Oram and Styris played beautifully; they never looked like getting out, and saw us home rather easily against a good attack. We played pretty good cricket that day and it was a good start to our campaign. It was certainly nice to get one over England, especially at such a big tournament as the World Cup.

Our first leg at the World Cup saw us based in St Lucia for the group matches against England, Kenya and Canada. And St Lucia was pretty quiet, a really pleasant place and very safe. There were other places, such as Jamaica, which were a lot more dangerous, where you had to be careful when you left the team hotel. But at St Lucia you could walk down the road and not be interrupted.

The next two games were about getting our guys into some good form. We never expected to lose those games; we just had to do what we had to do. And four of us posted some decent scores against Kenya, with Flem, Rosco, Styris and me all posting half-centuries in our total of 331–7. Kenya was never in it from there, struggling through to 183 before being dismissed in the 50th over.

We then ended our pool-play phase with a 114-run win over Canada. Again we batted first, posting a total of 363–5. Lou scored 101 and it was certainly good to see him in form. Flem scored 66 off 67 balls and the thing I remember most was him returning to the sheds after he had holed out, saying: 'I have just thrown away another hundred.' He got himself out when he was really just cruising.

But the happiness over some impressive contributions with the bat quickly evaporated once we started in the field. Canada put on 76 for the opening wicket before John Davison was dismissed in the 10th over. Four years previously and Davison had taken to our bowling at the World Cup in South Africa. He certainly slapped the ball around the field; he seemed to have a real liking for our bowling attack.

We leaked runs all over the show, although we were eventually able to mop up their tail pretty quickly. We might have won by 114 runs, but there was still a lot to work on. And we suffered another blow against Canada with Daryl Tuffey being ruled out of the tournament after injuring his right arm. He was eventually replaced by Chris Martin.

Throughout those final two matches our concentration was growing on our opening Super Eights match against the West Indies at Sir Vivian Richards Stadium, Antigua. The hosts had lost their opening second-stage match to Australia by 103 runs, with poor weather forcing the match into its reserve day just 24 hours before we were to take on the Windies.

And it was at Antigua where the lack of wisdom behind the tournament ticket prices really hit home for me. Just 5414 people turned up for our clash. Now there was something seriously wrong when a crowd of just that size would turn up at Antigua, which is Sir Vivian Richards' country, to watch the West Indies play.

Again we won the toss and bowled first, with Bondy bowling beautifully at the start of the match, swinging the ball at pace. He was just too hot to handle for guys like Chris Gayle. He also turned Shivnarine Chanderpaul inside out a few times. Scott Styris got Brian Lara out, a big wicket for us, and we ended up dismissing them for just 177 inside 45 overs.

We chased the total down within the 40-over mark, losing just three wickets in the process. But there was some worrying time for us, with the rain clouds threatening when I went out to join Styris in the middle at 77–3. I went out to bat knowing that the Duckworth-Lewis system looked to count against us if we lost another wicket.

With that in mind, Scott and I kept the score ticking over without taking too many risks. We put on 100 runs for the fourth wicket, with Styris ending on 80 not out and I added an unbeaten 33. It was a good, clinical win.

Our winning momentum continued against Bangladesh and Ireland. We won both matches relatively comfortably, without setting the world on fire. But our trip to Guyana for the 129-run win over Ireland certainly wasn't the happiest time for me. I got pretty crook three days before the Ireland game; I was basically vomiting for two days. I ended up having the South African doctor coming in and giving me an injection to stop me being sick. I got better the day before the first game against Ireland, and while I didn't train that much, I was announced fit to play the game.

After those two results it was time for our Super Eights section to get really serious. A clash with Sri Lanka at Grenada was the first in a tough-looking three-game section. Matches against South Africa and Australia, also to be played in Grenada, were to follow.

We had obviously played Sri Lanka so much in recent seasons that we didn't have to do too much scouting on them — we knew them inside out. They are the sort of team that we either play really well or really poorly against. And in the conditions at the World Cup, Sri Lanka certainly had the upper hand right from the start.

We didn't help ourselves by generally not batting well. If it wasn't for an impressive unbeaten 111 from Styris our eventual total would have looked a lot sicker than the 219–7 we were able to post in 50 overs. Unfortunately, no one else was able to back Scott up — I got out sweeping to Murali for just one.

The pitch flattened out by the time Sri Lanka batted, with Sanath Jayasuriya and Kumar Sangakkara batting well and making it look easy. Sri Lanka eventually enjoyed a pretty comfortable six-wicket win. We didn't get enough runs on the board — we didn't bowl well either.

We were now increasingly desperate to secure enough points in the Super Eights phase to enable us to secure a spot in the semi-finals. And while we obviously would back ourselves to beat Australia, especially after what we'd done to them in the Chappell-Hadlee Trophy series, we didn't want to go into our final Super Eights game against them, needing to win to make the top four.

With that attitude we took on South Africa in Grenada. We've always had good battles with South Africa. They are a team that we don't dominate, but we still manage to beat them at times.

We won the toss and there was little hesitation in opting to bowl first as the pitch at the National Cricket Stadium was fairly wet. It meant that for the first 15 overs the ball seamed and swung, helping our bowlers hugely. And Bondy bowled beautifully at the start, knocking over Graeme Smith early on.

But Jacques Kallis hung around, not scoring too many runs, as did Herschelle Gibbs, who was starting to open up after surviving Bond's spell early on. Dan ended up dismissing Kallis after he charged down the wicket to him. That was a huge wicket for us because once Kallis gets through those tough periods he is a very good player.

By this stage Gibbs was starting to bat pretty well, posing a pretty clear danger to us. One of my biggest frustrations while in the field for the Blacks Caps over the years was that I didn't think I was used enough as a bowling option. So it came as a bit of a surprise when Flem threw me the ball to bowl the 35th over.

My first over was OK, but in my second over I was hit for a four and I knew it was pretty much going to be my last over. But I managed to get Gibbs to chop on when he was on 60 — it was huge because he was their mainstay; if they were to get a big total he had to kick on. With a new guy coming in, Flem decided he would try to get a couple more overs out of me. Then I got Ashwell Prince to hit one down to long-off. In the next over I had Mark Boucher caught on the boundary too. All of a sudden I had 3–23 in five overs, ripping out the heart of South Africa's middle order.

At one stage it looked like they could get a decent total, but we turned it around, restricting them to a total of 193–7, a target that we could attain as long as we batted well. We ended up winning by five wickets, batting well and securing a semi-finals berth — a win over Australia in our final Super Eights clash might even secure us top-billing for the semis.

Australia had been by far the most dominant team at the World Cup.

Posing alongside fellow test centurians Mark Richardson (left), Scott Styris and Lou Vincent after scoring centuries in the test against India in Mohali in 2003.

Expressing differing views with Adam Gilchrist after my decision not to walk at the Gabba in 2004.

I shared a lot of good times with Daniel Vettori both on and off the field during my international career.

Blazing away during one of the most important innings of my career, scoring a defiant 89 against Australia at the SCG during the 2007 ODI tri-series.

Whenever I had the ball in hand I always had a degree of white-line fever, here leaving Mike Hussey under no illusion that I think I've dismissed him at the SCG.

Lashing out during my crucial innings of 52 during the Black Caps' win over Australia at Eden Park during the 2007 Chappell-Hadlee Trophy series.

Acknowledging the crowd after posting my record-breaking and match-winning century against Australia in Hamilton in 2007.

The Black Caps celebrate their stunning 3–0 clean sweep over Australia in the 2007 Chappell-Hadlee Trophy series.

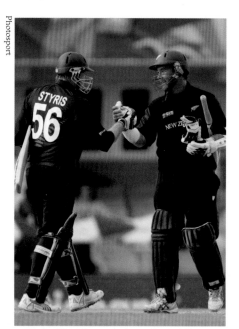

Scott Styris and I congratulate each other after guiding the Black Caps to victory over the West Indies during the 2007 Cricket World Cup.

Despite Mark Boucher using Gunn and Moore, who sponsored me for eight years, he seemed to like the look of my Kookaburra bat.

More time on the golfing fairways beckons following my international cricket retirement.

The retro Black Caps (left to right): Daryl Tuffey, Daniel Vettori, Chris Cairns, me and Hamish Marshall (lying on his team-mates) share a lighter moment during the 2005 Twenty20 international against Australia.

Pictured alongside some of my Kolkata Tigers team-mates in an ICL promotional poster.

Australian great Dean Jones, left, talks to me and Mumbai's Nathan Astle during the inaugural ICL tournament.

At home with Cherie, Lucie and Mitchell. Cherie has been a loyal and strong supporter — during good times and bad.

International retirement has provided me with much more family time with my children Mitchell and Lucie.

The McMillans: Kathryn, Lindsay, Judith and I share a rare moment together.

The Nelson cricket club in the Lancashire Leagues provided me with a great chance to start rebuilding my international career after losing my New Zealand Cricket contract in 2006.

Any hopes we had of toppling them, however, were dealt a massive pre-match blow when Shane Bond was ruled out with food poisoning.

In his absence, the Australian batting line-up just bullied us, led by opener Matthew Hayden who scored a typically brutal 103 off 100 balls. Ponting, Clarke and Watson also took their toll on some pretty ineffective bowling, as Australia went on to post 348–6.

It was just one of those days when we were totally outplayed. Our batting wasn't impressive either as we were dismissed for just 133 in 25.5 overs, losing by a huge 215 runs. It was the worst dress rehearsal we could have hoped for ahead of the semi-final against Sri Lanka at Sabina Park, Jamaica.

Although we knew what to expect from Sri Lanka, I was certainly nervous about playing them in the semis. In fact I would have preferred to have played Australia. With Murali and Lasith Malinga, they had two bowlers who had been constant dangers for us. The fact that we were playing in Jamaica made us think that the pitch would have more pace and bounce, something that we thought would help us. But it didn't, it was just like all the other pitches we confronted in the West Indies.

Sri Lanka decided to bat first after winning the toss. And while we were able to make an early inroad, with James Franklin bowling Jayasuriya in the third over, our bowlers didn't have a great day. Bondie, returning after missing the match against Australia, certainly didn't bowl well at the start. In fact, all of our bowlers struggled.

Basically, everything that could have gone wrong did, as Sri Lanka posted an impressive target of 289–5. That included me getting injured in the field. I was down at third man early on and dived to stop a ball. But I felt something in my lower groin go; it was a bit sore and I managed to stay on. But about 10 overs later I went running after a ball, pulled up badly and couldn't run and was forced off.

I wasn't sure what I had done; the pain was in a high, nasty region and it was something I hadn't done or felt before. Any movement through my groin hurt like hell. I couldn't run, so I pretty much sat on the sidelines watching the guys toil in the field with little reward. And, to be honest, in the break between innings we had the feeling that it wasn't going to happen for us.

When we turned up for the start of the match the weather was hot and dry. But at lunch it started clouding over and all of a sudden we were out to bat. The ball was swinging like crazy and our guys couldn't deal with Malinga and Chaminda Vaas.

The injury meant I was moved down to No. 7 in the batting order. I had some throw-downs during the break to see what I could do. But I couldn't really do much and by the time I went out to bat with a runner the game was well gone.

I managed to get a hold of Jayasuriya a couple of times — but it came at a cost to me. I kept forgetting what I could and couldn't do with my injury. Our physio told me before I went into bat just to nudge the ball around for singles, not to play any big shots. But I was facing spinners — it was like a red rag to a bull. If we were going to win the game we needed a lot of big overs. It was just out of instinct, but it certainly did hurt.

Unbeknown to me at the time, that ended up being my last one-day international innings for New Zealand. Our 81-run loss in the semi-final was really disappointing when I look back at it as it was my last game. It was an unsatisfactory game and we hadn't performed well in our last two games against Australia and Sri Lanka. In fact, three of our last four games were pretty poor.

John Bracewell: I don't think we would have beaten Sri Lanka on that day anyway, given the fact it clouded over and the ball started swinging when we went into bat. Earlier Jayawardene played such an outstanding innings — he picked one out of the box. I always remember going out to the wicket and Muralitharan was out there. He said, 'Made in Sri Lanka.' It was just one of those things.

We just got beaten by a better team on the day. We managed ourselves through to a beat. We beat England well; we knew that was a big game. We beat South Africa well; we knew that was a big game. We performed in that tournament, but we just didn't win it.

We really had no momentum through that tournament. Apart from Scott Styris, we didn't have any other batsmen who performed consistently. We weren't helped by the fact we lost Louie mid-tournament when he broke his arm facing Shane Bond in the nets. Louie hadn't been in the greatest form, but he was a guy who could win a match. And we were in need of match-winners in our side. It also shook up the team — we had lost one of our own, through one of our own. It was an accident, but it was so frustrating that one of our own had ruled a team-mate out.

John Bracewell: I thought the World Cup was as good a planned campaign as it possibly could have been. We lost Mills before the tournament which had an effect on our bowling attack in terms of balance, and then Nathan's retirement. But probably Lou breaking his arm affected the balance of the team more than anything, because of the dynamics of our starts.

We designed the programme pretty well, we followed the programme pretty well and we gave ourselves as good a chance as any of winning it.

The schedule was always going to be difficult and I thought we managed it better than some teams. I thought we scouted it really well; we had Ashley Ross who went over and checked out all the venues, practice facilities and the hotels.

It was scouted really well. We knew where we would be staying, how we would be staying and the distance between all the locations. I think the players were pretty disciplined, as disciplined as I have seen them given the length of the tour. And I think they trained really well.

The length of it was just the nature of it; we adapted and we rehearsed and we were ready. You can't change that. You can bitch and moan about the length of time and things like that, but we knew the length of time. We knew how long the piece of string was — we planned pretty well along the whole piece.

If the loss wasn't bad enough, our return travel arrangements added to the pain. We had two days to wait until we could get out of Jamaica. We had two days of reflection, thinking about what might have happened. The reality was that we were outplayed and didn't play to our best.

What happened at the end of the World Cup final, with all the uncertainty about the match rules among the officials, really summed the tournament up for me. To be blunt, it was a farce from start to finish. The tournament had the opportunity to be truly great — the West Indies is a great place to tour. But through the organisers, a lot of the mistakes they made really killed it. It certainly wasn't the spectacle it should have been.

The way the final finished was an absolute farce. From a New Zealand perspective, it was disappointing Jeff Crowe was in charge of it in his role as ICC match referee because he is a hell of a nice guy.

Crowe takes blame for light chaos
AFP, 28 April 2007

The match referee Jeff Crowe took the blame for the farcical finish to the World Cup final which saw Australia celebrate victory twice and forced Sri Lanka to bat in pitch-black darkness. But he suggested the third umpire Rudi Koertzen may have initiated the process leading to chaotic scenes at the climax of the game.

Crowe, despite heading up a team of officials which included the umpire Steve Bucknor, standing in a record fifth World Cup final, managed to overlook a basic playing condition which states that once 20 overs have been bowled in both innings enough cricket has been played to create a match. A result can then be declared under the Duckworth-Lewis system for rain-affected games.

Instead the teams, following instructions from Bucknor and Pakistan's Aleem Dar, came back on to bowl three more overs in gathering gloom. Both Mahela Jayawardene and Ricky Ponting rightly thought the game had finished. With the match gone from Sri Lanka, Jayawardene and Ponting came to an arrangement that it would finish with Sri Lanka facing slow bowling as a safety precaution after the umpires had incorrectly told them they would otherwise have to come back on Sunday's reserve day.

'In hindsight, I should have known the rules and said the game had been called

off. I'm very embarrassed for the playing control team today,' Crowe said after the officials had been booed during the trophy presentation ceremony. 'For me the real confusion has come from the fact we were talking about resuming the game tomorrow, which was technically wrong.'

Crowe said he and the on-field umpires, as well as Koertzen, were all involved in the discussion which left both sides stunned when, after Sri Lanka had gone off for bad light at the end of the 33rd over, they found themselves all coming back out again. 'Sometimes you get a stronger voice which says: "I know the rules — this is how it works",' Crowe said. 'Then you get a bit of confusion in the group itself, and no one wants to overrule the other. The match referee should have known and said, "That's not right — the game should be completed now".'

Crowe said the officials took 'collective' responsibility but suggested Koertzen had played a significant role. 'Rudi was talking about the allowances and talking about the possibility of tomorrow,' he said. 'I don't think it's Rudi's mistake, it's a collective mistake. The fact Rudi might maybe have suggested it early doesn't mean the other umpires couldn't have overruled him. The two on-field umpires are the ones who control the match.'

Asked if it was a resigning issue, Crowe said: 'I'll have to talk with my superiors on that. But I hope not.'

That wasn't the end of the comical scenes, though. Malcolm Speed was talking at the post-tournament press conference and the sponsor's backdrop fell down — it summed it up for the whole ICC. They had no idea about how to plan and organise a good tournament. It was way too long and there was far too much time between matches.

While it was a sad ending for us in the semi-final, it is still no mean feat to make the top four. We seem to be a little bit jinxed when it comes to World Cup semi-finals. But we still did well, especially considering that sides like India, Pakistan, England and the West Indies didn't get that far. I have no doubt that we will go further at some stage, and hopefully it will be at the next tournament because if you play in enough semis, you will win one sooner or later!

The World Cup was the longest I had been away from home, away from my wife and kids, for a couple of years. I found that really tough. It's sad to admit, but I don't look back on the 2007 World Cup with a lot of enjoyment. Unfortunately, that spark and burning desire which helped get me to the World Cup quickly started to dim.

Being judged by your peers

It didn't take long to find out some significant changes had been made within the Black Caps unit on my return to the team in the months leading up to the 2007 Cricket World Cup. And the changes weren't just restricted to different faces in the team unit.

Off the field things had also changed considerably. Gilbert Enoka was no longer with us — neither were some of the off-field initiatives he had helped develop.

'Leading Teams' was now the catch-phrase or current buzz word around the team. Where Gilbert once initiated things to help us get the best out of each other, we now had the very different services — and ideas — of Australian-based Kraig Grime. He's a director of Leading Teams Australia and his sporting CV included work with the Chiefs Super 14 franchise, the North Queensland Cowboys NRL team and the AFL's Hawthorn Football Club.

Kraig's approach was just so different from anything I had seen or experienced previously in the national team. He pretty much came and went from the team environment. He was in New Zealand for a week during the 2007 Chappell-Hadlee Trophy series and previously had spent time with the guys at Lincoln at a stage when I wasn't part of the squad. But even though I wasn't in the environment, I was aware that quite a few senior players were pretty unhappy with some of the stuff that went on during that phase.

One of the big initiatives in the new set-up was the introduction of peer assessments. The process would see the squad go into a team meeting and be told who was to be reviewed. At that stage the squad would be split in two. Each group had its own leader. Flem led one group, Daniel led the other.

The pair of players who were to be reviewed would be given a questionnaire to fill out, and had to come up with words that they thought best described them. The others inside the room would talk about the same thing then give feedback on the areas they thought the player needed to improve and work on.

Some guys got told they went out too much, others were told they drank too much. It was very much like being at school, being told what you can and cannot do. But everyone was an adult and understood what they had to do — we were all professional athletes. And our team in general does everything in moderation. I think we are very responsible in terms of how we conduct ourselves off the park.

> **John Bracewell:** What the Leading Teams philosophy does is take away the coffee group mentality. If you are going to say something to a guy, say it to his face rather than to little groups. I find that cricketers are some of the worst gossips and the least in your face, confrontational people that I have ever met. We don't mind sitting over a coffee and bitching and moaning about Craig not having gone for a run or eating crap food, but no one is prepared to go and talk to him about it. We seem to have this thing going: 'No, that is management; they should be dealing with those sorts of things.'
>
> Cricket is a game played by people. And management just manage people. In my opinion it is up to the team to have a certain degree of honesty about what they say. And if you can't say it to his face, don't say it at all. That really is the whole process of peer assessment. It is: 'This is an opportunity to say what I think to help you become a better cricketer. This is something I have been gossiping about for years but haven't had the balls to say to you.'

A lot of this process came from Bracewell's paranoia, in terms of his belief that there was gossiping and a coffee group mentality. That never happened. It was Braces' notion that there was supposedly something going on behind the scenes. When Steve Rixon was coach and Gilbert Enoka was our facilitator, we always had the saying, 'In the belly, not the back'. If there was an issue, if someone thought a team-mate wasn't preparing right for a game, things were said straight to him and not behind his back. As far as I was concerned, that was the attitude we should still have.

Maybe the whole Leading Teams initiative just gave Bracewell more reassurance of his position as coach.

Generally, a couple of players would be reviewed during each campaign. And I was to find out just how frustrating the whole process is after being selected alongside Hamish Marshall for an inter-squad assessment during our stop in Perth during the 2007 Commonwealth Bank Series.

It was all a new experience for me as I'd been out of the team when this process was first brought in. So it was with a fair bit of apprehension that I got a pen and filled in my own assessment form.

First of all was the job of coming up with three words which I thought the group would use to describe me — I chose 'competitive', 'stubborn' and 'distant'. The three terms I selected as those I wanted the group to be using were 'competitive', 'team player' and 'renewed'.

Under the heading of what I thought my team-mates would want me to stop doing I wrote: 'Being closed off.' Under the heading of start doing, I jotted down: 'Communicating more with how feeling or what thinking. Giving more time to younger guys.' Things that I felt my team-mates wanted me to keep doing including working on my fitness, different batting roles, listening to others and keeping a close eye on my fitness and health.

Even though I didn't believe I was closed off, I wrote it as I thought that is what some of my team-mates would have come up with. After filling in my form it was then time to wait outside as my team-mates passed judgement on me. After about 30 minutes it was time to go in and hear what people really thought about me.

Those who are being assessed are told they are supposed to be non-confrontational. I usually sit with my arms folded — it is just a habit — but apparently that is taken as confrontational. I was told to sit with my arms at my side — something that felt really weird and uncomfortable for me. You are asked if you are having a problem with something. Is that why you are sitting in a manner with closed body language?

During the feedback session, you are not allowed to challenge anything that is said. You have to just sit there and take it. And it's fair to say that the last thing I wanted to hear was some of the things my mates in the team had come up with.

Dan's group used the words 'talented', 'obstinate' and 'combative' to describe me. They also wrote I should stop sweating on the 'small stuff', not be guilty of selective hearing, share my experience with team-mates and for me to believe that I was world class and fulfil my potential. They urged me to keep: 'improving as a person, cricketer and athlete'.

I thought that was fair enough. But I certainly didn't share the views in what was to come in the review completed by the Fleming-led group.

The three words they used were 'competitive', 'stubborn' and 'self-centred'. I was judged to be guilty of only looking after myself and it was recommended that I started giving to others with both actions and attitude, be internally driven, look after my diet and fitness and open my mind to different points of view.

At the end of each of these sessions you are asked, 'Are you OK with what has been said?' It's fair to say I wasn't too happy with some of the things that were said about me, especially in the form completed by Flem's group. He was the one who was charged with writing my review and I challenged a few of the things he had brought up.

One of the biggest issues I had was that Flem hadn't actually seen me play in the past 12 months as I hadn't been in the Black Caps. I felt that if I hadn't made changes to the way I approached things, and made sacrifices, over that period of time, then I wouldn't have made it back into the Black Caps.

So I thought a lot of the stuff he was saying may have been relevant in my time previously in the Black Caps. But I thought that as a person I had made quite a few significant changes for the better. Flem hadn't been privy to that, so I thought he was right off the mark. I challenged what he said. He is not the easiest man to challenge at the best of times; he speaks so well he can quite often talk you around to his way of thinking, even if you are right.

What was written on Flem's form certainly got my back up. One of the things I was told in the meeting was that I wasn't giving guys enough throw-downs. At training, Flem was always the first into the nets when it was time to bat — he was captain so he got first use of the nets. And he always got twice as long in the nets as everyone else to work on his game. Quite often he would go and have a second or a third net. Maybe I hadn't been joining the queue to throw to him.

What they said about me being concerned only about myself just didn't wash with me. Cricket is such an individual sport in a team game. So, as a batsman, you have to concentrate on yourself to do the things that you need to do to get your game in order. And a lot of times we got told that by the coaches. Even Braces would say, 'Do what you have to do to make sure you are right for tomorrow.' Once I had done my work in the nets, I would do things like seeing if other guys wanted throw-downs or quite often go into the nets and bowl to someone. There would be a couple of net bowlers who weren't in great shape and one of our lower order guys would be batting and would want some decent bowling.

I left the room despondent, feeling that everyone had talked only about my bad points and weaknesses. It really was just a bit of a shit-fight — just name the worst things about a certain guy that you can. Then they tried to cover it up by saying, 'Well, we are trying to give you feedback so you can improve.' It was also uncomfortable listening to my team-mates telling Hamish what he should or shouldn't be doing.

To this day I don't know why I didn't throw my forms in the nearest rubbish bin — because that is what I felt like doing. None of the peer assessment sat well with me at all so I never bought into it. But I know some of the other guys did, especially the leadership group. I would guess it was in their best interests to do just that.

The whole thing they kept talking about was that it was 'team first'. They laid down all these key words and they were put up in the team changing room. I don't think many of the guys really bought into it. It was pushed by the captain, coach and a couple of the senior players. The issue I found frustrating about the 'team first' motto was that the various people who supported it were, at times, contradicting it.

> **Daniel Vettori:** I think what came of that was a group of guys who actually cared about him and wanted to find a way to make him as productive as possible and stay in the team as long as possible. And sometimes we get caught up in the emotion of the words and what they mean to you literally, whereas I genuinely believe they came from a group of guys who wanted Craig McMillan to be our best batsman and contributing to the side. I can understand there are frustrations with certain words, as they affect people in different ways, but I believe the majority of the guys were coming from a good place.

The motivational side of things was really started in the Black Caps by Gilbert Enoka. The 1999 tour was the start, with the phrase 'Better than Before'. It was a brilliant term and one that the whole team embraced — we wanted to create history and by the end of the tour that is just what we'd achieved. Ever since then it seems we were always looking for something else and everything has come and gone. Nothing has stuck by the team.

'Better than Before' is something that I believe could have remained a constant the whole way through. It doesn't matter who you are playing or what you are trying to do, you are always trying to be better than before. I don't believe a lot of the newer guys who came into the team from then on fully grasped the importance of what we were trying to achieve.

> **Gilbert Enoka:** My model has always been one of not being an imposing interference for them as people or cricketers. We had to do what we were going to do in a way which didn't interrupt to a huge extent their particular persona. Our reviews seldom lasted more than 50 minutes. The process they have got now, I couldn't think of something that would turn Macca off more than that. You can get paralysis through analysis. There is only so much you can do in that regard. People quite often say, 'Just let me get out and play, won't you?'
>
> I have also heard some say it is the best thing since sliced bread because it is making some people face things that they sometimes are not prepared to do. And our mate does suffer from that sometimes. As much as I love him, sometimes you have to really hammer hard to make a point heard. I mean that in the most endearing way because I love the guy.
>
> When I worked with the team, Craig would sit there and he would listen. If he thought it was bullshit, he would tell you. And I always felt that that was great. What you don't want is people sitting there, nodding just for the sake of it. It has to be bone deep and not skin deep. Craig was someone who only embraced things if they were bone-deep, not just niceties on the surface.

I did the minimal amount of work I had to do on the Leading Teams concept. I didn't like my team-mates coming up with that stuff about me. And I didn't even enjoy it when we were in the room talking about someone else in our team. One Black Cap was even told that he over-used humour to try to cover up certain things. You just want to play cricket and you had to put up with that rubbish!

Gilbert's system was far superior: it was more informal and if there was any problem it was taken upon the senior members to sort out. I remember when I was a junior member coming into the side, I couldn't think about misbehaving at all. You were so concentrated on cricket and playing well, off-field distractions didn't come into it.

Jesse Ryder's case is a classic example of this. If his indiscretions had been going on, then within the team set-up the senior guys would have stamped them out. They would have pulled him aside and said, 'Look mate, you are not giving yourself the best chance to perform. You need to pull your head in because you are letting your team and your team-mates down.' For Jesse to lapse like he did tells me that this Leading Teams thing is not working at all.

The peer assessments weren't the only new way that the Black Caps were asked to judge their team-mates during my final year in the side. Even more craziness was to follow in the World Cup in the West Indies.

We had to do player reviews after every game. The squad would be split up into three groups and each would be given five guys to comment on how they went the day before. Each team was tasked with judging the players in the group, giving them a rating from zero to 10.

The morning after every game we would wake up and marking sheets would have been slid under our hotel room door during the night. There would be a list of guys we would have to mark.

There were certain headings for various areas. With the bat it would include running between the wickets, shot selection and other areas. We were asked to mark our team-mates on energy they displayed on the field and the bowlers also had various areas that needed rating. If you had the perfect day you should get 10; if you had a bad day you should get zero.

Management were keeping the totals. So at the end of the year or campaign they would go through your totals and say, 'Right, these are the areas that you need to improve in.'

But the biggest problem to me was the whole system was just so selective. What you might consider to be an eight out of 10, another guy might consider to be a four. So depending on whether you had an easy marker or a hard marker, it was weird.

In our first game of the tournament against England I got 27 and holed out. So I was getting marks like five out of 10 along with comments from some team-mates saying: 'Only did half the job — should have seen it through.' The funniest thing was that Ross Taylor got a four-ball duck against England, yet he was getting marked at a five out of 10 by some people. I was sitting there thinking, 'OK, is no one allowed a zero in this team or what? Is it so PC that we just say he couldn't do much, got out first ball so I will just give him a four or a five?'

I just saw through it all and because of who I am, there were a couple of instances where I just gave guys a zero. I gave them the zero and said: 'Well, you didn't score any runs. How can you get a score? There is no point giving you a five when you are out first ball.' If someone got 25 or 30, they could get a five. But not if you are out for a duck!

So I sort of upset the whole thing with the marking. All of a sudden the marking questions came up and Flem said he wasn't too concerned about the marks, he was more worried about the response, the general feedback and the talk it created.

When we played the West Indies at Sir Vivian Richards Stadium in Antigua, I went into bat with Styris and it started spitting as I walked out to the middle. Under Duckworth-Lewis, if we'd lost another wicket we would have been in a lot of trouble. And at the time Scott was going really well. So my job was to hang around and get a partnership going with him. If we did that, we would win. That is just what we did: I ended up with 33 not out and we won. Scott ended unbeaten on 80.

It wasn't a pretty innings, but it was what was needed at the time. When we sat down and did the marking, Peter Fulton gave me a seven out of 10. Other guys were giving me nines or 10s. If there was a number that was askew, the leader of the group would ask: 'Why did you give him a seven because everyone else has given a nine?' Fulton said: 'Well, in my book no one can get a 10 and it wasn't his best innings.' I said to him, 'Well, what more could I do? I did the job, got 33 not out and we won.' The response was that everyone marked differently.

There was a real problem here. If you were keeping the scores for the coach at the end of the season, and you think you should get a nine but only get a seven, then you feel you are being ripped off.

John Bracewell: It wasn't about the numbers. What tends to happen is that people who are sensitive try to defend the numbers. It is as simple as that. But it ain't about the numbers at all. It is just a point of trying to find a difference. We have five players sitting in a circle; five of them have marked him as a seven and then all of a sudden someone has marked him as a two. Now there is a point of difference and you can ask, 'Why have you marked him as a two?'

That brings out a comment which is designed to help the guy get his game ready for the next game. And it provided me with a lot of stuff that I could use to tactically shift our guys at each practice. I could get a key onto what needed to be done at the next practice; it was quite invaluable to me. And most players who didn't defend the numbers actually found it of good benefit.

Guys who defended the numbers found it offensive and were defensive towards it. Just because of his nature, he was constantly on the alert for criticism. So a low number means a criticism, when in fact a low number just meant an observation that is designed to help you. Trying to get that change in mentality is quite difficult.

Like the peer assessments, I thought it was just bullshit. It was a friggin' nightmare. So I started marking it as brutally and honestly as I could. If guys did a job, like Styris did in the West Indies game, I would give them a 10. He got 80 not out and did the job. I got 33 not out, also did the job, and thought I should have at least got an eight or nine.

I truly felt that a lot of guys did the markings just to get through the meeting. They would rather put down a five or six so they weren't creating any conflict. There were cases when guys who were bowling were getting pounded and bowling wides and no balls, yet they were still getting six out of 10. It was so PC and guys were too worried to put down a zero on their mate — they were worried what their mate would think.

Daniel Vettori: I think Craig did actually believe in it, it was just his way of battling against it. If you sit down and talk to Craig, he has a good cricketing brain. The point of those reviews was to get good cricketing brains to the forefront and open up about a particular person's innings or what they did in the middle. While some guys might not like numbers, you do get a positive product of exactly what you do need to move forward. I know Craig was involved in some heated discussions — but that has been the nature of him for his whole career. I reckon he actually enjoyed them. He might put up a front that he didn't, but I think a lot of good stuff came out of them for him and for the team from him.

The other problem was in regards to senior guys like our captain Flem: it seemed that no one wanted to give him any low scores. It was all because he was the captain. But there were a couple of times when I gave him a two or three out of 10 because he had thrown his wicket away in different situations. That was what I thought he warranted. But the other guys weren't going to do that.

The whole scoring system that the management were keeping track of was so artificial and false. The only good thing about it was if a discussion came up afterwards and a couple of good points were raised. I can't say that wasn't always the situation. But some of the stuff discussed just saw us going around in circles.

Indian summers

In early November 2007 it was time to board a plane to India, and the debut Indian Cricket League Twenty20 tournament, just over a month after signing my ICL contract. It was a country I had toured three times previously, but this trip was far different from any of my visits dating back to the first time I toured India with the New Zealand team in the 1996–97 season under the coaching of Steve Rixon.

In so many ways it was a trip into the unknown, leaving New Zealand with high hopes but ultimately no real idea of just how this brave and exciting new era in world cricket would really go. But I didn't travel on my own when I boarded the plane to Mumbai; alongside me was my brother-in-law, mate and former Black Caps team-mate Nathan Astle, a member of the ICL's newly formed Mumbai Champs.

Once we arrived at Mumbai international airport it was amazing once again to be part of the recognition that cricketers get in India. It is almost as if nearly everyone watches cricket as we were spotted as soon as we started walking through the airport. The next couple of nights were spent in Mumbai, and wherever we went there seemed to be a real excitement directed our way. People knew what we were there for and, despite pessimism from some quarters, the ICL was being looked forward to.

I was the last to arrive in camp with the Kolkata Tigers, joining our coach, former South African batsman Daryll Cullinan and a variety of former international players including Rohan Gavaskar, Lance Klusener, Darren Maddy, Boyd Rankin, Upul Chandana and later on Nantie Hayward. The first week in camp was all about getting to know my new team-mates. While I'd played against a number of them, I didn't really know most of them very well. There were 15 Indian domestic players in our unit who I had never heard of. So it was a really good chance to see what they could do on the cricket pitch, learn their names and get a bit of team bonding going.

After the settling in period, it was time to head to Mumbai for a series of three matches against the Mumbai Champs, something which provided me with a good chance to catch up with Nathan again. Brian Lara was the big name in the Champs outfit, but he was missing from the practice matches, having turned up on the last day of the warm-up period. And even though he didn't figure in any of the games against us, it was virtually impossible to miss the impact he had in Mumbai once he arrived. It certainly was amazing to see the media contingent that followed him — he was like the Pied Piper. The media turned out in force to his welcoming press conference, and it seemed that everyone wanted to get a photo of him with their cellphones or cameras — they swarmed after Lara.

Our spirits were pretty high after beating Mumbai in all three warm-up matches. It was good to know we had a competitive-looking side — and off the field my pre-tournament nerves were also eased after talking to Tony Greig, one of ICL's key figures. He had played a huge hand in getting things organised, including scouting for international players for the debut season. It was really good to talk to him and get some reassurance about what was going on and what they were trying to achieve. After those warm-up matches, all the teams gathered in Mumbai and we had a dinner which doubled as the inaugural ICL launch. The main man behind the ICL, Subhash Chandra, came and spoke to the players. It was all done professionally and it was great to hear the vision behind the ICL.

With the pleasantries completed, all the teams headed for Chandigarh, with the northern city set to be our base for the next three weeks. While the debut ICL tournament had teams from six different regions, the pettiness of the BCCI had effectively banned our series from using any of its top-line stadiums from the regions which were represented in the ICL. So instead of each team having its own home ground, the first instalment of the ICL was to be played out at the Tau Devi Lal Sports Complex — a venue which five weeks before the first ball was bowled in the ICL resembled little more than a club ground.

The infrastructure we eventually had at the ground was effectively built up in little over a month before the action started — it seriously was built pretty much from scratch. A groundsman was hired from South Africa to work on the outfield and the pitch block. And the good thing about India is that you have a lot of helpers, people who are probably working below the minimum wage, and they got it done. It was incredible that they did everything like putting in a pitch block, laying the grass, erecting stands and putting up light towers in a month. But whether New Zealand's OSH laws would have given it a tick is another issue.

The Panchkula stadium is an overnight wonder
ICL website, 29 November 2007

The Tau Devi Lal Sports Complex cricket stadium, the venue for the ICL Indian 20:20 Championship has undergone a complete makeover in a matter of about five weeks.

'I have never seen things happen so fast. When I came here two days ago, there was nothing, just a lot of labourers. The stadium now has floodlights, stands, ground fencing, grass, a performance stage and an electronic screen is almost complete. This is amazing,' said a journalist from a leading Kolkata newspaper.

Rolls of grass were brought in by the organisers from nurseries neighbouring Chandigarh and Mohali also. Within a matter of hours they had been laid to give the place a lush green look.

The ground itself has a lush green look and the ICL management ensured the best in the business to do the pitches for the championship. 'We hired the best professionals from around the globe to do the square (pitches). I can assure you that the pitches will be extraordinary,' said Ashish Kaul, Executive Vice President of Essel group, which is promoting the ICL.

'We had a job at hand and we are happy to have accomplished that. Resources were never a problem but getting things are and putting them up was a race against time,' Kaul added.

The ICL took over the stadium in mid-October and was giving finishing touches to the entire stadium, a day before its 17-day championship gets under way. The stadium offers a beautiful backdrop of the Himalayan ranges.

The newly made media box with state-of-the-art facilities is unique too — it is housed in shipping containers converted into a luxury facility from inside. Foreign professionals could be seen lifting ladders, wires and other equipment to put things in place for the event along with the local labour force.

The work ethic of those involved in getting the ground sorted in time for the first match rubbed off on the players. At Chandigarh we stayed in the same hotel that the Black Caps had stayed in when I had last toured there in the 2003–04 season. It wasn't the flashest of hotels and we had a couple of guys who had to change rooms because there were rats running around.

As the countdown neared for the start the anticipation increased, but still there were some who weren't sure how it would play out. But everyone went with the flow, and whatever was organised we did. There had been so many stumbling blocks and hurdles put in the way of the ICL actually starting, for us to get to this point was a hell of an achievement in itself. We were there to make it work and be as successful as possible — we all had to roll our sleeves up and pitch in.

Signing with the Kolkata Tigers meant I had the chance to play in the same team as Lance Klusener, a guy who had won so many games for

South Africa against the Black Caps. And I had played in a lot of those games. It was great to be able to sit in the same changing room with him and talk about different aspects of our game. It was also great to be playing alongside some of the younger Indian players. They were like sponges; they just wanted to learn and play as much as possible. They listened and held onto any bit of advice you gave them. For them, it was a fantastic opportunity to be sitting in the same dressing room as a Lance Klusener or a Brian Lara. It is something I imagine they never thought they would ever be able to do in their wildest dreams.

It wasn't just the younger Indian players who had their eyes opened during the first ICL tournament. Some of the things they told me really stuck in my mind, in terms of the sacrifices and what they had given up to play in the ICL. A couple of the guys, including Reetinder Singh Sodi, who had played international cricket for India, went to watch India play a one-day international against Australia. But they were recognised as people who were aligned to the ICL and were barred from the ground. That is the length that the BCCI has gone to make life tough for those who are signed to the ICL.

They have also banned its players from training in the nets or any of the BCCI's other facilities. It has taken a lot of strength and willpower for the Indian players especially to have followed that path. It has been a hell of a decision for them to say, 'I am going to give up all of this and play in this new competition.' The thing is that they just want to play cricket. They are getting opportunities they wouldn't otherwise have got and their feeling is that they haven't been well treated by the Indian cricket authorities domestically. They don't feel any allegiance to the BCCI and have gone to this new organisation that they know will look after them better.

The debut ICL Twenty20 tournament was eventually won by the Chennai Superstars, with the Kolkata Tigers making it as far as the semi-finals. The ratings were great on Zee Television and it went out to about 150 countries. But it obviously wasn't broadcast in Australia and New Zealand. And I can't see it being shown in New Zealand with Sky's association with New Zealand Cricket — they won't want to give it any leverage at all, which is disappointing because I'm sure there is a market here.

The ICL was an exciting tournament and venture to be part of. As I packed up to return home to New Zealand in time for a very rare Christmas with my family, I did so with the realisation that I could see no reason why the ICL can't survive up against the BCCI's IPL. There has been talk about how there could be a merger between the two tournaments down the line, but there will be a lot of water which will have to go under the bridge before that can happen. There is just so much enthusiasm for cricket in

India and people who want to be associated with teams over there that I am sure the ICL will survive as long as its boss wants it to survive.

Christmas 2007 was the first time I had been able to spend the entire festive season with my family in 11 years. Two of the other New Zealanders involved in the debut ICL event returned to the New Zealand domestic scene, Chris Harris with Canterbury and Daryl Tuffey with Auckland. For me, a holiday in Queensland beckoned with Cherie and the kids. Then, before I knew it, it was time to return to India for the second Twenty20 instalment of the ICL. In the intervening months, the New Zealand contingent in the ICL had grown — Shane Bond had signed with the Delhi Giants after messy and very public negotiations with New Zealand Cricket, André Adams was joining me at the Kolkata Tigers and Lou Vincent had suddenly terminated his NZC contract to sign with the Chandigarh Lions after battling depression.

The arrival of that very talented trio was one of many changes as the ICL sought to show it was a sporting venture with credibility. That included an exciting expansion of the tournament — with teams being introduced from Lahore and Ahmedabad. The Lahore Badshahs are effectively an international side, featuring 14 past Pakistani internationals in their side. And, on paper, if they were to play the Pakistan national side at the moment, I have no doubt that they would quite comfortably beat them. Right across the board, the teams were strengthened for the second tournament. More Australians were added to the playing rosters, guys like Damien Martyn, Michael Kasprowicz and Jimmy Maher.

The expansion proved to be a massive success, with Lahore eventually losing the final to the Hyderabad Heroes. My beloved Kolkata Tigers made the semi-finals, eventually losing the play-off for third and fourth to the Chennai Superstars. A combination of the expansion and increased depth of talent contributed to the TV ratings going through the roof for the second tournament. The tournament was also picked up by Ten Sports, a huge move as it meant ICL action had the potential to be broadcast into 48 million homes in places such as Pakistan, Dubai, Sri Lanka, Bangladesh and Singapore. While the TV coverage worldwide increased greatly, New Zealand's Sky TV still had found no place for it. It's a move which means New Zealanders who want to taste some ICL action will have too do so via the internet.

Another initiative was the post-tournament triangular series between the Pakistan 11, the Indian 11 and the World 11. The week-long tournament is a key concept because it means the young Indian players we are playing with, and trying to develop, have something to achieve and aim for. Obviously, the BCCI has banned them from ever playing for India, so the goal of playing internationally has been taken away from them. Now the best Indian players in the ICL have the chance to play international cricket of sorts. That is something that is very important and something I think will be successful in the long term.

The other big difference during the second tournament was that we had three match venues, instead of just the one we had in Chandigarh for the first event. The organisers added Hyderabad and Gurgaon, near Delhi, as well as the original specially built venue in Chandigarh. It's a move which will take the ICL to an even bigger audience, allowing fans to feel more ownership of the teams when they get the chance to watch their regional team play in the flesh.

The ICL has received no lack of negative headlines, dating back well before the first match was played in late 2007. It has been said that the series wouldn't last, that no one would be interested and that too many of the international players signing up for the cricket venture were past it. But that negativity is missing in the environment where it is being played out — in fact in India there is a wealth of positivity surrounding the ICL. And it is a sporting venture which some of the most-famous names in the massive Bollywood film industry have taken notice of. A lot of Bollywood stars are coming on board with the ownership of teams — and the Kolkata Tigers are no different, with hugely respected Mithun Chakraborty taking on an ownership stake during the second ICL tournament.

The news was announced at a press conference in Kolkata, which a few of us on the team roster also attended. I've obviously been to a few press sessions during my career — but nothing like this! Between 120 and 130 journalists were on hand, as well as 30 to 40 TV cameras. Having Mithun Chakraborty on board will open a lot of doors for us — it certainly adds a lot of credibility to the brand. Everyone I talked to about him agreed that he was a massive star and a real hero from Bengal. The scenes at the press conference were full on. The 60-odd photographers were all shoving each other as they tried to get the perfect shot. Our table was being pushed around — and it was a little bit freaky until the security guards came in to settle the chaos. It just showed how big the Bollywood stars are in India.

Mithun Chakraborty picks up stake in Kolkata Tigers
ICL website, 27 March 2008

In a strategic move, the Indian Cricket League today announced its association with Bengal's favourite son and Bollywood icon, Mithun Chakraborty, at a press conference held in the city. As per the alliance, Mithunda will own a stake in ICL's Kolkata Tigers team and would be instrumental in endorsing and promoting the team.

Speaking on the occasion, the evergreen Bollywood actor Mithunda said, 'I always maintained that sport in Bengal needs a bigger and better platform for promoting sports people from Bengal. Keeping the millions of Bengalis in mind, I have associated with ICL to promote Kolkata Tigers. I would want to see more domestic players becoming national icons from my city of joy.'

Kapil Dev, Chairman, Executive Board, Indian Cricket League, said, 'It is heartening to see a living legend of Indian cinema promote sport. There is a lot of similarity in our vision and passion for sport. Mithunda's association with the ICL will greatly help in promoting the young domestic players from the eastern region. His support is going to help us display the best cricketing talent from the eastern zone.'

ICL is currently promoting the Edelweiss 20s Challenge which is being held in three locations: Hyderabad, Chandigarh and Gurgaon. The tournament promises 30 days of non-stop pulsating cricket from March 9th to April 7th, 2008. Two new teams — Ahmedabad Rockets and Lahore Badshahs — have also been added to the existing six teams, making the tournament more comprehensive and competitive. With international cricketers of high stature being added to the league, the quality of cricket is expected to be on par with international standards.

Kapil Dev was also there, along with the Sports Minister from Bengal who announced that he was going to allow our team to play at the famous Eden Gardens ground. That was fantastic news, especially considering the pressure the BCCI put on various ground owners not to allow us to play at their stadiums for the first ICL tournament. But the attitude was that as the IPL had been granted permission to play at Eden Gardens, there was no reason why it couldn't also be given to the ICL. It was huge.

In all my time of playing for the Black Caps and touring India, I had never got the opportunity to play at Eden Gardens. Watching on TV, and reading about the venue, it really is one of the world's great cricketing grounds. It was also announced that we would be renamed the Royal Bengal Tigers for the third ICL tournament, instead of just the Kolkata Tigers. That means that instead of just being consigned to Kolkata, we will represent the whole district. There will now be a lot more fans we can get to.

In terms of marketing and exposure in India, the ICL can't compete with the IPL — the latter is just on another wavelength. The amount of money being thrown at the IPL is unbelievable and it is not really an option for us to go head-to-head with the IPL. But one of the advantages the ICL has is that they will have three tournaments a year, whereas the IPL is all over in a month — within a few weeks each year it is done and dusted. The ICL will be there in three different slots throughout the year; it is continual and people will get to know that. The ICL is something that I believe a lot of people expected would fall over pretty quickly. But the more and more I have seen from playing in the tournament, the more I realise that this concept could continue on for a number of years.

I truly believe that the IPL is actually more of a threat to international cricket than the ICL. I base that purely on the fact that the ICL wants its players (such as Shane Bond) to be able to continue playing for their country. And when he is not playing for his country, well then he will play in the ICL. With the IPL you are seeing examples already of international tours being rescheduled. You have also seen the possibility of players from the West Indies preferring to play in the IPL instead of playing test cricket against Australia because of the amounts of money on offer. Those sorts of things are hugely damaging to the game.

I still struggle with the notion that the ICL is going to be harmful for international cricket. They have stated all along that they want players to still be playing international cricket. But, unfortunately, the guys can't because a lot of the respective international boards have banned them as they don't want to harm their relationships with the BCCI. I have no doubt that if that approach hadn't been taken by bodies such as New Zealand Cricket and the English and Wales Cricket Board, a number of the guys signed with the ICL would still be playing international cricket for their respective countries. And I think New Zealand is one of the best examples of that — guys like Lou Vincent and Shane Bond would still be eligible for the Black Caps.

On the same side

Stephen Fleming is a player who had more heaped on his shoulders in the 10 years I was associated with the Black Caps than any other player. Not surprising, as he was captain through this period, but at times the burden definitely dragged him down to his lowest point where he basically wanted to resign after the 2000–01 series against Sri Lanka.

Being the skipper of an international side at the age of 23 is no mean achievement. But right from the start, Flem had all the credentials to succeed. The Rixon/Graham management team was perfect for him, allowing him to grow into the job over a number of years.

He is very articulate, so getting a message across was never a problem for Flem, and he had the respect of the team because he was our best batsman. But there is no doubt that had his conversion rate been better over the years our success as a team would have increased. It could have been similar to what Steve Waugh achieved with Australia. A lot of their success was built around the hundreds he scored.

Despite not having the number of hundreds he would have liked, Flem has a huge number of records in New Zealand cricket and they will take a number of years for anyone to surpass. It's amazing that three of them are big double-hundreds. Once he got to 100 he could kick on.

He could make batting look so easy and those long levers made striking the ball effortless. But over the years he became very technical in his approach to batting. The media sure had a fascination with his conversion rate but after stints in County cricket it seemed that batting long periods and scoring hundreds wasn't a problem any longer.

At times I know I used to frustrate him. He couldn't understand why the likes of me and Nathan Astle wouldn't be hitting as many balls or putting the same amount of time into our games as he was. All I can say is that we were different from him. He felt comfortable and confident after hitting 300 balls — I would feel the same way after 30.

He used to bat sometimes twice as long as the rest of us in the nets, then he would have countless throw-downs at the end. He crunched his game up so tight, especially when he began opening in tests for New Zealand.

My last test was against Australia in Wellington. Bracewell told me Flem was moving back down the order and someone had to make way for him and, unfortunately, that was me. With that my test career was effectively over, even though my stats at that time were superior to others.

Flem went through different periods in which he chopped and changed where he wanted to bat — from No. 4 to No. 3, to opening to back to No. 4, then back to No. 3. His best position was definitely at No. 3, where he averaged 49.

When he let himself go he could be very destructive. His innings of 106 off 57 balls against the Fica World XI at Christchurch during the Tsunami Series showed how good he could be. Muttiah Muralitharan has never received treatment like that in his whole career from anyone — not Gilchrist, not Lara, not anyone.

The fact he wasn't considered good enough to be picked in the Black Caps side for the 2007 Twenty20 World Cup was a disgrace. He should have been there, full stop. We would have been a better side with him.

I found it amazing that he got Richard Boock, one of his (and my) most severe detractors to write his book. I guess it might have bought him some time from criticism from the author, but I bet he regrets it now after the disgraceful articles written by the author around the time Flem was being linked to the ICL. I hear they don't talk any more, but then most in the team don't like talking to the 'poison pen'. But unfortunately they have to.

I'm sure on retirement Flem will have job offers lined up all over the table. To me his career will be remembered for many things but maybe his best achievement was as someone who had the skills as captain to turn an average New Zealand cricket team into a very good international side who believed they could beat anybody.

Shane Bond is someone I have known since we played primary school cricket together and against one another. To be honest, there were no real signs at that early age that Bondy would end up being one of New Zealand's greatest-ever fast bowlers. And cricket didn't figure prominently for him until he took time out from his career with the New Zealand Police and committed fully to the game.

The number of injuries and setbacks he has suffered over his career has been horrific. His career has been shorted by many years; it's incredible to think he only played 17 tests for the Black Caps.

It also amazes me the criticism he has endured about the injuries. Just how many of those voicing their opinions have had their spine fused back together? Not many I'm guessing!

Shane was probably the most professional guy in our team in terms of the amount of fitness work he did. Despite his run of injuries, he worked so hard. It must have been so demoralising dealing with setback after setback, having to start from scratch again.

Looking back, it really amazes me that he stuck at it as long as he did. Many others would have thrown the towel in long ago.

And when he played he gave us a point of difference, genuine pace with swing. During the 2002 VB ODI tri-series in Australia he was unplayable. The way he had the Aussies on the back foot was sensational and Flem suddenly had a weapon he could navigate.

The rest of our attack became better bowlers overnight as batters took more risks against them rather than Shane. His best performances always seemed to come against the best teams — he certainly had a knack for stepping up and Australia really bore the brunt of Bondy at his best.

I think part of his success was that when he came into cricket he was a pretty well rounded individual; cricket hadn't been the be-all and end-all of his life to that point.

I think it's a great shame that the last two or three years of Shane's career will be played out in India, instead of for the Black Caps. What a pity New Zealand Cricket couldn't have worked out something to have kept our best player in the game here.

After the injuries he suffered, his top speed probably dropped by between 5 and 10 kph. But he made up for that with some subtle variations that made him the complete article, matched by being ranked the world's No. 1 ODI bowler at the time of his parting from NZC. And he will be more useful in years to come with passing on his knowledge of fast bowling to young up and comers than New Zealand's only other great fast bowler.

Kyle Mills' game has grown unbelievably over the last three years, a period in which he has been our best one-day bowler. He has been in and out of the side over the years, but is now an established member of the Black Caps in both forms of the game.

His batting is underrated but will be very important over the coming years. And the insecurity and paranoia of earlier years are gone. The key to Millsy is he swings the ball, maybe not at great speed, but swing gets good players out and that's what Kyle does.

People think Cantabs are one-eyed. Well, they should meet Kyle. He is a self-confessed Auckland rugby expert who is blindly loyal. And Mr Rugby is very funny to be around. At the 2003 World Cup in South Africa we decided to have a World Series of Pool over 11 games. Our team room had a pool table that kept us entertained for the duration of the tournament.

I'm no Stephen Hendry but I was still sharp enough to take the spoils, much to Kyle's disgust. We played a second tournament as I was worried the loss had upset him so much that it might affect his cricket. Luckily, he won the second! Man it was competitive and the sledging was certainly as piercing as anything I heard on a cricket pitch.

He is regarded as one of the snazziest dressers in the New Zealand side, but that's just an Auckland thing. It is great to see Kyle getting the credit he deserves for his performances after overcoming some fairly serious injuries.

Chris Harris was once a regular in the New Zealand side, going back to 1990 when he actually had hair. And for much of his 14-year international career he was the people's poet — the punters loved him as he was so often the battler who always got New Zealand out of a tough position. Well, almost always.

He loved playing it up on the field: he used to make the simplest catch or stop look ridiculously hard and the public would buy it. Among the team we used to wet ourselves when he would do this, it was so theatrical.

Of course, there were many, many times when his athleticism was outstanding on the field — some of his fielding was freakish. At his peak he was as good a fielder as South Africa's Jonty Rhodes; both were great stoppers of the ball, their one weakness was they didn't hit the stumps that often.

We sometimes wondered why Harry took a bat out with him as invariably he would get hit on the pad first ball. No one in the changing room would take the bet on him using his bat first up.

I have no doubt Harry could have been a very good test player, if only he had the self-belief he has when he bats at first-class level. He never transcended that into his test game, which was sad. When we would bat in the nets on a tough practice wicket most of us would struggle to lay bat on ball, but not Harry, who would be smashing everyone to all parts. I used to wonder how he couldn't do this in test matches.

There's no doubt too much sugar for Chris was a really bad thing for his team-mates. He just couldn't sit down; he was your typical dressing room pest. Harry also loved the camera: Harry Vision was right up his alley. He used to follow us around everywhere with his camera, putting on a special voice when he was filming — it was classic.

In the last of his 250 one-day internationals against Australia in 2004 he suffered a horrific shoulder injury while fielding. I was 12th man so got to field the last 30 overs when Harry was off the pitch. Despite the serious nature of his injury he still came into bat during our run chase, dropping down to No. 11 and batted one-handed against Brett Lee while Kyle Mills nearly won the game for us. It was one of the gutsiest things I've seen.

The shoulder injury was so bad he was out of cricket for over 12 months. When he came back the furthest he could throw was 25 metres. That was just shattering for someone once regarded as one of the best fielders in the world. He had lost his mojo.

Being the battler he is, he can now throw almost from the boundary and at the age of 38 he is still an amazing cricket player. We always said he'd still be playing for Canterbury at 40. Well, it wouldn't surprise me if that was 45 now, he loves playing so much.

Nathan Astle and I have known each other for years and now that we are brothers-in-law we will be spending a lot of time together in the future. Our kids are the same age and already enjoy one another's company.

I'd hate to think how many games we have played together over the years from club to international cricket. His dropping from the ODI side in the 2006–07 season no doubt hastened his retirement from the game in the lead-up to the 2007 Cricket World Cup. He should have been having a final hurrah and opening for us at the World Cup in the West Indies, where his experience of three previous tournaments would have been invaluable.

His decision to retire was so understated, but that is just Nath. His enjoyment had gone so he felt it was time to move on — no fuss; it was just time to go. I had known for a while he wasn't enjoying his cricket, especially under the Black Caps' management regime. But I did think he would guts it out to the World Cup. Bracewell and Co never regained his trust after he had been dropped.

The one good thing about his retirement was that at least it got him out of his room for a change and we had a great night on the drink at a local pub in Perth celebrating (if that's the right word!) his decision. Nath's nature is very quiet: on and off the field he didn't say boo. His bat was the only thing that did the talking.

Later in his career he became more vocal off the field, maybe because he could see more things going wrong. I'm sure his friendship with Flem meant at times he wasn't as loud as he wanted to be as the things being put in place had to be favoured not only by the coach but the captain as well.

We would often talk and the frustration of making a simple game hard by too much talk was evident. Inadvertently, when he made a century we more often than not won games. Nathan was a proven match-winner. His ODI record will mean he will go down as probably our greatest ever limited overs player. The other part of Nathan was his nagging medium-pacers that always seemed to secure a wicket and his fielding. His one-handed catch against the West Indies in 2006 was an absolute gem.

There was a downside to Nathan, though, and that was rooming with him. He was a nightmare as he was an absolute tidiness freak, almost to the point where he had a problem. The room was virtually divided in two. His side of the room looked very different to mine, clothes separated, folded neatly, shoes next to one another in a row. That was just the way things had to be for him.

The boys used to love opening his cricket bag and roughing up his whites from the systematised way they were folded. Nath didn't find that funny but there was a chuckle from most in the changing room.

We toured Sri Lanka in 1998 and man it was hot. Six of us — Flem, Dan, Cairnsy, Hornet, Nath and me — decided it was so hot that we would each get a No. 1 haircut. It was a big surprise when Nath agreed as we knew how important his all-round look was to him, and even more important was his hair.

Off we went to Dan's room and out came the clippers, Dan and I being the youngest we went first, followed by the oldies. Flem was doing a bit of back tracking at the sight of the first three cuts but was persuaded by Cairns that he would still look great so he went through with it. That left only Nathan. Well, not only was he back tracking but he was reversing out the room as fast as he could, much to the disgust of his team-mates. No convincing could get him to cut his locks and the same haircut he had on debut 13 years ago still sits proudly on his head!

Nath could also be very stubborn. The only thing harder than getting Nath to change his hairstyle was getting a round of drinks out of him! In the next few years cricket will be still be a big part of our lives playing in the ICL, and hopefully the enjoyment and fun will return to the level at which it all started.

Scott Styris has been a useful player for a number of years for New Zealand, especially in the one-day arena. Even though he started as a bowler, who batted a bit, he always had the tools to become a batsman. At the 2007 Cricket World Cup he found a rich seam of form and was outstanding throughout the tournament.

His bowling was a big part of his game and it's only recently that it has dropped off to the point where he now bowls more fast off-spinners than medium-pacers. I'm sure this has had an adverse affect on his batting, as he was at his performing best when heavily involved in a game.

His retirement from test cricket puts a lot more pressure on him to keep performing in one-day internationals, especially with his limited bowling these days. I'm sure a job in the Sky commentary team will be chased when he does retire.

Brendon McCullum is really just beginning to show how good he is going to be over the next five or six years. I'm certainly one of those who are glad he is finally opening for the Black Caps in ODIs, as this is the position in which he will win many a game for New Zealand.

When he first made the New Zealand side in 2002 he got thrown in the deep end opening and wasn't a success. But he was very raw and his game hadn't developed to where it is now. He's a better player now for batting down at No. 7 or No. 8 and learning how to win games. I love the confidence he brings to the crease — the opposition know they are in for a battle.

His maturity as a person has translated into his game to the point where he will be the dominant figure in New Zealand cricket for a number of years to come. He's a man in a hurry in a lot of ways.

I have no doubt that at some stage he will captain the Black Caps, his rise to the side's vice-captaincy has just been so rapid. After Dan, he is the logical replacement.

Confidence has never been a problem from the first day Baz arrived in the Black Caps. And that's vital for the wicket-keeper in your side because they set so many of the standards that the team revolves around.

His wicket-keeping has got better and better over the last couple of years to the point that, technically, he would be the best around. The odd lapse that plagued him, including dropping Rahul Dravid at the 2003 World Cup, has disappeared. I know Steve Rixon has played a big part in this.

Keepers are showmen: they love hearing their voice on TV through the stump microphone. Parore was the same and Baz is no different. He's one of the few who is prepared to chip away at the opposition, giving anything to get an edge or create an opportunity for a wicket.

The thing I like about Baz is that he is a gambler. He's prepared to take risks on the field and I've always thought that brings bigger rewards. He's one of the guys I enjoyed spending time with, either on the golf course or around the card table.

Daniel Vettori and I first came across each other on the New Zealand under-19 tour to England in 1996 and our friendship has been firmly entrenched since then. We were coached by John Bracewell and there were other New Zealand players-in-waiting on that tour — Jacob Oram, Gareth Hopkins and Matthew Bell.

Dan stood out from an early stage. There was nothing to him and he looked like a twig (I mean that in a good way mate!) that would have been 55 kg ringing wet. He looked anything but a cricketer but within a year he was playing test cricket for New Zealand.

To be thrown into international cricket at the age of 18 is a daunting prospect and the way Dan's career has progressed to this point is testament to his amazing skill and determination. He comes across relaxed, but inside he is fairly intense and fiercely competitive.

He's also a statistics freak — not quite in Richard Hadlee's class, but not far behind! — who knows not only his own stats but everyone else's. He's our 'Mr Cricket' if you like and he's the only guy I know that travels with the *New Zealand Cricket Almanack* in his cricket coffin. Any cricket question game played while watching a day's play is usually dominated by Dan!

Dan's action has changed dramatically over the years due to his ongoing back problems. When he first started I remember him being a big turner of the ball, with a big hop and bound in his action. Despite losing some of the turn, experience has taught him the use of flight and varied pace. The only thing properly still the same is the sight of his tongue!

He is such an important part of the attack through the middle overs of a one-day international and so well respected that for a couple of series the Australians didn't attack him at all. They just nudged him around, which was completely against the Aussie style of play, but testament that they rated him. They played Dan very circumspectly and were content to stop him from taking wickets, hence putting the rest of our attack under pressure.

His changes of pace and flight are so subtle now that you very rarely get a bad ball from him. He can tie up an end while the seamers attack from the other. Dan really is a true all-rounder now with his batting such an important part of the New Zealand lower order. He hits the ball to some parts of the field that the ball just shouldn't go to, in the process frustrating opposition teams.

On our tour to Australia in 2001–02 we were playing a test match and the team player profiles came up. We had been ribbing each other for a while about whether I would get a ball next to my name or him a bat next to his. Needless to say he was less than impressed on seeing a red round thing next to my name and no brown bat next to his. I reckon this was his motivation to develop his batting to the point where I don't mind admitting now it has leap-frogged my bowling!

Being a deep thinker of the game, it came as no surprise that he developed as the successor to Flem. I'm sure the challenge of captaincy had always been a goal of his. In all honesty, I wish he had just been the one-day international captain for a year or so and then he could have learnt more from Flem before taking over the test captaincy.

I reckon he has taken a bit of a hospital pass with all the retirements and loss of players and the next couple of years could be tough for him, especially in the test arena. As long as his back holds together he will break all appearance records for New Zealand plus many more records. Being a spinner he could play for another eight or nine years. Time will tell whether he lasts that long but New Zealand cricket will be stronger if he does.

Jacob Oram is an entertainer who has amazing power with the bat. He certainly adds a nice balance to the team when he plays.

Big Jake was also the prime reason for the early end to my test career and was a Bracewell favourite from the start. He has been labelled the next Chris Cairns, which I'm sure at times has put extra pressure on his shoulders to perform. He could end up being a better batsman than Cairns, but he won't touch him on the bowling front. He has also had a very injury-prone couple of years where he picked up injuries out of nowhere.

Jake was supposed to bat at No. 3 in a Bracewell experiment at the ICC World Twenty20 tournament, but that lasted all of one ball after he was hit in the head by a Brett Lee bouncer in a warm-up game. I'm sure over the next few years Jake's contributions with the bat will win some important games for New Zealand and then the tag 'match winner' will sit more comfortably than it does at present.

Jake has a great sense of humour that spares no one, including himself, and can defuse tense situations. Funnily enough, he was told at a peer assessment review to cut back on his humour and not to use it as a front. Some people just didn't quite understand that it is just his personality. But I did get the feeling that at times he is too quick to try and please too many people

Hopefully, he will be a major contributor to New Zealand cricket's success over the next few years.

Ross Taylor excites me every time he bats. I love the way he believes he can hit every ball for four and I hope that belief doesn't get coached out of him or disappear after a few failures fuelled by criticism.

He can dominate and change the course of a game in overs and that can't be coached. I see a lot of myself in Ross at that age when I watch him bat — an aggressive approach that is far from bulletproof, but one that will be entertaining and exciting. But it won't work all the time.

Ross has had a great start to his international cricket career; the only blip has been his catching. I have never seen someone go through an extended period of dropping catches. The strange thing was I fielded with him at training and he wouldn't drop one and many were a lot harder than the ones he was shelling in games.

As one of our quickest and best fielders he was put in positions where the ball was more likely to go. Unfortunately, when we tried to give him some breathing space in quiet areas it still managed to find him. He seems at home at first slip and has taken some beauties there recently so the blip is well and truly over.

While at the 2007 World Cup in the West Indies we had a few dinners where we chatted about batting and his eagerness to learn will hold him in good stead in the coming years where he will become a dominant force in the New Zealand line-up.

Mathew Sinclair is a strange fellow. I have known 'Skippy' since we toured Australia in 1995 on an under-19 tour. To be honest, he hasn't changed one little bit.

Things he was being told on that tour are still being told to him. I'm sure his inability to listen and make changes to his batting has cost him plenty of games for New Zealand over the years.

One thing about Mathew is that when he gets in he is tough to get out, something shown by the two test double-hundreds he has scored. That amazing 214 on debut against the West Indies should have booked his ticket for years to come. But, unfortunately, it was followed by a consistent run of failures.

I remember players and coaches talking to Skippy about the need to play with soft hands and to be able to rotate the strike. Yet year after year he would be trying to trash the ball through the off-side. We used to sit in the changing room shaking our heads at how many times Mathew would hit good shots to fielders.

At Canterbury we would put up 'the great Wall of China' on the off-side of the field and he would try to hit the ball harder and harder through the gap, of which there was none. This hitting of the fielder created pressure on his partner at the other end and I'm sure it is a reason he is not considered a real ODI option. His strike rate isn't high enough and that's from his inability to get a single to get off strike.

He had an extended run in the test team during the 2007–08 international season and couldn't make the grade. I don't think there will be any more chances coming his way.

Peter Fulton is a laid-back sort of fellow and has struggled due to inconsistency from the selectors. His best position is at No. 3 in both forms of the game and that is where he was told he was going to bat before a late change of thinking from the selectors saw him dropped to No. 6.

He never seemed to recover from that. You have to realise there's a big difference between the two positions. At No. 3 you have the advantage of being able to score quickly by just playing normal cricket shots due to the fielding restrictions, but at No. 6 you need to be a bit more of a risk taker by scoring at better than a run a ball and having the ability to hit the ball to the boundary is a must.

Peter showed glimpses of this during the 2007 Chappell-Hadlee series in New Zealand. But there's no doubt that New Zealand will get the best out of him at the top of the order. He's also a good fielder who is deceptively quick over the ground. He loves his Coca-Cola and has a sharp sense of humour.

Roger Twose brought so many things to the New Zealand dressing room. He was a showman who loved entertaining. He had a great cricket brain from many years of playing professionally in England for Warwickshire and he was an exhibitionist who loved confrontation. He also loved being on TV.

Twose became one of the best one-day international batters in his latter years while unfortunately never coming to grips with test cricket. He bagged a pair at Edgbaston, his home ground for Warwickshire, on our England tour in 1999 before eventually being dropped.

When he was batting, he used to shout calls even when he was blocking the ball; it was a real show of his intent to the opposition. It was so loud I'm sure everyone in the crowd could hear. He also used to cop it from the Aussies about being a Pom playing for New Zealand, but he always gave as good as got.

When he went out to bat he used to wear a body armour suit that, to be frank, looked bloody ridiculous. It was like he was heading into battle and if he had the suit on he was going to be OK. Teams used to bowl short to him, thinking he was poor at playing it and he did wear a few on the body.

Twose became a one-day specialist after finishing with test cricket. It was like he turned over a new leaf and he carved up many a side in one-day internationals when they bowled short to him. The transformation was truly remarkable.

He had a real swagger about him and his sense of humour was vital to the team at times. His one-day international shirt number was 77. He chose this number because he reckoned it made him look thinner on TV! I guess 11 would have been his first choice but Dan Vettori had nabbed that number. He would have been great at Twenty20 cricket.

Mark Richardson's move from left-arm spinner to left-hand opening batsman was an amazing transformation. You certainly had to admire the changes he made.

And to do it with the diligence and reach the standard that Rigor did, there had to be a certain amount of compulsiveness and selfishness. Many in the side would say he was one of the most selfish cricketers we played with, but he added real value to the test team and made the rest of our jobs a little bit easier.

New Zealand Cricket has been looking for a replacement since his retirement and it's fair to say no one has come close. Rigor would spend more time than anyone batting in the nets or getting throw-downs to the point that others waiting for their turn to bat would be frustrated.

His mental toughness was his strength; he knew his limitations and played to them religiously. He knew where he could hit the ball and where he couldn't.

The only time things got complicated was when one-day international cricket got thrown into the mix. Playing limited overs cricket meant expanding his game and range of shots which he just couldn't do. It was a source of discontent for him, but his game was so regimented that by expanding it he risked it falling apart completely. But at least he got the coveted black ODI shirt that he longed for.

I've never seen someone as angry on getting out as Rig; he just loved batting. He would go nuts when he played a loose shot, as he did once when he threw his bat 20 metres in disgust after running a quick single — his expression was priceless.

He was one of the most negative people you could come across, very nervous before he batted but steady as a rock once in the middle. At times he could be a character; the beige suit and running races against the slowest member of the opposition took on their own importance. It was like he had an alter ego.

In hindsight perhaps a career in the media wasn't surprising. I loved talking to him because we could debate things for hours. In the end, though, I would have to walk away after reaching a stalemate. He could be defensive and stubborn, traits I guess an opener needed.

We had many a chat on the Australian tour of 2004. I wasn't getting picked so was feeling low and he wasn't in a great frame of mind with a real feeling of anger and frustration towards the media and, at the end of his career in particular, our Sky commentators whom he felt should have had a more balanced view, being ex-players.

That said, he slipped into the seat next to them pretty quickly; I guess things are different when they're paying the bills. We had disagreements on things he was saying and I for one certainly felt he should have stuck up for us more when the others were delivering their usual degrading views. He had just left the set-up and knew as a team what we were trying to achieve.

His reply was that he was being paid for an opinion and that was what he was doing — fair comment, I guess. It's not until you leave the game that you understand that. When you're a player you tend to take things personally; we both probably did that.

I actually think Rigor is a pretty good commentator now. He seems a lot more comfortable and at ease and is a more positive now than he was as a player. He thinks about the game deeply and I hear a real passion in his voice. I just hope he doesn't get too technical or try to compete with the others.

He would always be the first picked in my test side.

Lou Vincent would always make my side and he is probably the most-talented cricketer I have seen. He had all the shots against any bowler, he could destroy attacks, he could also bowl and he has kept for New Zealand as well.

The only thing that held Lou back was his self-belief, or at times lack of it. I sat there puzzled sometimes wondering how he could go from one of the best players in the world one day, to someone that looked like they hadn't picked up a cricket bat for months.

I guess his recent revelations about depression explain a lot of the ups and downs, along with his constant changing up and down the order and in and out of the team by the selectors. None of this has helped him become the cricketer he should have been.

How someone can score 224 in a test batting at No. 4, then next test be moved to open, defies logic. He got a bum rap for that one. Even though he was a replacement for Styris who was injured, Lou had every right to bat No. 4 in the next test. Styris should have been moved or not made the side — that's what happens when you get injured, you give someone the opportunity to take your spot.

Lou often listened to a lot of people and I think this confused him on how he should play. I always said to him, 'Just play mate', because I knew that if he kept it simple he would be successful.

His fielding behind point was electric and many a time he kept us in the game with a run out. I think fielding was his outlet to show the public who Lou Vincent was. And he was definitely the showman in our side.

As good and quick as Lou was in the field, he sometimes had the odd case of the 'dropsies'. I remember him dropping Inzamam ul-Haq in a test in Lahore in 2002 just after he had got a hundred. When we next met up at drinks he quipped that he hoped Inzie didn't get a double-century. Much to our disgust he got 334 and we fielded for three days!

He fancied himself as a cameraman on tour and some of the material he produced was hilarious. My lasting impression of Lou will always be during one of many periods of down-time at the 2007 Cricket World Cup. He ran around behind our coach John Bracewell, who was being interviewed by Mark Richardson, virtually naked, imitating Borat in a lime green bathing suit. There was always some laughter to be had around the Black Caps whenever Lou was nearby.

Dion Nash couldn't be beaten when it came to being a driven and competitive cricketer. He had a real fire inside that used to burn strong on the cricket field — it had to for him to overcome the many injuries he suffered throughout his career. For someone that was so physically fit, and strong, it must have been so frustrating.

Not only did Dion have to overcome the injuries but he also had to cope with a massive change in his bowling action that had crept in and got to the point where his bowling had become largely ineffective. He changed this and became a vital part of the New Zealand side with the ball.

The one positive of the injuries was that he spent a lot more time on his batting to the stage where Dion was a genuine all-rounder at the end of his career. I always left the changing room on Dion's dismissal — you could see the red mist coming from his ears as he left the ground and his gear generally went flying all over the place!

He loved playing the Aussies: there were always verbals when Dion was around, and I think he dragged the rest of us along with him. He also played a big part in our success on the England tour in 1999, showing then that he was someone who loved leading the way. Dion would have been a very good international captain but, unfortunately, his opportunities were limited due to Flem's long reign.

Off the field, he played a big role in the creation of the Players' Association. Dion was a strong voice for the players during that turbulent period and he made it very clear during that time that he was never afraid to stand up and commit to something he believed in.

Now it is great that he is on the Black Caps' selection panel. We need more younger people like him in those positions, instead of some of the older generation that we go for as a safety net.

Chris Cairns will be remembered as one of New Zealand's best all-rounders. When not bedevilled by injury, he was as close to the complete cricketer as you could find. His batting was good enough that he could have made the side on that alone, but Cairnsy always had to be bowling to feel the part.

He saw himself as an entertainer and tailored his batting to do just that. Chris probably hit the ball as hard and long as anyone in the game and bowling to him in the nets was at times terrifying. Some of the shots he played against Shane Warne when Australia toured New Zealand in 2000 were out of this world; he was probably at his batting peak around this time.

Chris' bowling was at times quick and, with the invention of a quality slower ball, he was good enough to be New Zealand's third-highest test wicket-taker. I've got no doubt that the appointments of Steve Rixon as Black Caps coach and John Graham as manager were instrumental in getting the most out of Chris.

He was an immensely talented player who sometimes struggled with those who weren't so gifted. Unfortunately, like a lot of New Zealand's leading bowlers in recent seasons, he missed a lot of games through injury. But when he was in the side, he gave us a real presence.

Like Astle, he didn't enjoy the treatment from Bracewell towards the end of his career and I believe he probably retired from international cricket a year or two too early. When he was occasionally called on to captain in Fleming's absence, it seemed to add a real spring to his game. He was definitely more prepared to take risks than Flem — he loved rolling the dice.

Chris had obviously played so much cricket from an early age that at times you got the distinct feeling that he wanted to be somewhere other than on the cricket field. There were times when you could swear he looked uninterested in proceedings.

The only time I really saw Chris beaten on the field was when Andrew Symonds took to him in the second Chappell-Hadlee Trophy match in Wellington during the 2005–06 season. Symonds was on fire, carving up all the bowlers and, at the end of his 9th and 48th over, Chris stormed to fine leg, refusing to bowl the last over. Instead Vettori had to take to the bowling crease.

It was a bit sad really and not a good look for the team. Chris and Kyle Mills were our death bowlers and it was their job; it was a tough day at the office but we needed them. Chris just wasn't used to receiving the bashing that Symonds dished out to our bowling attack.

Off the field, he always seemed to find himself on the social committee with a couple of the younger guys to arrange team events on each tour. The youngsters always complained that they did all the work and Cairnsy took all the credit! He always had a protégé or two under his wing, his two favourites were Andrew Penn and Hamish Marshall.

The ultimate team-mate

There has been one constant during my professional cricket career — the love and support I've received from Cherie. She's been on hand to see some of my best moments in the Black Caps. She also provided the support I needed during the dark times in 2006 when the Black Caps selectors deemed I wasn't good enough to secure one of its contracts for what they believed are the nation's 20 best cricketers.

I've been with Cherie right from when I started coming up through the national age-grade sides in my teens. We first met through mutual friends — my mate, Nic Sargisson, had gone to primary school with her. During our secondary school years, I went to Shirley Boys' High and she went to Marion College, which is basically across the road. Generally, what sixth and seventh formers did was hang around the front gate just checking out who was floating around going to college before we went to class. We ended up getting together and it has gone from there — it seemed to click right from the start. Nine years after we first started going out, Nic was on hand to be my best man when we got married.

Cherie McMillan: We got together when we were in seventh form in 1994. And here we are now, we have two children and Craig has played international cricket for 11 years.

When we first got together he was playing for the New Zealand Youth team and he was always going away. Some of those youth tours were up to two months long. The first year we were together he was selected in the Canterbury team and then he was going away for one-day and four-day stuff — that was almost heart-breaking for me. Four days without Craig seemed huge. Then as he went further up the ranks and made his way into international cricket it became weeks and months away from home.

Cherie travelled as much as she could during my early days in the Black Caps. Early on, it wasn't really that hard. She worked as a travel agent and could take holidays and managed to go on a couple of tours, including to the West Indies in 2002. A year later we got married.

> **Cherie McMillan:** It was a Wednesday and I had just come home from work. Craig had got himself dressed up in a suit and I just came in and brushed it off. I thought he must be off to a cricket function that I had forgotten about. Then I saw a big bunch of roses on the bench. Soon after Craig did the traditional thing, got down on the one knee and said all the niceties. The ring was around our dog Chloe's collar. That was really special because we have had her since she was five weeks old — and she was always comfort and security when Craig was away. We got her long before we had our children.
>
> We got married on 12 April 2003. We had a few cricketers there, including Dan, Flem, Chris Harris — Millsy came along later. We got married at the church at St Andrews College and had the reception at the Clearwater Resort. It was a fantastic day.

It became a lot tougher for Cherie to come on tour once we had Mitchell. When we toured England in 2004 she came over with our little boy. I would leave the hotel at 8 am and normally would not get back to our room until 8 pm after the day's play. By that time, Mitchell was already asleep in bed so we couldn't really talk or watch a movie because he was sleeping in our room. It was really difficult to try to go on tour with the children.

We are really lucky that we both have very supportive families; they have been there for us whenever we have needed help. The support network I know has been huge for Cherie when I have been away on tour. I am sure it did make it a little easier for her. That group includes her sister Kelly, who is married to my former Canterbury and Black Caps team-mate Nathan Astle.

> **Cherie McMillan:** A lot of my friends always say they don't know how I've done it, especially as they now have children of their own. You just get used to it because you have to get used to it. You don't have the choice. I have always supported Craig and I would never have wanted him to retire before he was ready. While it was hard when he was away on tour, I have always done my best to encourage and support him.
>
> I guess I am lucky that I have had Kelly there. Of late it was a bit hard when Nathan retired in early 2007 and Craig was still travelling and playing. Kelly and I used to joke about being each other's secondary husband. I'm also friends with Tracey Bond and Ellissa McCullum. We all get together quite a bit, all being Christchurch girls. There are a lot of things I would talk to Kelly about that my

other girlfriends wouldn't understand. She knows exactly what it is like to get up every day when your husband is away on tour. If I didn't have her I would have been a lost cause sometimes.

Both of our sets of parents have been very supportive. Craig's sister Kathryn has also been great. I am just so lucky that I have such a good support crew when Craig has been away. Kelly and I have always been close sisters, but having husbands doing the same thing and having children at the same time has meant we could bounce everything off each other. She has understood everything I have gone through; it has been huge. She is my best friend.

I don't think Kelly and my parents were wholeheartedly upset when Nath and Craig retired. As much as they loved following their careers, they had many days and nights spent between our houses helping us out as only your parents know how to and when to. They have been more of a rock than they will ever know and I could never thank them enough.

The advent of the ICL has been a great thing for our family. It's allowed me to still play a form of professional cricket, but also spend far more time with my family. Being a New Zealand player you really have to commit yourself to nine or 10 months duty a year, whether that is playing domestically or travelling. Even when you are in New Zealand you really don't get to spend many nights in your own bed. There is very little cricket played in the South Island, most of it is played up north. So it is nine or 10 months when you are hardly at home. To me, now going away up to three times a year for three or four weeks makes a huge difference.

There are big gaps in the scheduling of the ICL tournaments in India. I was always going to retire from international cricket in 2007, but the way the ICL is structured meant it really was a perfect formula for us. There are a lot of things you take for granted when you are on tour with the Black Caps. But one thing you can never replace is what you miss out on when your kids are growing up — there are a lot of things you really wish you could see.

Since retiring it is amazing the things you notice in your kids' development. It's also brought home just how much I've missed out on by following my cricket path. They are things like kids saying their first words, taking their first steps and learning how to swim — all things that you can't put a price on.

Since announcing my retirement, it has been great to be able to spend quality time with Cherie and the kids. Mitchell and Lucie needed their dad around. And after 11 years on the international cricket merry-go-round, I think Cherie really needed her husband around too. Something I am really looking forward to over the next few years is the chance to spend real time with them. I can't wait to watch my kids grow up and develop.

You don't actually realise until you spend a stretch of time at home that parenting is such an ongoing thing; it really is 24/7. You get up at 6.30 each morning and go through the same routines, seven days a week. When I retired I understood and respected what Cherie has done much more. During my absences she had done far more than I had previously comprehended. I don't think we realise sometimes how tough it is on our wives back home who are looking after the kids and unable to get a breather.

Mitchell loves going out into the backyard to play cricket or golf. When I'm around I'm also able to take him to his tennis lessons. When I take him to a cricket ground and he is throwing a ball around, people will come up and say, 'Oh, you must have taught him how to do that.' To be brutally honest, I haven't because I have been away from home so much.

Mitchell has been like a different boy since I have been home. And from my point of view, it has been great to be around and spend the sort of quality time that I need with my son. It must have been hard on him, to have me at home for a week, then go away for another eight weeks. It's difficult for kids to understand why their dad keeps coming and going. Being able to concentrate on the family has been fantastic for everyone. And I'm loving being part of it all.

With Lucie, I am now being able to watch her development. What I missed out on when Mitchell was younger, I am now able to see with Lucie. Being able to be around the family when Lucie is so young is fantastic. It has just reinforced that the decision I made to move on from the Black Caps was the right one to make.

Cherie McMillan: It's fantastic to have him home. A lot of people think about the kids' side of it. But, for me personally, just to have a husband around and a normal married life is great. There has been so much time apart and when he has been at home, in the back of your mind you know there is another tour coming up. For him to be gone for five or 10 weeks a year now, compared to before when it could be for more than five months a year, is just huge. The difference in the kids, with their temperament and everything, is amazing. I have really missed having him around. To have him here to do everyday things with, even just to sit down with him and watch TV after the kids have been put to bed, is great.

Cricket has always been there for us. It is almost like we are now learning to live together. For years I have had things in place, especially for the kids, and he is now learning to fit into our lifestyle. Since having Craig at home we are now focusing on doing things as a family. That is what appeals to me the most now with having Craig around. Everyone thinks of the kids missing Dad; for me, sometimes it felt like you didn't have a husband. You were married, but when your husband is away for weeks on end it is like you are a single mum. It was really tough, especially when you tried to get out and about for the sake of the children. But being around other families it wasn't only me that felt it tough that dad wasn't there — you could see it on the kids' faces.

Mitchell used to get quite upset at me that Craig was away. He always asked when his daddy was going to come home. Whenever there were tears, he wanted Daddy. That was pretty hard to deal with and explain as kids have no concept of time. With Lucie being a bit younger, she used to wave at photos of Craig around the house and kiss his photo goodnight. It was hard for the kids; one day he would be here and the next he would be gone.

Craig is just a normal person. Like all professional sportspeople he is confident, but he is not arrogant to the point that some of the media have portrayed him to be. Maybe when he was a bit younger he went through it a bit, but he has never been above himself. He is very level-headed. He is down to earth. When he is at home he is a TV buff: any sport is worth watching. He loves being at home. He is very family-orientated, relaxed, easy going, a fantastic hands-on dad and a very doting husband. You take him as you get him and he certainly wouldn't change the way he is for anyone. I don't think he is confrontational as such, but he will stick up for what he believes in. And that is something that I respect. I really look forward to the years ahead in our somewhat 'new cricket lifestyle'. Having him around more is fantastic for all of us and we treasure the times we have as a family.

Cherie has been a great support for me. She has been my sounding board a lot of the time and I realise things have been tough for her being at home when I've always been travelling. But she has always been there to listen to me when I've gone through my frustrations — and always been there to give a calm, balanced view. Cherie is a very strong woman; she has had to be to keep the family going when I've been away for long periods. She's very loyal and is my best mate.

Life after cricket

My life certainly hasn't slowed down too much since announcing my retirement from international cricket in October 2007. I've played in the Hong Kong Sixes, two ICL tournaments, signed up for a new six-a-side tournament, had a well-earnt and overdue family holiday in Queensland and at the time of completing this book I'm playing for the Nelson club in England's Lancashire League. And all the while one thought has stuck in my mind — my decision to walk away from international cricket was the right one to make.

It certainly is one decision that I made during my career which I don't regret in the slightest. I loved my tenure in the Black Caps, even though it has cost me precious time with my family. Now being able to spend time with Cherie, and see our kids grow up, is priceless. And that is one of the great things about my time in England, the fact my family are over here with me.

The ICL has also been ideal for my family. It has provided me with some financial security and allowed me to continue playing, but not at the expense of being away from my family for more than six months of the year. I have a two-year contract with the ICL, plus the option of taking up a third year. And that would be ideal, by the end of the contract I would be 34 and with the kids the ages they are, I think I will probably be dusting off the CV that I got done in 2006 and will go job-hunting again.

I envisage still playing a bit of club cricket and I would like to play in the New Zealand domestic Twenty20 cricket competition, whether that is for Canterbury or another New Zealand association. It is a tournament which is played over just a three-week period. If it was spread out over a season it wouldn't have such an attraction. With my commitment to the ICL, I really need to keep playing to keep my skill levels and fitness up. You can't just take six months off and then head away to one of these tournaments and be back to your best. That is why I went back to England in the middle of 2008, to keep things ticking over.

Since taking a step back from the grind of the international cricket circus, I've had plenty of time to think about my career, the places it took me, the things I achieved, the ordeals I have been through and the people I met and played alongside and against along the way. Obviously, things didn't always pan out the way I hoped they would have. But I can say I have no major regrets — possibly the biggest regret I would have had is if I had quit after missing out on a New Zealand Cricket contract in 2006.

At times I think the world did see the best of me in the international arena. I finished with a batting average of 38.46 in my 55 tests and 28.18 in my 197 one-day internationals. Sometimes stats can be misleading, and you can use them for whatever you want. When I look purely at the numbers, my one-day average isn't flash. But to me it was not so much about the batting average as about what I could contribute to the team winning. There were a lot of times when you have to sacrifice yourself because that is often the best thing for the team overall. It would be nice to get an unbeaten 30 or 40. But when you come in and need seven or eight runs an over throughout a prolonged period, such as we did against Australia at Eden Park in 2007, that is just what you have to do.

On a lot of occasions it won't come off — you will be caught out for four or five and that damages your personal stats. You can't be questioned about the role you are playing. As long as people know the role you are playing, and understand it, then it is fine. But a lot of the time the general public don't understand, but the guys in the side do. They know what you are trying to do for the team.

In terms of test cricket, I think I have a very good record. While I am happy with it, I would have loved to have the average stay above 40. It slipped under that mark because my last few tests weren't that flash. The only regret I have in my test career is not scoring a hundred in Hamilton against Pakistan in 2001, the match when I hit a world record of 26 runs in an over off Younis Khan. I look back on that and think it would have been the icing on the cake to have finished that innings off with a century, as I was hitting the ball so well. But I was caught by Waqar Younis, who was fielding at third man, two overs later off the bowling of Fazl-e-Akbar. If Younis hadn't leapt up and sensationally pulled the catch off, I would have hit a six and recorded another test century. It just showed the fine line in cricket between success and being unsuccessful.

After finishing their careers I think every batsman would say that they wished they had scored more centuries. I reached triple figures six times in test cricket and three times in one-day internationals. I got to play 55 tests and 197 one-day internationals — that is a lot of cricket over a long period of time. I'm pretty comfortable where it has ended up.

So where to from here? To be totally truthful, I don't know. But what I am sure of is that it will be a decision that I will make after a lot of careful consideration because I have already been burnt in the business arena once before.

During the 2002–03 season I invested a considerable sum into securing a Carnivores franchise, alongside former All Black Greg Feek and a mate, Graeme Moody. At the time I had been looking for an interest out of cricket for a while. For me, cricket was never going to be the be-all and end-all in life. And I was conscious that at the end of my career I needed to have some sort of qualification or interest that I could get into.

One of the lucky things about being a professional sportsperson, regardless of the sport, is that you get to meet a lot of important people from a lot of different areas. And it is important that you can utilise some of that networking. One of my favourite lunch stops in Christchurch was a business called Carnivores. They made great chicken sandwiches. I was on first-name basis with the owner and after a while I asked whether he had ever thought about franchising or selling his store. He said that was something he had thought of and if anything came up then I would be the first one he would contact.

Sure enough they decided to franchise and were going to move into the malls. We got the franchise for Northlands Mall in Papanui. But what started out with high hopes certainly ended up as being one hell of a learning experience, right from the start with the contractual negotiations. At the time maybe I wasn't ready for what we got into. Over a period of 18 months we lost a fair bit of cash, leading up to having to consider closing the doors and going into receivership. That option would have resulted in us leaving a fair bit of debt, which, considering our profiles, would not have been a great look.

We went about making sure we paid off all creditors, got everything back to zero and effectively gave it back to the franchisor. I felt things the toughest financially. I had the biggest shareholding of the lot, holding 45 per cent, and lost quite a bit more money than everyone else. We had some bad luck, being at the wrong place at the wrong time. In the end I lost just under $200,000 on that venture — it was pretty devastating for a long time.

Because I have always been a bit of a gambler, it was one of those things that we went in with good intentions and the attitude that you never know unless you try. It didn't work out the way we wanted. The business was something that I had looked at as a venture for when I finished playing cricket. But it didn't eventuate and it was a bloody hard lesson to learn. It certainly opened my eyes. And it definitely isn't an experience I would like to repeat. I now feel really gun-shy about putting at risk any amount of money that could have a bearing on our quality of life, especially with our young family.

Being an international cricketer dominated my list of aspirations as a youngster. I didn't go to university, pretty much slotting into the cricketing 'workforce' straight from high school, so I don't have any qualifications from a tertiary base or the 'real' workforce.

Some of the things we fought for during the 2002 contract wrangle with New Zealand will certainly ensure the young guys coming through the grades now won't be faced with the same degree of uncertainty when their careers end. The current crop is fortunate due to some of the initiatives put in place by the players' association. They're given advice and have workplace and career specialists on offer for them — they can do work experience and study. And in the next year or two I would like to look into some of those things.

On occasions people ask me what I am going to do down the track. It does worry me that I can't give them a straight answer — I can't say I want to do this or that. It's something I've thought about for the past three or four years but still can't come up with an answer. It is something that I am going to have a look at.

I want to be in a job where I have some sort of freedom. I couldn't see myself being behind a desk for 40 hours a week — that just is not my nature. I could see myself as a rep for a company, maybe working on the road a bit and interacting with other people. Something along those lines could suit my nature quite well. And I'm sure I wouldn't have a problem working for someone else.

There are plenty of different opportunities in India, including commentary. My breakfast stint on Radio Sport certainly has opened my eyes to the world of broadcasting. And if it was an area that I looked at getting into in greater depth, I would have to say that radio commentary would be the thing that appeals the most. I've always enjoyed listening to radio commentaries; there just seems to be a lot more scope to expand on what you are witnessing out on the cricket pitch.

One area I don't really see myself going into is coaching. I did some coaching as a teenager when I first made the Canterbury team and it wasn't something that I really enjoyed.

From my point of view, when I do go out and try a few things it will be the true test and will tell me what I am into and what I am not. It will help give me the chance to make a definitive 'Yes' or 'No' on what I want to do. And I've confronted, and won, enough tests in my life so far to know that I won't be found wanting.

About the writer

NEIL REID has been a full-time journalist for 15 years, and is presently the Rugby Editor of the Yahoo!Xtra website. Previously he worked in the *Sunday News* sports department for eight years, including a four-year tenure as Sports Editor, during which time he covered two Olympic Games (Sydney 2000 and Athens 2004), the 2002 Manchester Commonwealth Games, David Tua's unsuccessful heavyweight world title fight against Lennox Lewis in Las Vegas and numerous Black Caps, All Blacks and Kiwis tours. He has also covered the All Blacks' last two Rugby World Cup campaigns in Australia and France. He was on the Basin Reserve embankment to watch Craig McMillan score his first test century, against Zimbabwe in 1998, and has followed his career with interest right up to McMillan's international retirement in 2007. This is Neil's first major biography. In 2007 he co-authored *The Year That Was* with Peter Leitch, a look at the Kiwis' dramatic 2006 Tri-Nations campaign.